Deconstruction and Philosophy

Deconstruction and Philosophy

The Texts of
Jacques Derrida   *Edited by John Sallis*

The University of Chicago Press • Chicago and London

John Sallis is the Arthur J. Schmitt Professor of Philosophy,
Loyola University of Chicago. Among his many books are
*Delimitation: Phenomenology and the End of Metaphysics; The
Gathering of Reason; Being and Logos: The Way of Platonic Dialogue;*
and *Spacings—of Reason and Imagination in Texts of Kant, Fichte,
Hegel* (the latter also published by the University of Chicago
Press).

The University of Chicago Press, Chicago 60637
The University of Chicago Press, Ltd., London
© 1987 by The University of Chicago
All rights reserved. Published 1987
Printed in the United States of America
96 95 94 93 92 91 90 89 88 87   5 4 3 2 1

Library of Congress Cataloging-in-Publication Data

Deconstruction and philosophy.

   Papers presented at the international conference
held at Loyola University of Chicago, Mar. 22–23, 1985.
   Includes bibliographical references and index.
   1. Deconstruction—Congresses. 2. Derrida,
Jacques—Congresses. I. Sallis, John, 1938–
B809.6.D43 1987   149   86-19236
ISBN 0-226-73438-2
ISBN 0-226-73439-0 (pbk.)

Contents

Acknowledgments   vii

Note on Translations   ix

Introduction   xvi

1   *Deconstruction and the Inscription of Philosophy*

   1. Infrastructures and Systematicity   3
     Rodolphe Gasché

   2. Philosophy Has Its Reasons . . .   21
     Hugh J. Silverman

   3. Destinerrance: The Apotropocalyptics of
     Translation   33
     John P. Leavey, Jr.

2   *Deconstruction and the History of Metaphysics*

   4. In Stalling Metaphysics: At the Threshold   47
     Ruben Berezdivin

   5. Doubling the Space of Existence: Exemplarity in
     Derrida—the Case of Rousseau   60
     Irene E. Harvey

6. Regulations: Kant and Derrida at the End of
   Metaphysics   71
   Stephen Watson

7. A Point of Almost Absolute Proximity to Hegel   87
   John Llewelyn

3   *Deconstruction and Phenomenology*

8. The Economy of Signs in Husserl and Derrida: From
   Uselessness to Full Employment   99
   John D. Caputo

9. The Perfect Future: A Note on Heidegger and
   Derrida   114
   David Farrell Krell

10. Deconstruction and the Possibility of Ethics   122
    Robert Bernasconi

4   *Deconstruction—in Withdrawal?*

11. Following Derrida   143
    David Wood

12. *Geschlecht* II: Heidegger's Hand   161
    Jacques Derrida

Notes on Contributors   197

Index   201

Acknowledgments

The papers collected here were presented at the international conference "Deconstruction and Philosophy: The Texts of Jacques Derrida" held at Loyola University of Chicago on March 22–23, 1985. I would like to thank all those at Loyola University who helped make the event possible: first of all, Francis Catania, Dean of the Graduate School, also Fr. Lawrence Biondi, Dean of the College of Arts and Sciences, as well as my colleagues Thomas Sheehan and John Bannan. I owe thanks also to the Mellon Foundation, which provided financial support for the conference.

My thanks especially to those who spoke at the conference. Most of all, I am grateful to Jacques Derrida for his generous and unstinting participation in the conference.

John Sallis

Note on Translations

Most passages cited in English translation have been translated directly from the original texts, though available English translations have in most cases been consulted and reference made to them in the notes.

Introduction

Especially since what is at issue is deconstruction and philosophy, I would have liked to introduce Jacques Derrida by recourse to the paradigmatic figure of the philosopher, the figure delimited and enacted in the Platonic dialogues, inscribed there for the entire history of metaphysics, the figure of Socrates.

After all, if one reads the dialogues carefully, one cannot but notice that the deconstruction of the privilege of presence has a certain parallel there, that its schema, even if limited or diverted by other schemata, is already traced in the very turn by which Socrates comes to be the philosopher. For when, inscribed in the *Phaedo,* Socrates comes to narrate his own history, he tells of his fear of being blinded by looking at things directly, as people sometimes look directly—or rather, almost directly—at the sun during an eclipse. And he tells of how, instead of turning directly to things, he turned rather to λόγοι in order to examine there the truth of beings. For λόγος one can, of course, say εἶδος, ἰδέα, going on then to recite the series of words that serve to constitute metaphysics as logocentrism. But perhaps, on the other hand, one could still say for λόγος simply language; and perhaps also one could find in the Platonic text certain resources that would inhibit the all-too-familiar metaphysical translations. Then one could, within the limits of those resources, rethink the Socratic turn as a displacement from presence to language. Socrates—on the way to language. A deconstruction of the metaphysics of presence traced in the very gesture by which metaphysics would have been founded.

Can one be assured that this way is secured? Or might one not suppose instead—even if only by isolating a certain stratum of the Platonic text—that it is the way of someone who admits that he does not know where he is going?

The words that I have just cited come from a text presented by

Jacques Derrida at the opening of a thesis defense in 1980.[1] Let me—in order to mark perhaps another direction—also excerpt from that text another passage. It occurs at a point where Derrida has just been outlining a certain range of interests pursued in his work after 1968. He continues:

> My interest . . . continued to relate to the same question: how is it that philosophy finds itself inscribed, rather than inscribing itself, within a space which it seeks but is unable to control. . . . How is one to name the structure of this space? I do not *know;* nor do I know whether there can even be what may be called *knowledge* of such a space.[2]

The space of philosophy's inscription, the space of a certain non-knowing, a space in which a philosopher cannot but enact a certain kind of ignorance that it would not be entirely inappropriate to call Socratic, even though Socrates ventured at least a name for this space, the name πόλις. Because the space of philosophy's inscription was named πόλις, the dialogue named πολιτεία not only draws the figure of the philosopher but also enacts the education of the philosopher, this entire discourse on the philosopher being inscribed, as the middle books of the dialogue, within a discourse on the πόλις.

And yet, is there not a decisive limit that must be observed in introducing Jacques Derrida by recourse to the Socratic figure? Is not deconstruction set apart from philosophy, decisively separated, by its writing? Recall the epigraph at the beginning of the first chapter of *Of Grammatology,* the chapter entitled "The End of the Book and the Beginning of Writing." The epigraph is taken from Nietzsche, and it reads: "Socrates, he who does not write." Antipodes, it would seem, in this respect, the respect for writing. The philosopher who does not write; and now, in the transgression of philosophy, the beginning of writing. Thus, deconstruction would announce the liberation of writing from the repression enforced by/as metaphysics, its release from subordination to speech and thereby, finally, to presence.

And yet, one might still wonder—especially if one rereads a passage in *Was heisst Denken?* in which Heidegger broaches the disruption of presence, broaches it as withdrawal (*Entzug*). In this passage Heidegger ventures to characterize thinking as being in the drawing

---

1. ". . . for this is what I hold and what in turn holds me in its grip, the aleatory strategy of someone who admits that he does not know where he is going." "The Time of a Thesis: Punctuations," *Philosophy in France Today,* ed. Alan Montefiore (Cambridge: Cambridge University Press, 1983), p. 50.

2. Ibid., p. 45.

into withdrawal, as being drawn along in the withdrawal. And then, in relation to this transgressive figure, he introduces the figure of the philosopher who does not write.

> All through his life and right into his death, Socrates did nothing else than place and maintain himself in the draft of this drawing [*in den Zugwind dieses Zuges*]. This is why he is the purest thinker of the West. This is why he wrote nothing. For anyone who begins to write from out of thinking [*aus dem Denken*] must inevitably be like those people who take refuge from the all-too-strong draft.[3]

Perhaps today it is precisely this inevitability that ought to be put to question: the inevitability that would require that the scene of writing be a refuge, a shelter from the gale. What about the texts of Jacques Derrida? Are they not written out in the open, exposed utterly to the draft of withdrawal? Is that not perhaps what the beginning of writing is, a liberation of writing to the draft, or rather to the whirlwind, writing in withdrawal? A scene that is perhaps not entirely unlike the one pictured on the now well-known postcard, a Socratic scene of writing, a figure of Socrates writing.

At the event itself—the conference on deconstruction and philosophy held at Loyola University of Chicago on March 22–23, 1985—the above introduction immediately preceded the final paper, Derrida's "*Geschlecht* II." As the title indicates, Derrida's paper is linked to an earlier text, one already published;[4] it is linked also to another, a still unpublished continuation that did not go entirely without discussion at the conference. At the time of the conference the subtitle given to "*Geschlecht* II" was "The Hand of Man according to Heidegger."

Now—after the event—to introduce also the others who spoke at the conference, who had, in fact, already spoken when the above introduction was finally interjected, would be, in a sense, quite superfluous; for they, too, spoke of deconstruction and philosophy, even if in various regards, the texts of Jacques Derrida regulating indeed all the discourses prepared for the conference. One could, then, propose for each the prospect of writing in withdrawal, the figure of Socrates writing.

And yet, there is perhaps also something to be said for retracing, if ever so lightly, a certain trajectory which, following Derrida, they

3. *Was heisst Denken?* (Tübingen: Niemeyer, 1954), p. 52.
4. "Geschlecht: différence sexuelle, différence ontologique," *Martin Heidegger,* ed. Michel Haar (Paris: L'Herne, 1983), pp. 419–30; translated as "*Geschlecht:* Sexual Difference, Ontological Difference," *Research in Phenomenology* 13 (1983): 65–83.

traced out. One trajectory, probably not the only one, certainly not one simply programmed, most likely a mixing of prospection and retrospection.

One thing, however, was certainly a matter of program: Deconstruction was to be considered in thematic reference to philosophy, not to literary theory, theology, politics, the human sciences, etc., even though one would, of course, want to observe the precaution of not overly insisting on these disciplinary distinctions. Correspondingly, at the outset deconstruction is situated in a certain positive way with respect to philosophy, as an attempt to give an account (λόγον διδόναι), namely, to account for certain "constitutive 'contradictions'" by means of various arche-syntheses or "infrastructures." This is not to overlook the peculiar torsion that belongs to such an account, that it is precisely such as to put in question the very procedure of giving an account; but it is to say that, at least within certain limits, the deconstructive double of the philosophical text needs to be read *from* the philosophical text. Bringing philosophy to a certain close, opening the discourse of philosophy to an other that is no longer simply the other *of* philosophy, no longer simply a nonphilosophy to be, in the end, (re)appropriated, deconstruction marks that other, nonetheless, as the *limit of* philosophy, as the other in which philosophy comes to be inscribed.

Within such space of inscription, within the space of a certain non-knowing, radical disorientation is inevitable. Among other things, deconstruction cannot but put radically into question the orientation of philosophy toward that place where it has so customarily been inscribed and, in a sense, grounded, namely, the university. To expose philosophy's inscription, to expose philosophy to inscription, is to set it adrift in a way not unlike that in which a text is set adrift in being translated, reinscribed. If philosophy cannot but be inscribed, if it cannot but submit to writing (signifier of a signifier), then it is always already a matter of translation, "the handwork of Babel," as Derrida's translator says.

Deconstruction has especially retraced the inscription in the history of metaphysics. First, at the threshold, where what Heidegger once marked as a transformation of truth is heralded by the issue of ψεῦδος, deception, spreading into images and the indeterminately dyadic—here metaphysics is shown to be installed in such a way as to be always already stalled, disseminated. Metaphysics nonetheless runs its course, follows its trajectory, for example, to Rousseau—an example whose exemplary value will have been contested—who repeats in an exemplary way the metaphysical reduction of writing, repeats it within a repetition of the metaphysical privileging of presence, presence now taken, however, as the self-presence of consciousness or feeling. Metaphysics is trajected on to the advent of critique: consciousness now, as reason, doubling back upon itself, turning into critique, opening thereby a space of heterogeneity that threatens the very presence whose recovery critique would assure. Behind the back of reason, in the space where (self-)critique turns, there will always have been a certain operation; and metaphysics would, finally, inscribe itself in the economy of that reason more cunning than critique could ever have recognized. Or, exceeding the end, overshooting the mark, toward a play by the other of reason, that refuse whose very refusal constitutes the delimitation of metaphysics, its delimitation beyond all dialectical opposition, the scene of differance, almost an outside of the Hegelian text, the refuse, the remains, *ce qui reste du savoir absolu*.

Deconstruction has also traced the reinscription of metaphysics in phenomenology, its translation. Phenomenology is the most rigorous renewal of metaphysics, an exemplary translation of the metaphysical privileging of presence, its translation into the principle of all principles. Also a translation of the secondariness that metaphysics must then accord the sign: At the very outset phenomenology reduces expression, which would be the very essence of language, stripping it of everything by which it would otherwise be taken to signify, denuding it until there is nothing to be said or heard, only silent soliloquy. On the other hand, phenomenology thickens the present; it closes, if ever so briefly, the eye of temporality by exposing the retentional function that serves to install at the very center of presence a non-presence, a non-presence that is not simply a symmetrical opposite of what it would displace. Time, becoming ecstatic, is spread out beyond presence, is the "beyond" of Being as presence, ἐπέκεινα τῆς οὐσίας. *Destruktion* becomes deconstruction, perhaps even at the cost of much of what has come to be regarded as essential to the project of *Being and Time*. Perhaps also at the cost of the future ethics onto which *Being and Time* sometimes was taken to have offered an opening. Perhaps at the cost of displacing ethics too beyond Being, toward an impossible discourse on the very law of laws.

What, then, of the promise of deconstruction? What of its promise for philosophy, or, rather, for a writing in withdrawal that would somehow be the heir of philosophy, that would, even if in the most unheard-of way, resume the trajectory that Western thought has followed, the voyage of the West, the voyage that is the West, the voyage west?

Such was at least one trajectory broached on the occasion of the gathering in Chicago.

Deconstruction and the Inscription of Philosophy

1

Infrastructures and Systematicity

1

Rodolphe Gasché

One of the more persistent misunderstandings that has thus far fore-stalled a productive debate with Derrida's philosophical thought is the assumption, shared by many philosophers as well as literary critics, that within that thought just anything is possible. Derrida's philosophy is more often than not construed as a license for arbitrary free play in flagrant disregard of all established rules of argumentation, traditional requirements of thought, and ethical standards binding upon the in-terpretative community. Undoubtedly, some of the works of Derrida may not have been entirely innocent in this respect, and may have con-tributed, however obliquely, to fostering to some extent that very mis-conception. But deconstruction which for many has come to designate the content and style of Derrida's thinking, reveals to even a superficial examination, a well-ordered procedure, a step-by-step type of argumen-tation based on an acute awareness of level-distinctions, a marked thor-oughness and regularity. Of course, the methodical aspect of decon-struction, if it is recognized at all, could still be viewed as the minimal coherence of a merely private and anarchic project, closer, in its aberra-tions, to literature than to philosophy. All adequate comprehension of the nature and implications of the order characteristic of deconstruction is, indeed, possible only on the condition that one also develop a sense of what deconstruction is to achieve. As long as its goal is believed to promote the above-mentioned licentious free play, nihilistic canceling out of opposites, abolition of hierarchies, and demystification or de-ideologization of Western philosophemes, deconstruction's definite and logical procedure cannot be grasped in all its specificity. To make out the goal pursued by deconstruction requires, indeed, not so much a familiarity with certain corpora within the history of philosophy (such as, for instance, the philosophy of Hegel and the phenomenology of Husserl and Heidegger) as a keen awareness of the most elementary and most essential topoi and exigencies constitutive of philosophy since its incipience. The background of these fundamentals of philosophy alone provides the means to establish what deconstruction intends to achieve. How, then, are we to define deconstruction?

Deconstruction must be understood, we contend, as the attempt to "account," in a certain manner, for a heterogeneous variety or manifold of nonlogical contradictions and discursive inequalities of all sorts that continues to haunt and fissure even the *successful* development of philosophical arguments and their systematic exposition. What is this nonhomogeneous manifold for which we claim that deconstruction provides, in a certain manner, the unifying principle, origin, or ground? These dissimilarities are to be located, first, in concept-formation; second, on the level of the strategies of philosophical argumentation; and third, on the level of the textual arrangement and disposition of the different parts of a philosophical work. We limit ourselves to one schematic example for each such level.

(*a*) All major philosophical concepts (being, essence, the good, the One, truth, logos, etc.) are values of unbreached plenitude and presence. Yet concepts are not pointlike simplicities, because in order to be what they are, they must be demarcated from other concepts to which they thus incessantly refer. In addition to such referentiality to other concepts with which they form binary oppositions, they are, moreover, caught in systems and conceptual chains. The aimed-at conceptual homogeneity is, thus, "contradicted," in a certain manner, by the concepts' constitutive relation to other concepts.

(*b*) The inconsistencies characteristic of the level of philosophical argumentation can best be illustrated by the discrepancies in philosophical texts between the philosopher's explicit declaration of what he wishes to argue and how he argues in fact—for instance, between Saussure's declaration that writing must be condemned and his simultaneous assignment to writing of a predominant, even constitutive role when determining the structure of speech. Or when Plato argues in writing that writing must be reprehended. These are discrepancies owing to inequalities between strata and moments (temporal) of argumentation, which, however, in the philosopher's eye do not at all inhibit the validity and well-foundedness of the argument.

(*c*) The inconsistencies that can be found on the level of the textual arrangement are more complex and comprise a heterogeneity of possibilities ranging from lexicological inconsistencies owing to multiple and variegated uses of one key word, signification, theme, or even signifier (such as, for instance, the letters *i* and *r* in Mallarmé's writing), to discrepancies between a preface, or the title of a work, and the main text—all of which, once again, do not, in the philosopher's eye, put the unity, coherence, and wholeness of the philosophical discourse into question. Yet these discrepancies are there. In complicated active and passive manner they contribute to what is perceived as the philosophical discourse's accomplished sense-unity. Hence, these discrepancies, as well as all the others mentioned, need to be accounted for.

Deconstruction accounts for these *constitutive* "contradictions" through the construction of arche-syntheses, or infrastructures, as we will call them hereafter. These infrastructures represent laws of distribution and disposition, economically minimal clusters of concepts, predicates, or possibilities of these "conflicting" concepts, levels of argumentation, or heterogeneous instances of discourse. Because of the incommensurability of the material possibilities that enter these syntheses and the specific structural arrangement of their features (a problem we cannot broach here), these arche-syntheses are non-unitary. Their type of accounting can, therefore, not simply be translated as a grounding, constituting legitimation and justification. It remains, however, that it must *first* be understood in terms of accounting and the classical problem of the λόγον διδόναι, which here becomes applied not to the homogeneous manifold that philosophy makes it its task to reflect into its own, but to a forever-irreducible plurality. Examples of such arche-syntheses are the arche-trace, differance, supplementarity, the re-mark, iterability, to name a few. With such a determination of deconstruction, the latter's indebtedness to the basic operations and exigencies of philosophy comes clearly into view. Although the nonlogical contradictions and discursive inequalities that it is concerned with are not specifically philosophical, since they are "presuppositions" (of sorts) of the successful philosophical discourse, deconstruction yields to the philosophical demand of accounting for such heterogeneous manifoldness by means of quasi-synthetic constructions. Deconstruction submits to these elementary philosophical demands even where it can be demonstrated that the singular task of deconstruction ultimately displaces and limits these very requirements, since they themselves are dependent as to their possibility on infrastructural clusters.

The judiciary thrust of deconstruction—deconstruction as an operation of "accounting"—alone explains and provides the horizon for the logical layout of all its distinctive steps. It appears as a meaningful operation only if it is construed as a search for minimal syntheses that

regulate the noncanonical and nonphilosophical problems that haunt
the philosophical discourse as such, and that, although they do not
destroy the possibility of philosophizing, significantly limit that possibility. As a result, all philosophy in the aftermath of deconstruction
will have to live with this new type of finitude that is brought to light
by deconstruction, and which is the result not of a constitutive human
weakness, but of structural qualities owing to the discursive nature of
the philosophical enterprise.

Now, deconstruction has been explicitly construed by Derrida as
an attempt to shake and reinscribe philosophy's endeavor to account by
itself for itself by knowledge's systematic and system-forming self-
exposition. When we said that deconstruction accounts for a plurality
of discursive and other discrepancies that breach the accomplished philosophical discourse, we implied that these discrepancies limit in an essential way the totality and the system in which this discourse seeks its
self-legitimation. The possibility of self-justification through totalization and system-formation is limited by these discrepancies, because
that very possibility carves itself out in the non-unitary system of these
discrepancies. In short, totalization and system-formation are dependent upon them. But does such criticism of philosophy and its systematic intentions imply that deconstruction's own systematical aspects are
restricted to the methodical order of its argumentational set-up? Is it
itself reduced to merely point-like, punctual, fragmentary reasoning? In
short, is Derrida's philosophy antisystematical as is often assumed? And
is his interrogation of the classical demand for system-formation tribu-
tary to the obviously complicitous form of the antisystematic practice of
the fragment? These are some of the questions that we will now begin
to address.

It would not be difficult to show that Derrida has insistently and
repeatedly rejected the concept of "the fragmentary" to thematize his
approach. As the notion of the antisystematic in general, the fragmentary is based on resources within the codified interpretative possibilities
of philosophy itself. But if Derrida has rejected the concept and the
notion of the fragment, and through it all other forms of antisystematic
thought, it is primarily because he recognizes philosophy's demand for
systematicity and system-formation as an unsurpassable and indispensable demand to which antisystematic thought (as Romantic thought
amply proves) remains profoundly committed. To deconstruct "*the
greatest totality*—the concept of the *episteme* and logocentric metaphysics" (*OG* 46), as Derrida puts it,[1] can, thus, not consist of simply
doing away with that essential requirement. First, a certain mimicry and
a pretension to systematicity is already required if deconstruction is to

find a foothold in the discourse it seeks to deconstruct. Something else than mere antisystematical thought must, consequently, be at stake for deconstruction. Would we say that in a Heideggerian fashion it is bent to thinking systematicity in a more originary manner? Although Derrida would certainly acknowledge that such an operation is indispensable, deconstruction, as its definition suggests, cannot be determined as a search for essences, however originary. Deconstruction is concerned, on the contrary, with determining the limits (the conditions of impossibility) of the possibility of systematicity and system-formation. It amounts to a meditation on those structural features which the indispensable demand for systematicity and system-formation must unavoidably presuppose to achieve its goal, but which, because they cannot be interiorized in the system which they make possible, also limit the possibility of systematization as such. Deconstruction, from this perspective, represents a meditation on what we want to call the *general system*. The *general system* is not the universal essence of systematicity; rather, it represents the ordered cluster of traits of possibilities which in one and the same movement constitute and deconstitute systems.

In order to get a better hold on the thought of the *general system*, let us circle back again to the problem of the infrastructures. We said that they represent arche-syntheses that draw together a variety of concepts, strata, and heterogeneous agencies. Any careful analysis of several such infractructures reveals that they are not point-like, fragmentary constructions, but rather that they form a certain system of concatenated chains. Overlappings, recoverings and intersections between these differing structures can easily be made out. Derrida refers to them occasionally as "a system which is no longer that of presence but that of differance" or as "a system of ciphers that is not dominated by truth value" (*SP* 147, 149). There is, undoubtedly, something systematical about the infrastructures, as their interrelations prove. But they do not form a homogenous body. Owing to the constituting arrangement of their features, they form a fanned-out volume resembling scenes, stagings, synopses, rather than a closed-off system. Their total arrangement is not governed "by the unity of a focus or of a horizon of meaning which promises it a totalization or a systematic adjoinment."[2] Although they are linked in different ways, and can enter into multiple combinations, their chains cannot be gathered once and for all upon themselves in some ideal purity. Derrida remarks that they "can never be stabilized in the plenitude of a form or an equation, in the stationary correspondence of a symmetry or a homology" (*P* 46).

The non-unitary system, or nonsystem of the "system" of the infrastructures, the ordered cluster of arche-syntheses, can be construed as what we called the *general system* because it comprises the main traits of possibility that all systematicity and system-formation must indeed presuppose: relation to Other in the case of the arche-trace, repeatability in the case of iterability, difference and differentiality in the case of differance, and so forth. Among the several reasons that explain why all these arche-syntheses or infrastructures cannot be fully reunited in one well-rounded-off system, let us mention only that, as conditions of successful idealization, they themselves escape idealization and, a fortiori, system-integration as well. Although all these infrastructural conditions thus make systematicity and system-formation possible, the *general system* also represents that which falls out of the reach of what it makes possible. The *general system* of the conditions of possibility and impossibility of systematic thought is, indeed, an articulation "older," so to speak, than the involute knowledge of *prote philosophia* and *episteme,* older than the system by which that knowledge becomes accomplished. In short, instead of being involved in antisystematic thought, deconstruction is better described as geared toward the exhibition of a more encompassing system than the system of knowledge, even if this more complete system must be said to be essentially, and that for structural reasons, radically incomplete. Even if this more encompassing system is no system at all (considering what system has always meant), it is from a philosophical point of view a more appropriate characterization of the goal of deconstruction than the concern with antisystematicity. Antisystematic thought might at best be called a representative *within* the metaphysical discourse of the *general system.*

In what follows, we will try to refine the nature of the *general system* a little bit—that is, refine that (almost) systematic set of features without which systematicity would not be possible, but which also serves to explain why it can never be fully attained. In order to do so, let us recall again that systematicity and system-formation are fundamental philosophical exigencies. In the system, knowledge lays itself out, and thus comes to know itself. The system as a complete and in-itself necessary order of foundation in which philosophical truths acquire their required internal coherence and unity, is a function of the philosophical desire for self-conceptualization. As we remember, infrastructures were said to be economically and strategically minimal distributions or constellations—arche-syntheses—of essentially heterogeneous predicates. The principle articulated by each singular infrastructure applies to itself as well, and, although each one of the by right infinite number of infrastructures can be replaced (or supplemented) by another, they are not synonymous with or even identical to one another. One can, thus, clearly see how infrastructures contain the *possibility* of tying elements together into a totality of foundation, as well as of self-thematization and of element-combination and transformation.

However, since infrastructures combine heterogeneous predicates and apply to themselves only the better to unground themselves, they also appear to be strangely ambiguous or ambivalent. Yet it is not the sort of ambiguity that would be witness to an absence of clarity in the process of their determination, to the negativity of a lack of precision, to vagueness or looseness of terms—in short, to semantic confusion— nor is it an ambiguity concerning the meaning of the infrastructures, owing to some polysemic richness. Ambiguity in these senses is always a function of presence, that is, of an ultimately self-identical significa- tion, as is demonstrated by the possibility of the dialectical sublation of ambiguous meanings, whereas the ambiguity of the infrastructures is not the positive sign of a dialectical or speculative state of affairs. Final- ly, this ambiguity does not signify the enigma of all truth as an uncon- cealing. Indeed, the ambiguity of the infrastructures is not univocal in a higher sense. It does not simply coincide with what Heidegger calls *"zweideutige Zweideutigkeit,"* an ambiguity grounded in a gathering (*Versammlung*) or unison (*Einklang*), whose unity itself remains un- speakable.[3] The specific ambiguity of the infrastructures cannot be sub- lated or made to sound in unison. If determinacy requires self-identity then the ambiguity of the infrastructures has no boundaries.

For all these reasons, it is advisable to avoid the term *ambiguity* altogether in characterizing the infrastructures. By analogy to Gödel's discovery of undecidable propositions, Derrida suggests that infrastruc- tures be qualified, provisionally, as undecidables. In an essay, *On For- mally Undecidable Propositions of Principia Mathematica and Related Systems,* Gödel demonstrated that metalogical statements concerning the completeness and consistency of systems any more complex than logical systems of the first order cannot be demonstrated within these systems.[4] Derrida, in *Dissemination,* transcribes Gödel's theorem in the following terms: "An undecidable proposition, as Gödel demonstrated in 1931, is a proposition which, given a system of axioms governing a multiplicity, is neither an analytical nor deductive consequence of those axioms, nor in contradiction with them, neither true nor false with re- spect to these axioms. *Tertium datur,* without synthesis" (*D* 219). To call the infrastructures undecidables is, thus, not merely to stress the essential incompleteness and inconsistency of their level of formaliza- tion. Without denying the philosophical ideal of exhaustive deduc- tivity—in other words, of the possibility of determining every element of a multiplicity as either an analytic consequence or as a contradiction of a system of axioms said to govern that multiplicity—the undecidability of the infrastructures questions that ideal from a structural point of view. Finally, as Derrida remarks in *Positions,* to call infrastructures undecidables is to stress that they are "unities of simulacrum, [of] 'false' verbal properties (nominal or semantic) that can no longer be included within philosophical (binary) opposition, but which, however, inhabit philosophical opposition, resisting and disorganizing it, *without ever* constituting a third term, without ever leaving room for a solution in the form of speculative dialectics" (*P* 43).

Before continuing our analysis, let us recall that Derrida emphasized that infrastructures were to be called undecidable only by analogy. The notion of the undecidable, he remarks, in his *Introduction to the Origin of Geometry,* in its very negativity, "has such a sense by some irreducible reference to the ideal of decidability." Its revolutionary and disconcerting sense "remains essentially and intrinsically haunted in its sense of origin by the *telos* of decidability—whose disruption it marks" (*O* 53). Yet what is being thought under the title of the infrastructures transcends the project of *definiteness* itself. Therefore, "undecidability" must be understood not only as essential incompleteness and inconsistency (bearing in mind their distinction from ambiguity), but also as a pointing to a level vaster than that which is encompassed by the opposition between what is decidable and undecidable.

As "originary" syntheses, or economic arrangements of traits, the undecidables constitute the medium or the element between the binary philosophical oppositions and between philosophy and its Other, as well as the medium that encompasses these coupled terms. They are undecidable because they suspend the decidable opposition between what is true and false and put all the concepts that belong to the philosophical system of decidability into brackets. By virtue of their position as constituting a space in between conceptual dyads and, at the same time, comprising them, the infrastructural undecidables are "the medium in which opposites are opposed, the movement and the play that links them among themselves, reverses them or makes one side cross over into the other" (*D* 127). Their undecidability, their "floating indetermination," permits the substitution and the play of the conceptual binary oppositions which, by turning into one another, become incapable of denominating and defining the medium from which they emerge (*D* 93). Thus, if one terms infrastructures "ambivalent" or "ambiguous," it is in the sense that they do not offer themselves to mastery in terms of simple and clear-cut distinctions. Indeed, conceptual couples, and their play, are essentially nothing other than the attempt to bring the play of the medium of the undecidables to a stop, to make rational

what, according to their implicit and explicit ethos, can only be irrational, to appropriate it, to identify it by forcing a self-identity upon it.
The restricted play of the philosophical conceptual couples proceeds to
this task by trying to reconstitute the undecidables as dialectical contradictions susceptible of eventual dissolution, but, notes Derrida, undecidability "is not contradiction in the Hegelian form of contradiction" (*P* 101). The undecidables, on the contrary, are what suspends
decidability in all its forms, particularly in its dialectical form (i.e., a
mediation of contraries *and* that in which decidability and definiteness
carve themselves out). Above all, the "ambiguity" of undecidables is
rigorously irreducible and irresolvable because of its essentially *nonse-
mantic* character. Speaking of the "hymen," Derrida holds:

> "Undecidability" is not caused here by some enigmatic equivocality,
> some inexhaustible ambivalence of a word in a "natural" language, and
> still less by some "*Gegensinn der Urworte*" (Abel). In dealing here with
> *hymen*, it is not a matter of repeating what Hegel undertook to do with
> German words like *Aufhebung, Urteil, Meinen, Beispiel,* etc., marveling
> over that lucky accident that installs a natural language within the ele-
> ment of speculative dialectics. What counts here is not lexical richness,
> the semantic infiniteness of a word or concept, its depth or breadth, the
> sedimentation that has produced inside it two contradictory layers of
> signification. . . . What counts here is the formal or syntactical *praxis* that
> composes and decomposes it (*D* 220).

The undecidability of infrastructures results from the *syntactic arrangement* of their parts. Yet what does Derrida mean by syntax? As
opposed to semantics (and pragmatics), as another major aspect of the
grammatical construction of sentences (and of the general theory of
signs), syntax refers traditionally to the formal arrangements of words
and signs, to their connection and relation in phrases or sentences, as
well as to the established usages of grammatical construction and the
rules deduced therefrom. However, Derrida's use of the concept of syntax is not simply a reference to the formal properties of language insofar
as these are traditionally considered to refer to the articulation of the
signifieds. Form, indeed, is just another name for presence, Derrida
notes. His use of "syntax," precisely does not imply the traditional sub-
jection of syntax to semantics. In distinction from the grammatical opposition of the syntactic and the semantic, of form and content, and so
on, Derrida's use of "syntax" is intended to systematically undo these
oppositions. Syntax is conceived by Derrida as irreducibly in excess of
the semantic and, consequently, as disequilibrating that traditional

grammatical and philosophical distinction. How then are we to think such an "irreducible excess of the syntactic over the semantic?" (*D* 221). Such an excess takes place where it can be shown that the formal properties of language are not simply a function of signifieds, of the content of the words, but that these formal properties are themselves arranged and intrinsically dependent on a syntax of their own. Yet, if it can be demonstrated that formal syntactic properties can be syntactically composed and decomposed, a *syntax of syntax* comes into view, along with the problem of the simulacrum, which, as we have seen, is no longer subject to truth or, in the case of syntax, to the content of the words. In "The Double Session," Derrida has shown that the writing of Mallarmé is precisely such an attempt to explore the possibilities of syntactical excess. It is, therefore, a literature in which "the suspense is due only to the placement and not to the content of words" (*D* 220).

Now, the syntactic excess responsible for the infrastructures' undecidability stems from the fact that their formal arrangements, dispositions, distributions, or constellations of predicates refer to a supplementary mark. The infrastructure of re-marking or of the double mark demonstrates this essential character of infrastructures in general, which consists of their being folded upon themselves in such a manner that they themselves become a paradigm of the law they represent. Infrastructures apply to themselves. The arrangement that they represent is always rearrangement by themselves. For this reason, they are in constant displacement, incapable of assuming any stable identity. By re-marking the syntactic disposition with a supplementary syntactic trait, the infrastructures can no longer be brought to a semantic halt. They seem to be purely syntactic; yet, since these purely "formal" or syntactic structures, or knots of intersections, are their own paradigm, they also, unquestionably, signify and are not, for that reason, purely syntactic.

> Through the re-marking of its semantic void, it in fact begins to signify. Its semantic void *signifies,* but it signifies spacing and articulation; it has as its meaning the possibility of syntax; it orders the play of meaning. *Neither purely syntactic nor purely semantic,* it marks the articulated opening of that opposition (*D* 222).

The infrastructures, thus, float indefinitely between the possibilities of the semantic and the syntactic, of meaning, in short. Though not purely syntactic (nor, for that matter, purely semantic), they are in a position of anteriority and of possibility to both aspects of language, precisely because of the excess of the syntactic over meaning, that is, of the re-marked syntax, of a syntax that arranges (itself). It is in this sense that we will continue to speak of the infrastructures as syntactically undecidable. After having demonstrated in "The Double Session" that the infrastructure "hymen" is undecidable because of syntactic re-marking, Derrida writes:

> What holds for "hymen" also holds, *mutatis mutandis,* for all other signs which, like *pharmakon, supplément, différance,* and others, have a double, contradictory, undecidable value that always derives from their syntax, whether the latter is in a sense "internal," articulating and combining under the same yoke, *huph'hen,* two incompatible meanings, or "external," dependent on the code in which the word is made to function. But the syntactical composition and decomposition of a sign renders this alternative between internal and external inoperative. One is simply dealing with greater or lesser syntactical units at work, and with economic differences in condensation (*D* 221).

Because of this undecidability, the infrastructures can serve as "originary" syntheses, without, at the same time, lending themselves to a movement of (teleological or archaeological) reappropriation: "these points of indefinite pivoting . . . mark the spots of what can never be mediated, mastered, sublated, or dialecticized through any *Erinnerung* or *Aufhebung*" (*D* 221). If they mark dialectics with sterility by undercutting the possibility of a reduction of their undecidability through sublation, how much more do they evade nondialectical philosophy and its reflexive oppositions!

As undecidables, infrastructures *resemble* syncategoremata. Like those secondary parts of discourse—distinguished in grammar and logic by writers ranging from the medieval William of Shyreswood to Husserl in *Logical Investigations*—which, in contradistinction to categoremata, are unclosed expressions that have no determined and fixed meaning, undecidables also predicate jointly. They cannot function as terms and, thus, are not of the order of the φωνὴ σημαντική. Similar to syncategoremata such as "and," "or," "not," "if," "every," "some," "only," "in between"—expressions that cannot be used by themselves but only in conjunction with other terms—infrastructures are essentially used together with predicates, categoremata, or concepts, with respect to which they exercise a specific organizational function. Yet syncategoremata, which are considered logical constants determining the logical form (as already with Buridan), never relate to themselves in the complex manner that we have said to be decisive for infrastructures. If they never signify their own semantic quasi-void, it is because the ethical orientation of grammar, giving priority to categoremata, cannot afford to blur its hierarchical and clear-cut distinctions. However, as Mallarmé's texts reveal, syncategoremata, such as "in between," or "or," lend themselves to an operation of re-marking. Speaking of "*entre,*" "in between," Derrida stresses that "it can be nominalized, turn into a quasi-categorem, receive a definite article, or even be made plural" (*D* 222). If in the following we will continue to speak of the infrastructures as syncategoremata, it is in this sense of a nonreflexive doubling of their incomplete meanings.[5]

For the remainder of these reflections it is imperative to recall that Derrida's references to syncategoremata occur in the context of "The Double Session," that is, in an essay that sets out to prove the irreducible excess of syntax over semantics. This demonstration is framed by a critique of thematic criticism and its overevaluation of the role of the word, in both philosophy and literary criticism. As the totality of Derrida's work clearly indicates (in particular, but not exclusively, *Of Grammatology*), this critique of thematic criticism is aimed at the mainstream of Western philosophy, which until recently ignored and trivialized the difference between words and sentences, between semantics and syntax, by confining the latter to, at best, a lateral role. All of Derrida's work is engaged in a systematic critique of the status accorded to the word, the noun, in order to question the mere secondariness of the syntactical; it is perhaps the most radical attempt ever made at allowing syntax a sort of independent form. As is well known, Derrida's criticism of the word, of semantics, in favor of the forms of syntactic construction, is also aimed at what he perceives as phenomenology's (in particular Husserlian) continuation of metaphysics. Yet, what still needs to be developed is that this critique is linked to Derrida's *complex* continuation of Husserl's project in the *Logical Investigations* of a universal and a priori, in short, a "purely logical grammar." Derrida continues this idea, which Husserl never developed, in a complex manner, because his critique of phenomenology, of the values of presence that it shares with metaphysics in general, of form as another name for presence, of semantics, thematism, and so on, also radically displaces what he calls in *Positions* the "remarkable project of a 'purely logical grammar' that is more important and more rigorous than all the projects of a 'general reasoned grammar' of seventeenth- and eighteenth-century France, projects that certain modern linguists refer to, however" (*P* 32).

Before elaborating on this project, a brief note on Derrida's indebtedness to Husserlian phenomenology may be appropriate. Not infrequently, one hears the opinion that Husserlian phenomenology is a dead end and that, consequently, any attempt to continue the questioning of that philosophy is, from the start, doomed to failure. Certainly, what is true of other philosophers is true of Husserl as well: by evading what is question-worthy in their texts, they all become dead ends. As far as Derrida is concerned, his relation to Husserl is at least threefold. First, it is a relation, to use Gérard Granel's words, to "simply the greatest philosopher who appeared since the Greeks."[6] To put it differently, it is a relation to the philosophical as a battle of gods and giants about being (γιγαντομαχία περὶ τῆς οὐσίας), as Plato calls it in the *Sophist,* or, in a less inflated manner, to the philosophical in all its technical and thematic richness. Second, Derrida's relation to Husserlian thought is radically critical of the metaphysical implications of the project of phenomenology itself, as has been amply documented. Third, it is a continuation and radicalization of a number of motifs in Husserl's own works that are capable of unhinging the major metaphysical themes at center stage in his philosophy, such as, for instance, the idea of a primordial axiomatical grounding, the ideal of deductivity in general, the idea of evidence, and the idea of the idea itself. Yet, to contend, as we do here, that Derrida continues Husserl (and this is true of his relation to Heidegger as well), precisely on those issues that foreground the classical ethico-theoretical decisions constitutive of philosophy as philosophy, is also to say that such a continuation is at the same time a decisive break with the idea of tradition, continuity, Oedipality, and so forth. Indeed, since the motifs in question are of such a nature that they themselves are radically more fundamental than the possibility of continuity, and since, moreover, they cannot be developed *within* the philosophical discourse as such, their continuation is possible only from a perspective that is marginal with respect to the history of philosophical development. From this standpoint, the fact that Derrida may have discovered these motifs in Husserl's works is, in a certain way, a radically contingent datum.

Now, let us recall, in as succinct a manner as possible, what the project of a purely logical grammar corresponds to. The *Logical Investigations,* in which this idea is set forth, are preliminary investigations required by Husserl's anticipated project of a pure logic or theory of theory, that is, a logic thoroughly different from what one commonly calls epistemology or theory of science, which would govern the implications of the very *possibility* of an idea such as knowing. In these preliminary examinations, Husserl is soon led to the insight that such a pure logic would have to include, as one of its parts if not as its foundation, a purely logical grammar, a logic that would be a purely formal mapping out of the *primitive* essential concepts or the ideal singulars a priori contained in the very content or meaning of certain genera, such as knowing. Indeed, if such a pure logic investigating what constitutes the idea of knowing anterior to its objective validation and "intentional fulfillment" would also, necessarily, have to investigate the laws related to these primitive concepts, laws that organize the ideal singulars constitutive of the genera, then the task of fixing these a priori laws would be incumbent on a discipline such as a pure logical grammar. This grammar must not be mistaken for a "universal science comprehending all particular grammars as contingent specifications," Husserl warns us in his *Logical Investigations*.[7] Contrary to such a science, which would still be empirical, the pure logical grammar is exclusively concerned with that field of laws relative to the pure semantic forms a priori contained in the idea of knowing. Such laws affect these forms insofar as they regulate their compoundings and modifications and watch over their meaningfulness even before these forms and their possible combinations enter the truth relations that are the object proper of logic in a pregnant sense. The sense or non-sense of these forms is based on these laws, independently of the objectivity and validity of these forms which itself depends on their prior semantic fullness. The purely logical grammar is thus a form-theory of meaning or intentionality prior to all possible objective validation of meaning or intentional fulfillment. The task of this meta-empirical logic is to provide traditional logic with "the abstractly possible forms of meaning, whose objective value it then becomes its first task to determine."[8] It is important, here, to mention that, on more than one occasion, Husserl conceived of these forms of meaning, of the laws of essence that regulate the primitive meaning elements and structures, as *trivia,* as obvious commonplaces. Yet these trivia, which are "intrinsically prior in the sense of Aristotle," behind whose obviousness "the hardest problems lie hidden," and which have never been thematized by the logicians, become the true object of the project of a pure logic, if not, with Husserl, of philosophy in general, especially since philosophy could be called "paradoxically, but not unprofoundly . . . the science of the trivial."[9] Now, what are these trivia, these forms of meaning, which, although they make no knowledge possible, are still full of meaning because they obey certain rules? What are these trivia which are the a priori conditions of the intelligibility of discourse?

The primitive forms of meaning that constitute the whole semantic realm are the formal laws that govern "the formation of unitary meanings out of syntactical materials falling under definite categories [and that] have an *a priori* place in the realm of meanings, a formation according to syntactical laws which are likewise fixed *a priori,* and which can be readily seen to constitute a fixed system of forms."[10] Thus, the pure logical grammar or form-theory of meaning faces the task of fixing in a system the categorical and syntactical primitive laws a priori built into the general idea of meaning. As Husserl had pointed out, this system of categorical and syntactical laws following from the generic essence of meaning as such, which is constitutive of the articulation of its elements, is an ideal framework and, as the essence of all speech as such, holds a prime place over against all actual languages and their empirical grammar. For that reason, it is to be called a "pure logical grammar."[11]

After what has been developed up to this point, it should not be difficult to see, by analogy with the trivia in Husserl (and with what Heidegger has thematized under the name of the most obvious or most simple), that the infrastructures continue, to some extent, Husserl's (and Heidegger's) research into the a prioris of meaning (that of Being included). However, in discussing Husserl's project of a purely logical grammar in *Speech and Phenomena,* Derrida also points out that its formalizing power does not cover the whole field of possibility for language in general, to the extent that it "concerns only the *logical a priori* of language," and that "it is *pure logical grammar*" (*SP* 8). In spite of its interest in the system of rules that make a discourse, properly speaking, a discourse, and not non-sense, before any objective fulfillment of the meaning-intention, the pure logical grammar remains "governed more or less immediately by the possibility of a relationship with objects" (*SP* 71). Indeed, "the purification of the formal is [itself] guided by a concept of *sense* which is itself determined on the basis of a *relation with an object*" (*SP* 98). Derrida, apart from insisting that there are modes of sense which do not point to any possible objects, also sets out to demonstrate that the rigorous distinction in Husserl between meaning-intention and its possible fulfillment by an intuition of an object is itself possible only because all meaning-intention is structurally testamentary. In other words, it functions only because it is always already supplementing a lack of actuality. The discovery of the infrastructures thus extends Husserl's project of a purely logical grammar. The expansion of its formalizing power implies a reinscription of the logical as merely one of a plurality of linguistic functions. Whereas, in Husserl, the primitive laws of essence of all meaning prior to its validation are all laws concerning the unity of meaning, thus giving priority to the categorical over the syncategorical and the syntactical, the infrastructures question the very *differences* between the a priori and the world they open, as well as the difference between the categorical and the syncategorical, between the semantic and the syntactic. In this sense, the infrastructures and their system are anterior, in an unheard-of way, to a phenomenology of meaning, that is, in short, to phenomenology. Reflecting on those unthematized differences, the system of the infrastructures precedes, "by right," the discourse of phenomenology.

Having established that much, let us now circle back to the *general system*. After the foregoing developments it becomes possible to determine it as a system of undecidables, of syntactically re-marked syncategoremata articulating prelogical and lateral possibilities of logic. To put it differently, the system can be viewed as a syntax of an infinity of "last" syntactically overdetermined syntactical objectivities.

To characterize the *general system* in these terms serves to indicate a decisive point at which this system leaves the philosophical horizon of phenomenology. This point is that of a radicalized, no-longer-phenomenologizable notion of syntax. As we will try to suggest in these concluding remarks, Derrida's concept of a re-marked syntax undercuts, deconstructs, in fact, Husserl's distinction, toward the beginning of *Ideas,* in section 11, of formal ontological syntactical categories and formal ontological substrative categories. This distinction is important to the whole project of *Ideas* since it will allow Husserl to make the syntactical forms and their categories depend on what he terms the *"ultimate content-laden substrata* as the nucleus of all syntactical constructions."[12] As a result, "syntactical objectivities appear in the formal region of objectivities in general, as *derivatives* of these ultimate substrata, that is, of objects *which are no longer constructions of a syntactico-categorical kind,* [and] which contain in themselves no further vestige of those ontological forms which are mere correlates of the functions of thought."[13] As *ultimate terms,* which no longer contain in themselves any residue of syntactical formation, they are "pure and syntactically formless individual units," and/or "ultimate substantive [*Sachhaltiges*] essences."[14] In one of the most classical gestures, Husserl, after having opened the radical formal province of pure objectivities, makes syntactical categories secondary with respect to those last terms, which as εἴδε or τόδε τι (as essences or individualities) link substance (οὐσία), in the fullest and most primary sense, to presence. The re-marked and undecidable infrastructures "as such" are the outcome of a deconstruction of these hierarchical distinctions in the purely formal region of the logical, distinctions by which form is subjected to content, syntax to semantics, purely formal forms to nonformal forms, that is, to singularities or identical subject-matters (*Sachverhalte*). The system of these infrastructures as one of syntactically re-marked syncategoremata is a system that escapes all phenomenologization as such; it constantly disappears and withdraws from all possible presentation. In privileging the syntactical in the sense that has been developed, that is, in the sense of

re-marked, doubled syntactic structures no longer suspended from semantic subject-matters of whatever sort, the *general system* spells out the
prelogical conditions of logic, thus re-inscribing logic, together with its
implications of presence and evident meaning, into a series of linguistic
functions of which the logical is only one among others. Derrida remarks in "Limited Inc.":

> The matter we are discussing here concerns the value, possibility, and
> system of what is called logic in general. The law and the effects with
> which we have been dealing . . . govern the possibility of every logical
> proposition. . . . No constituted logic nor any rule of a logical order can,
> therefore, provide a decision or impose its norms upon these prelogical
> possibilities of logic. Such possibilities are not "logically" primary or
> secondary with regard to other possibilities, nor logically primary or sec-
> ondary with regard to logic itself. They are (topologically?) alien to it,
> but not as its principle, condition of possibility, or "radical" foundation
> (*LI* 235).

As the system of these impure and non-ideal grounds, grounds so
different from what they ground as to be thoroughly alien to it, the
system of the infrastructures is also the exposition of what we termed
elsewhere "heterology." The *general system,* then, is the system of what
is Other to the λόγος—Other, however, not in the sense of absolute,
that is, abstract opposition, or in the sense of the Other of the same,
but, rather, in terms of what is alien to its own self-thematization. It is
the system of what, in spite of its thorough alterity to the self-understanding of thought, is presupposed by such thought, precisely insofar
as thought's handed-down goal is to secure its own foundation in itself
and by itself.

By taking the classical exigencies of philosophy to their logical
end, without, however, giving in to its ethico-theoretical, ethico-
ontological, ethico-teleological, ethico-political, etc., decisions, Derrida
brings philosophy to a certain close. This, however, is an accomplishment in an unheard-of sense. Opening the discourse of philosophy to
an Other which is no longer simply *its* Other, an Other in which philosophy becomes inscribed, and which limits its ultimate pretension to
self-foundation (a pretension independent of philosophical orientation)
is an accomplishment that marks not the end but the structural limits of
philosophy's autonomy and autarchy. Philosophy comes to a close, paradoxically, because the system of its heterological presuppositions constitute it as, necessarily, always incomplete.

Notes

1. References to the works of Jacques Derrida are included within the text under the following abbreviations:

OG   *Of Grammatology,* trans. Gayatri Ch. Spivak (Baltimore: Johns Hopkins
         University Press, 1976).
SP   *Speech and Phenomena,* trans. David Allison (Evanston: Northwestern
         University Press, 1973).
P   *Positions,* trans. Alan Bass (Chicago: University of Chicago Press, 1971).
D   *Dissemination,* trans. Barbara Johnson (Chicago: University of Chicago
         Press, 1981).
O   *Edmund Husserl's "Origin of Geometry": An Introduction,* trans. John P.
         Leavey, Jr. (Stony Brook, N.Y.: Nicolas-Hays, 1978).
LI   "Limited Inc.," *Glyph 2,* trans. Samuel Weber (Baltimore: Johns Hopkins
         University Press, 1977), pp. 162–254.

2. Jacques Derrida, "The Retrait of Metaphor," trans. F. Gasdner et al., *Enclytic* 2, no. 2 (Fall 1978), p. 18.
3. Martin Heidegger, *On the Way to Language,* trans. P. D. Hertz (New York: Harper & Row, 1971), p. 192.
4. Kurt Gödel, *On Formally Undecidable Propositions of Principia Mathematica and Related Systems,* trans. B. Meltzer (New York: Basic Books, 1962).
5. See also in this context the reference in "The Double Session" to the rhetorical figure of the syllepsis (*D* 220).
6. Gérard Granel, *Traditionis Traditio* (Paris: Gallimard, 1972), p. 71.
7. Edmund Husserl, *Logical Investigations,* trans. J. H. Findlay (New York: Humanities Press, 1977), vol. 2, p. 527.
8. Ibid., p. 522.
9. Ibid., p. 528.
10. Ibid., p. 513.
11. Ibid., p. 526.
12. Husserl, *Ideas,* trans. W. R. Boyce Gibson (New York: Humanities Press, 1969), p. 74.
13. Ibid., p. 70.
14. Ibid., p. 74.

Philosophy Has Its Reasons . . .

2

Hugh J. Silverman

If there cannot be a pure concept of the university, if there cannot be a pure and purely rational concept of the university on the inside of the university, it is simply because the university is *founded*. An event of foundation cannot be simply understood within the logic of that which it founds.

> Derrida, "Mochlos ou le conflit des facultés"[1]

As far as I know, nobody has ever founded a university *against* reason. So we may reasonably suppose that the University's reason for being has always been reason itself, and some essential connection of reason to being. But what is called the principle of reason is not simply reason. We cannot for now plunge into the history of reason, its words and concepts, into the puzzling scene of translation which has shifted *logos* to *ratio* to *raison*, reason, *Grund*, ground, *Vernunft*, and so on.

> Derrida, "The Principle of Reason: The University in the Eyes of Its Pupils"[2]

Beware of the abysses and the gorges, but also of the bridges and barriers. Beware of what opens the university to the outside and the bottomless, but also of what, closing it in on itself would create only an illusion of closure, would make the university available to any sort of interest, or else render it perfectly useless. Beware of ends; but what would a university be without ends?

> Derrida, "The Principle of Reason: The University in the Eyes of Its Pupils"[3]

Whence the necessity, for a deconstruction, not to abandon the terrain of the University at the very moment at which it is taking responsibility

21

for its most powerful foundations. Whence the necessity not to
abandon the terrain to empiricism and therefore to whatever force
comes along.
        Derrida, "L'Age de Hegel," *Qui a peur de la philosophie?*[4]

At a time when the European university was already established and
even renowned in certain key centers, Blaise Pascal delivered an outline
of his collected thoughts to the gentlemen of Port Royal. When he died
in the mid-seventeenth century, he left the text of his Apology for
Christianity in the form of a *Pensées*. Among them is the celebrated one
that states: *le coeur a ses raisons que la raison ne connait point: on le sait en
mille choses.* (The heart has its reasons which reason doesn't know at all;
a thousand things declare it.)[5] By a simple substitution, this maxim
might well read: Philosophy has its reasons which Reason doesn't know
at all. It would then go on to state: "a thousand things declare it." And
furthermore: philosophy "loves the universal Being, and itself naturally,
according to its obedience to either; and it hardens against one or the
other, as it pleases."[6] The replacement of the "heart" with "philosophy"
is not terribly outlandish considering that the heart is a kind of metonymy in which love is at issue. The heart stands for love. And love has
access to domains that are inaccessible to reason. But philosophy is love
(φιλία, not *caritas*): a love of wisdom. Even Socrates in the *Symposium*
goes out of his way to report the Diotimanian claim that the path from
ἔρος to φιλία (the love of wisdom) is a series of steps. The passions of
the body can become the passions of the soul. The soul, when properly
directed—by its own—can come to love and know the ideal forms according to which all things are fashioned. As the love of the heart replaces the love of wisdom, philosophy takes over the affairs of the heart.
Pascal's heart is a heart of devotion, wagered conviction, subtlety in the
face of the infinite. Pascal's heart has perspectives, justifications, conditions of understanding that are inaccessible to reason, that are outside
the competence of reason, that reason cannot know. Philosophy—as
another kind of love—bears these same characteristics. But this is curious, since the very concern of philosophy has to do with the affairs of
reason. The simple seventeenth-century dichotomy between reason and
passion is not so easily constructed. In that philosophy is both a love or
passion and the proper employment of reason, philosophy itself becomes indecidable.
    Philosophy is an indecidable as the φάρμακον is both remedy and
poison, as communication is a message and an action, as difference is
differing and deferral, as spacing is spatial and temporal, as the sign is

meaning and expression, as trace is the present mark and the designated absence, and so forth. Jacques Derrida has gone to lengths to demonstrate that the indecidable is neither conjunction nor disjunction, neither the unity of a duality nor the duality of a unity. The indecidable affirms and negates, brings together and separates, posits connection and disconnection, establishes a difference without decidability. The indecidable is left with the indecision.

Now what of philosophy? In *Archaeology of the Frivolous,*[7] Derrida demonstrates that metaphysics is (in good Aristotelian language) first philosophy. But when Condillac (following Locke if not Aristotle) practices metaphysics, he is certainly concerned with it much later than Aristotle. And even Aristotle places metaphysics *after* physics. Metaphysics is at best alongside physics—first philosophy second. Metaphysics requires that physics (the concern with nature) be displayed before metaphysics so that metaphysics (as philosophy) might comment upon it, discourse about it, render judgment on it. But these are only the beginnings of philosophy. Philosophy begins in wonder, for it has to have something to wonder about. At the other extreme, much has been said about the end of philosophy—by Hegel, by Heidegger, by Derrida, by Sallis, and so on (endlessly one might suspect). Yet the beginning and the end are not the respects in which philosophy is an indecidable—at least not for the present inquiry. Inserting philosophy, it would seem, at some place between the discourse of beginnings (first philosophy) and ends (where it all comes together for the once and final time) is the substitution of philosophy for the heart. With Pascal, one might say, philosophy can't decide whether it is first or last, whether it is finite or infinite, whether it appeals to the *esprit de géometrie* (as it did for Descartes) or the *esprit de finesse* (as Montaigne might have seen it). With Pascal the difference is to be clear (perhaps not so distinct—for both are of the *esprit*). The heart knows what reason does not, reason knows what doesn't belong to the heart. Philosophy knows (has its reasons) and reason has nothing to say about it. Like the heart, philosophy can stand outside reason while at the same time having its own reasons for being rational and employing reason. As long as philosophy is a love, it cannot be reason itself. But can it be the principle of reason?

To the extent that philosophy is at once passion (love or heart) and reason, it is a poor substitute for the heart as such. Yet as a poor substitute, it is also a good substitute in that it demonstrates the indecidability of philosophy itself. Philosophy is that which sets reason in motion. Philosophy gives weight and force to reason. Its very energy and enthusiasm is what takes it beyond what is simply accepted knowledge (*scientia*). In this sense, philosophy both generates and regulates reason. It is the principle of reason and the passionate exercise of reason. Here reason is both a power and a human faculty. As a power, reason can bring order, sequence, continuity, justification, support, and even understanding. As a human faculty, reason can overcome the passions, desire, aimlessness, confusion, and even ignorance. As a power, reason can persuade, deceive, cloud over, cover up, and even overpower. As a human faculty, reason can dry up emotion, enthusiasm, excitement, decisiveness, and even action. To the extent that philosophy is above all that, it can prevent itself from submitting to the desiccation of passion and the deceits of reasonableness. It is not that philosophy (like Nietzsche's *musiké* which is neither the excessive passion of the barbarian Dionysian nor the overwhelming rationality of Apollonian individuality) is a harnessed frenzy, an opposition held in tension. Rather philosophy is quite straightforwardly indecidable.

There is no *Aufhebung, dépassement,* superseding, surpassing, uplifting, conserving, or preserving here. Whatever is uplifting about philosophy—like the puffing up of leavening in bread—is deflated by the indecision. If only the love, the passion, the heart of philosophy could be unequivocally uplifting, the work would no longer be like work. It would be a *par-ergon.* And besides, something that ought to be like work (and isn't) should surely be suspect. And there are those who suspect philosophy. Philosophy is suspect because it looks like fun. It requires leisure (σχολή). But what is leisurely can't be scholarly, for what is scholarly is hard work. And those who practice the scholarly work that has been associated with philosophy since medieval times are charged with overlooking intuition—the kind of clear and distinct apprehension that Descartes associated with the rendering of absolute ideas. But if Descartes is right, such apprehensions cannot be the direct product of work. Work will ultimately bring about the passage (or bridge) from relative ideas to absolute ideas. The work is not in the intuition—this was Plato's view of νόησις as it was Descartes's impression of the *intuitio.* Intuition comes only at the end of work (education, dialectic, method). Philosophical intuition occurs—if it is to happen—when all the work is done, energy expended, exercise and practice maintained. Philosophical intuition (*Anschauung*) is neither scholarly (the meticulous exercise of reason) nor available to those who make sport of it (philosophizing with a golf club). If only Nietzsche could philososphize with a hammer. If only Wagner's hammering against an anvil could fashion more than a magical Rheingold ring. But such *Leitmotive* typically just pass into cultural history—and some are even too loud and tempestuous to hear in one's leisure. Heidegger tried to philosophize with a hammer—because paradigmatically and pragmatically *zuhanden.*

To construct with a hammer is hard work. Destruction with a sledge hammer goes a bit more easily. Neither can be done leisurely—they must both be done out of school.

But what kind of philosophizing can be—should be—done in school, in the academy, in the university? The question of the nature and essence (*Wesen*) of philosophy has now become a matter of the ethics of philosophy. What it means to philosophize—when, where, and how it can be done—also has implications for what it ought to do. The problem for philosophy is to deal with its own indecidability. Philosophy cannot simply speak from the heart. At the same time, reason is not the heart of philosophy. Philosophy has its reasons which reason does not know at all. There are domains of philosophy which are not simply translated into reason. Philosophy is neither reason nor passion. Philosophy has its own reasons. That which is philosophy's own seeks to define itself, to delimit itself, to say what it is, to produce a discourse about itself that it finds comfortable—that fits into its system, that is consistent with its style of practice, that articulates its very principles, that undoes its very presuppositions, that opens up a space in which it might operate, that offers hope and sometimes the revelation (apocalypse) of despair. Philosophy's own has many shapes. To presume to catalog them would be futile. Its aspiration is to be grounded in some sort of principle of reason—it wants passionately to achieve such an end. It would be so uplifting, elevating, and—if the sun is right—enlightening for it to be grounded in some sort of principle of reason. It is not that philosophy—like metaphor—is heliotropic, though it may well be that the ethics of philosophy—as Plato's allegory of the sun would show—will require an identification of the good with the sun. But then if we could only see what philosophy sees, or what it ought to see, or what it would love to see. . . . Imagine the light it would bring. The light would illuminate the ground—like a medieval manuscript— while some principle of reason might stand in the clearing, unveiled, disclosed, and available for the sort of careful reading that it would require. Such a principle of reason would have its own rules—as Kant claimed, properly it would be "only a rule." Opening up at the ground, what sort of gathering (as John Sallis has noted) would the principle of reason be able to achieve? What range of regulation could it achieve from the ground? Leonardo had the idea long before Kant: wouldn't some *"pensée de survol"* be more effective? One can see so much more from a flying machine, an airplane, or even a missile. But Merleau-Ponty's warnings about thinking from on high ought to be heeded. Bird's-eye thinking sees far, extends to the very horizons of sight, and surveys the breadth of the terrain, but it relies upon reflection. It is so far from the ground. And if philosophy is to operate in terms of a principle of reason, it must be grounded. Too much high-flying, high-fallutin' philosophy will go nowhere. The reasonable place within which to ground philosophy—for centuries the chosen place—is the university.

Inside the university, standing solidly on the university grounds, keeping out of the clouds and off the ivory towers, philosophy can do its work. Philosophy is comfortable within the university. It is sometimes so comfortable that it can and has become—in some instances—its own technology. Its reason for being (sometimes its sole *raison d'être*) is to provide tools for critical reasoning—and the hammer is rarely among them. Critical skills depend upon argumentation and the proper application of rules for "clear thinking." But logical tools have little to do with λόγος. To *serve* the academic community, philosophy need not involve thinking. To understand discourse, to read texts, to examine the unexamined limits of *what is* requires thinking, illuminating, grounding. Derrida has elaborated upon the groundedness of "basic" research. "Fundamental" research has foundations—even some which are below the ground. "Oriented" research is applied. When philosophy becomes "oriented" research, it reaches out beyond its ground. It thereby extends out beyond the comfortable zone. It performs its services, but it loses the comfort that comes from playing with its tools. Basic research in philosophy sticks close to the base. Theory, criticism, and history—the pillars of its *domus*—need to stand firmly on the ground. These pillars of philosophy need to speak from the ground, they need to shine in the light, they need to dispel the shadows—so that a peripatetic stroll through the στοά, around the quad, from one building to another, will be both pleasant and productive. Philosophical production demands that it be derived from a ground, that it speak from the ground, that it be a *Satz vom Grund*. Without the *Satz vom Grund*, theory, criticism, and history remain in the dark. The university is the "natural" place for the establishment of a ground for basic research in philosophy, for the university is purely a *cultural* institution.

The university's foundations are cultural. In Europe, they derive from the State. In America, they are more varied. Their funding (*les fonds*) may be church-related, privately endowed, or legislature-dependent. The success or failure of the American university may depend upon the virtues of its financial base. Whether its authority comes from church coffers (derived from one sect or another, one order or another), from granted land and legislative whim, or from successful alumni and friends, the achievement or failure of philosophy may remain substantially independent. Philosophy may be instituted by the

Church or it may be a component of a general education requirement. There may even be endowed chairs that support a philosophy program. But the practice of philosophy will generate itself in accordance with the power struggles at work among its practitioners. On occasion, its achievement may be related to the virtues of enrollment, the popularity of its subject-matter, and, albeit more rarely, the integrity of its thinking. But these concerns—financial and political—barely touch the principles upon which philosophy is based. From an administrative point of view, any philosophy will do. The content is irrelevant. Within the university it is important that there be philosophy, because philosophy has always been *in* the university. The normal review processes will be invoked to ensure "quality"—whatever the content, whatever the practice, whatever the production. The standards are those set by the reviewers and the reviewers are chosen in accordance with recommendations from those who seek to be confirmed—or by those who seek to disconfirm. But all this is like rafts tied to one another in the middle of the sea. There is no ground, no mooring, no principle of reason, no base from which to speak, no foundation upon which to build. How can philosophy build itself in the university when the building must be without ground? Philosophy has its reasons which reason does not know at all. If reason can't do the job, philosophy must appeal to its *own* reasons.

What must philosophy do when founded upon an abyss? In "What Are Poets For?" (*Wozu Dichter?*, 1946), Heidegger writes:

> Because of this default, there fails to appear for the world the ground that grounds it. The word for abyss—*Abgrund*— originally means the soil and ground toward which, because it is undermost, a thing tends downward. But in what follows we shall think of the *Ab-* as the complete absence of the ground. The ground is the soil in which to strike root and to stand. The age for which the ground fails to come, hangs in the abyss. Assuming that a turn still remains open for this destitute time at all, it can come some day only if the world turns about fundamentally—and that now means, unequivocally: if it turns away from the abyss. In the age of the world's night, the abyss of the world must be experienced and endured. But for this it is necessary that there be those who reach into the abyss.[8]

Heidegger is speaking (philosophically) about the poet who might reach into the abyss, who might call for the need to establish or reestablish a ground. But will it not, of necessity, be the philosopher who must reach into the abyss to find the ground? The sea is a kind of fathomless abyss. Derrida's reading of Cornell University as situated on the edge of an abyss (a gorge, whose grounding remains unthought) points to the place at which the ground (*Grund*) meets the abyss (*Ab-grund*). The abyss is away from the ground. The task of philosophy is to found the principle which founds the ground. Just as the university needs to be founded, erected, instituted on solid terrain, it needs to appeal to philosophy in order to found itself—to establish itself on a firm footing. It needs a theory of the university.

For the philosopher to reach into the abyss, into the *Ab-grund,* the philosopher must nevertheless stand somewhere. There must be some standpoint. A full-scale foundation is not necessarily called for, although foundations sometimes make philosophical activity possible. Just as the Renaissance goldsmith or the court painter drew strength from the support of a patron, so too the philosopher can often make good use of a grant or fellowship offered by a foundation to conduct the sort of research that will establish another ground outside of the abyss. But is it necessary for the philosopher to form a base from which to work? Must the philosopher speak or write from a ground? If not, what sort of standpoint is possible? Temporary supports like grants and fellowships only call attention to the need to speak from a ground (*Satz vom Grund*). They fill a gap, a leave, a sabbatical. But then they are a ground away from home. The *Stiftung* constitutes a building or erecting of an institute. What is instituted is not a full-scale institution, but rather a permanent impermanence, a granting agency that allows for the development of many different perspectives, different studies, different inquiries. The foundation as granting agency (private or public) establishes the principle of continual substitution of points of view. A new investigator will receive the grant the next year. However, the philosopher as investigator still requires a ground. Even the very principle of application requires that one apply *from an institution* and, once funds are granted, that they be placed in the institution's research foundation. It seems then that foundations are "all over the place." But like the sea for Coleridge's ancient mariner, there are foundations everywhere, but "not a drop to drink." Even when philosophers are able to benefit from foundations, there are few *real* foundations for thought. The philosopher seeks principles of reason just as the scientist seeks grants. And when *on* a foundation grant, the philosopher is still looking for foundations. And so the philosopher is always operating at the edge of an abyss—not quite able to fall in and not quite able to stand on solid ground.

The philosopher's responsibility is to survey the abyss, to seek after *terra firma,* and to operate in those places which are most the philosopher's own. These are the places in which the abyss looms ahead and the ground stretches out behind. The hope is for a bridge—*faire le pont*—it would clearly be the most effective way. Derrida says of the bridge at Cornell:

> A matter of life and death. The question arose . . . when the university administration proposed to erect protective railings on the Collegetown bridge and the Fall Creek suspension bridge to check thoughts of suicide inspired by the view of the gorge. "Barriers" was the term used; we could say "diaphragm," borrowing a word which in Greek literally means "partitioning fence." Beneath the bridges linking the university to its surroundings, connecting its inside to its outside, lies the abyss. In testimony before the Campus Council, one member of the faculty did not hesitate to express his opposition to the barriers, those diaphragmatic eyelids, on the grounds that blocking the view would mean, to use his words, "destroying the essence of the university." What did he mean? What *is* the essence of the university?[9]

The bridge is a linking function. It brings together elements that are different—at least spatially, if not in kind. But a bridge over an abyss is a dangerous going across. Nietzsche's "man" is a rope stretched between beast and overman. The bridge is not stable ground. It is not a place to stay. Rather a bridge is an *on the way (unterwegs)* to another place—a transport or a transition, an interruption of location, passing from an old place to a new one. Indeed the very metaphor for the metaphor of transportation is already a bridge between two places. The philosopher's responsibility is *to be a bridge,* to link ideas, concepts, points of view, practices, and so on, and to show how and that they are different. The philosopher as bridge is a passage, or link between differences. When it is most its *own,* philosophy practices differencing. The bridge crosses over the pit. It names difference; it even inscribes difference. At Stony Brook, when the main campus was being developed, there was a bridge, built from the union toward the library. But it was never completed. It passed over a road which leads in and out of the campus. At many universities, the union—in principle the gathering place for students and campus activities—is centrally located and sometimes even includes (as at Iowa and Indiana for instance) a hotel and many restaurants. The union is the center of life on campus. At Stony Brook, the bridge leading out from this center was commonly called "the bridge to nowhere." For a campus beginning its second decade in the early seventies, this appellation designated a sort of uncertainty that comes with a young but rapidly growing university. By the end of the seventies, a Fine Arts center had been constructed and the bridge was extended to connect up with both this new edifice and the library, thereby leading onto the main buildings of the campus. With its completion the "bridge to nowhere" became a "bridge to somewhere." Psychological services on campus were then called "the bridge to somewhere"—the bridge no longer simply traversed a road that passed in and out of campus. Now the bridge itself, along with the university and its students, was finally going somewhere. The bridge to somewhere was the hope that the university itself was not an abyss, but rather a groundwork for a determinate direction. The bridge became the symbol of a *vita nuova* for the university, a new vitality, a new reason to be. The bridge to somewhere was not a passage to anywhere in particular, but simply a bridge to somewhere.

Philosophy as a bridge does not necessarily bring the outside in relation to the inside and vice versa. By setting apart and marking off the ground from the abyss, philosophy may well establish its principle of reason at the limits or borders of the university—where the university defines itself as a system of disciplines and practices in relation to one another. The statement from the ground can at best be a statement in relation to the nonground. The philosopher's responsibility is to establish the bridge between them.

Some bridges identify *internal* relations (the Hertford College bridge at Oxford, the Memorial Bridge linking Harvard Square with the Business School in Cambridge, Massachusetts, the passageway between Lewis Tower and the Marquette Center at the Loyola Water Tower Campus). Others make the connection between the two different campuses of the same university—a bus links the old SUNY/Buffalo campus with the Amherst site, the University of California/Santa Cruz with UC/Berkeley, and the Chicago Loyola Water Tower campus with the Lake Shore location. Some bridges are tunnels like those that permeate the University of Alberta and Brown University. Some bridge-tunnels connect the outside with the inside, such as the one linking the British Rail station with the university at Sussex, ascending right up through the heart of the campus—resembling as well the ascent up the Faculty of Letters at the Université de Nice in Southern France. In such cases, the impression of steps leading upward is itself inspiring. The universities of San Diego, San Francisco, Duquesne, Montreal, Tübingen, and Perugia are even built on a hill. Those which aspire to the heights of church steeples (like Pittsburgh, Stanford, and Essex) offer no illusions about the expectations of their cathedrals of learning. But to turn bridges into towers is to entertain the often dreaded conflict in which the philosophy faculties must distinguish (and defend) themselves from aspiring theological (not to mention legal and medical) faculties. But what is philosophy's role in all this? Is there a bridge within philosophy, as philosophy might be the bridge within the university, and as the sciences might be a link with the world at large?

Philosophy has a responsibility to speak from the bridge. Philosophy has a responsibility to straddle the various intellectual concerns within the university *and* to provide an overarching view of them. Philosophy has a responsibility to provide a set of views on literature, the arts, science, the individual, and society. It must also devise its own methods, styles, and modes of self-expression, self-representation, self-articulation, and self-understanding. Philosophy has a responsibility. It is most its own (most *eigentlich*) when it both looks out and looks in on itself. It needs to look *out* onto the spectrum of disciplines and concerns that constitute our world. And it needs to look *in* on its own essence, meaning, structures, and activities. It needs to look into the λόγος of the universe and its own λόγος, the passion to know (*la volonté de savoir*) and its own reasons for being (*raison d'être*), the commitment to search out the nature of things and the obligation to "check itself out," to assess its own essence and practices. Philosophy's own indecidability (its deconstructive strategies and positions) is the bridge between its being and its objects, its passion and its reason, its place within the university and its view onto the world abroad. The textuality of philosophy is the elaboration of this indecidability: its texts are its views, and its views are its texts. Philosophy becomes itself when it is most something other. Its otherness is its textual identity.

The bar (*barre*) or barrier between what philosophy signifies and its signifying keeps it from becoming other than itself, keeps it from losing its identity, keeps it *for* itself. As philosophy establishes its own texts, it founds itself and its place within the university as that which is not itself, as that which is entirely other, as that which has no place in the leisurely, hallowed halls of the contemporary university. Philosophy has its reasons for being in the university and for justifying its degrees of otherness from itself—its Ph.D.'s and its D.Phil.'s—but it also has its reasons for looking in on the university, for its concerns about the well-being of the university with all its fields and domains. Philosophy has its reasons for wanting to know beyond, across, and between what it itself is and what it is not. Philosophy has its reasons for examining its own foundations as well as those of everything else. Philosophy has its reasons for being itself as well as being *other* than what it is. These are the reasons that make up the text of philosophy. They are the reasons that reason doesn't know about; *car la philosophie a ses raisons que la raison ne connaît point*—philosophy has its reasons which reason doesn't know at all.[10]

Notes

1. Jacques Derrida, "Mochlos ou le conflit des facultés," *Philosophie,* no. 2 (April 1984), p. 50.

2. Jacques Derrida, "The Principle of Reason: The University in the Eyes of Its Pupils," *Diacritics* 13, no. 3 (Fall 1983), p. 7.

3. Ibid., p. 19.

4. Jacques Derrida, "L'Age de Hegel," in *Qui a peur de la philosophie?* (Paris: Flammarion, 1977), p. 106.

5. Blaise Pascal, *Pensées* (bilingual ed.), trans. H. F. Stewart (New York: Modern Library, 1947), pp. 342–43.

6. Ibid., p. 343.

7. Jacques Derrida, *The Archaeology of the Frivolous: Reading Condillac,* trans. John P. Leavey, Jr. (Pittsburgh: Duquesne University Press, 1980).

8. Martin Heidegger, "What Are Poets for?" *Poetry, Language, Thought,* trans. Albert Hofstadter (New York: Harper & Row, 1971), p. 92.

9. Derrida, "The Principle of Reason," p. 6.

10. I am grateful to Jacques Derrida for reminding me, on the occasion of the presentation of this essay, that Heidegger, in *What Is Called Thinking?,* made the link between thinking (*Denken*) and thanking (*Danken*), that thinking involves "taking to heart." But if philosophy, here, takes the place of the heart, then the question, Derrida's question, as to the difference between thinking and philosophy becomes crucial. Making the bridge between philosophy and thinking, taking the place of the heart and taking to heart, inscribes the difference that might, one would hope, bring philosophy and thinking together.

Destinerrance: The Apotropocalyptics of Translation

3

John P. Leavey, Jr.

"*Tu as raison, nous sommes sans doute plusieurs.*"
Derrida, *La carte postale*[1]

I begin in epigraphy, since translation is always already, *toujours déjà*. My dispatch is divided, without destination and without message; rather I should say my dispatches, "for you are right in your reason, we are doubtless several." I begin then in *destinerrance,* not so much by choice, but in recognition of the chances of any writing. *Destinerrance* is itself several, the word that silently stitches together so many of the concerns of Derrida: his "readings" of Heidegger, Kant, Freud, Lacan, of the Apocalypse, Blanchot, and nuclear criticism. The plurality of *destinerrance* decimates, disseminates.

I want to begin by citing another translator—John Sallis—or at least his translation of an "essential" Heidegger text, "On the Essence of Truth" (1930). This text, Heidegger's text, serves, according to William Richardson in *Heidegger: Through Phenomenology to Thought,* as the first of three pivotal essays in Heidegger's "reversal," a turning from the focus on Dasein to Being as such.[2] This citation, which I extract from all its contexts, first within the essay itself and then from what might be called the Heideggerian corpus, is to serve in the manner of a plural epigraph. First, I want this citation to indicate a recognition of thanks to John Sallis for his work in translation, for his support of translations, and for many of mine in particular. I also want this extract to indicate the crossing of so many tongues, hands, and interests in this conference on "Deconstruction and Philosophy." In addition, this citation indicates a problematic I can only allude to, first by reason of my incompetence (my German is less than skilled), and second by reason of time: the place of Heidegger in *destinerrance.* Finally, by the chance of

translation, here in particular by the chance translation of *wendig* by
"adroitly" by Sallis, this epigraph indicates some of the manners, man-
nerisms, and hand play in "*Geschlecht* II," which as translator I have
already read and must provide an introduction to. I should say then
that, for Heidegger, errance seems to be the proper of man ("in the eksistence of his Dasein man [*der Mensch*] is *especially* subjected to the rule
of the mystery [*Geheimnisses*] and the oppression of errancy"[3]), like the
monstrous hand in its less than adroit warning and showing (also a
translation problem), in its apotropaic and apocalyptic signing.

The citation with which I will have begun is taken from section 7,
"Untruth as Errancy," which follows the section called "Untruth as
Concealing [*die Verbergung*]," both sections forming, according to
Richardson, "a unity." He continues, "The mystery (concealment of
concealment) is commonly forgotten, we are told, in the everyday state
of ek-sistent in-sistence. Now we examine in closer detail this forgotten-
ness of the mystery and give it a name all its own, sc. 'errance' (*die
Irre*)."[4] I would like the citation to be the pedal point that the trans-
lator's tattoo in its rhythm interrupts as a tonic or dominant possibility.
The citation:

> The insistent turning toward [*Zuwendung zum*] what is readily available
> and the ek-sistent turning away from [*Wegwendung vom*] the mystery
> [*Geheimnis*] belong together. They are one and the same. Yet turning
> toward and away from is based on a turning [*Wende*] to and fro proper
> [*eigentümlichen*] to Dasein. Man's flight from the mystery toward what is
> readily available, onward from one current thing to the next, passing the
> mystery by—this is *erring* [*das Irren*].
>
> Man errs. . . . Errance [*Die Irre*] is the free space for that turning
> [*Wende*] in which insistent ek-sistence *adroitly* [*wendig*] [my emphasis]
> forgets and mistakes itself constantly.[5]

Adroit is said of one "dexterous in the use of the hands" (Webster's). So
at least here we might read errance as that adroit handling of forgetting
and error in the movement of truth. That is to say, errance and the hand
are in the movement of truth. After thanking John Sallis for drawing
attention to a passage on the hand in the seminar on Parmenides, Derrida in "*Geschlecht* II" will say of Heidegger's hand in this seminar: "The
hand comes to its essence (*west*) only in the movement of truth, in the
double movement of what hides and causes to go out of its reserve
(*Verbergung/Entbergung*)" (p. 178 below). Heidegger uses much the
same words and manner concerning errance in the continuation of this
citation from "On the Essence of Truth":

The concealing [*Verbergung*] of the concealed being as a whole holds sway in that disclosure [*Entbergung*] of specific beings, which, as forgottenness of concealment, becomes errancy [*Irre*]. . . .

. . . In the simultaneity [*Im Zugleich*] of disclosure and concealing [*der Entbergung und Verbergung*] errancy holds sway. Errancy and the concealing of what is concealed [*Die Verbergung des Verborgenen*] belong to the primordial essence of truth [*das anfängliche Wesen der Wahrheit*] . . . the rule of the mystery [*des Geheimnisses*] in errancy.[6]

Here ends the epigraph I want to resound and interrupt with the task of the translator, the destinerrance in errance.

My task then, the task of the translator, is to translate three terms: destinerrance, apotropocalyptics, and translation. The third, translation, is itself, you are right, several, of several hands at least, the several dispatches (*envois*) of destinerrance and apotropocalyptics. But translation first.

In "The Task of the Translator," Benjamin, after speaking of the demand for literalness in translation, whose justification is right at hand (*auf der Hand*), states that this demand "must be understood in a more meaningful context [*aus triftigeren Zusammenhängen*],"[7] or should I translate, following the French translation, "on the basis of more pertinent correlations [*à partir de corrélations plus pertinentes*]."[8] I am tempted by a more impossible translation, by the word *triftig* itself, as a marine term, "adrift, drifting." The demand for the literal, for the word-for-word translation, "must be understood in a more drifting context, in a more adrift context." The double comparison that follows (*Wie . . . so, so . . . wie*) then is more adrift than might first seem evident. In the comparison Benjamin appeals to "a greater language [*einer größeren Sprache*]" as the vessel of fragments that makes it possible to recognize the idiomatic debris adrift as fragments and as fragments of that greater vessel of language that the hand must lovingly put together, since this dual comparison is adrift and waiting for the hand:

> Just as [*Wie*] the debris [*Scherben*] of a vessel which are to be glued together must follow one another in the smallest details, although they need not be like one another, so [*so*] a translation, instead of resembling the sense of the original [*anstatt dem Sinn des Originals sich ähnlich zu machen*], must lovingly and in detail incorporate in its own language [*in der eigenen Sprache*] the original's mode of meaning [*Art des Meinens*], in order then, just as [*wie*] debris [*Scherben*] are made recognizable as frag-

ments [*Bruchstück*] of a vessel, to make both the original and the translation recognizable as fragments of a greater language [*als Bruchstück einer
größeren Sprache*].[9]

For Benjamin the hand here is the "*intentio*" of the original, because the loving hand is what recognizes the fragments and at the same
time the vessel those fragments contain. But this hand must be, not
adroit, but adrift, lightly caressing, if we follow the first fragment of
Benjamin in recognizing the context of his layered comparison. Thus
translation becomes fragmented in its translation, insofar as Benjamin's
intentio, the guarantee of recognition, fragmentation, and the recon-
structing hand, remains clandestine in the fragments themselves. Translation is always already more adrift.
    Derrida also translates Benjamin. In "Des Tours de Babel" (a title
the translator of Derrida's text does not change in the translation from
French to English, since the title drifts in various ways: "*Des* means
'some'; but it also means 'of the,' 'from the,' or 'about the.' *Tours* could
be towers, twists, tricks, turns, or tropes, as in a 'turn' of phrase. Taken
together, *des* and *tours* have the same sound as *détour,* the word for
detour."[10]), Derrida sets Benjamin adrift in the Babel scene, which forbids language the possibility of being off-scene of languages. Translation is precisely what marks this detour of language in languages, this
drift and this refusal of the off-scene in the *intentio* of the "pure
language":

> What is intended, then, by this co-operation of languages and intentional
> *modes* is not transcendent to the language; it is not a reality which they
> would besiege from all sides, like a tower that they would try to sur-
> round. No, what they are aiming at intentionally, individually and
> jointly, in translation is the language itself as a Babelian event, a language
> that is not the universal language in the Leibnizian sense, a language
> which is not the natural language that each remains on its own either; it is
> the being-language of the language, tongue or language *as such,* that uni-
> ty without any self-identity, which makes for the fact that there are lan-
> guages and that they are languages.
>   These languages relate to one another in translation according to
> an unheard-of mode. They complete each other, says Benjamin.[11]

Translation, the handwork of Babel, is always already the adrift detour
refusing any off-scene to language as Babel, that is, to translation.

What of the apotropocalyptic? What does it translate in love? The term is the uneasy alliance of the apotropaic and the apocalyptic. As you know, the apotropaic is a means of defense that incorporates a small part of what it wants to defend against in order to defend against the whole from which the part is taken (to some extent, then, we might say Benjamin's *einer größeren Sprache* and the clandestine *intentio* are an apotropaic against destinerrance, translation against translation, Babel against Babel). Derrida examines the apotropaic first in a long note to "Hors livre" in *Dissemination* concerning the short essay of Freud on "Medusa's Head." Part of this note is taken up as a tattoo in the Hegel column of the dual-column text *Glas*.[12] Surrounding that tattoo or niche in the text is Derrida's elucidation of the logic of the apotropaic:

> the Jew effects (on) himself a simulacrum of castration. . . . By first incising [*entamant*] his glans, he defends himself in advance against the infinite threat, castrates in his turn the enemy, works out a kind of apotropaic without measure. . . .
>
> The logical paradox of apotropaics: to castrate oneself *already*, always already, in order to be able to castrate and repress the threat of castration, to renounce life and mastery in order to secure them; to put into play by ruse, simulacrum, and violence just what one wants to preserve; to lose in advance what one wants to erect; to suspend what one raises: *aufheben*. The relief [*la relève*] is indeed life's apotropaic essence, life as apotrope. Now being is life, being is *Aufhebung*. The Medusa provides for no off-scene [*hors-scène*].[13]

In the tattoo, Derrida recites Freud's examples of the apotropaic: Medusa's head, castrated, covered with snakes, and her wide-open mouth turn the spectator to stone, reassure him that he is not castrated, that he has a penis in becoming stone (Medusa's head as the display of the female genitals); the display of the penis or its stand-ins intimidates by its possession: I have a penis. Display of the genitals in singularity or excess is apotropaic. *And* apocalyptic: Ἀποκαλύπτω, I disclose, I uncover, I unveil, I reveal the thing that can be a part of the body, the head or the eyes, a secret part, the sex or whatever might be hidden, a secret thing, the thing to be dissembled, a thing that is neither shown nor said, signified perhaps but that cannot or *must* not first be delivered up to self-evidence."[14]

But the apocalyptic is not simply the disclosure of the genitals. In an analysis of Kant's "Of an Overlordly Tone Recently Adopted in Philosophy," John's Apocalypse, and certain of his own texts in a *galatic* (revelatory) display,[15] Derrida isolates the apocalyptic as "a transcendental condition of all discourse, of all experience even, of every mark or every trace":

> One does not know (for it is no longer of the order of knowing) to whom the apocalyptic dispatch [*envoi*] returns; it leaps [*saute*] from one place of emission to the other (and a place is always determined *starting from* the presumed emission); it goes from one destination, one name, and one tone to the other; it always refers to [*renvoie à*] the name and to the tone of the other that is there but as having been there and before yet coming, no longer being or not yet there in the present of the *récit*.
>
> And there is no certainty that man is the exchange of these telephone lines or the terminal of this endless computer. No longer is one very sure who loans his voice and his tone to the other in the Apocalypse; no longer is one very sure who addresses what to whom. But by a catastrophic overturning here more necessary than ever, one can just as well think this: as soon as one no longer knows who speaks or who writes, the text becomes apocalyptic. And if the dispatches [*envois*] always refer to other dispatches without decidable destination, the destination remaining to come, then isn't this completely angelic structure, that of the Johannine apocalypse, isn't it the structure of every scene of writing in general?[16]

In other words, the apocalyptic provides for no off-scene. The catastrophic overturning of the apocalypse then is, Derrida continues, the apocalypse of the apocalypse, "the self-presentation of the apocalyptic structure of language, of writing, of the experience of presence, in other words of the text or of the mark in general: *that is, of the divisible dispatch for which there is no self-presentation nor assured destination,*"[17] the apocalyptic *destinerrance*.[18]

So the apotropocalyptic allies (the alliance of the wedding band, the *hymen*) the apotropaic warding (off) and the apocalyptic (dis)-closure. There is no off-scene apotropocalyptic. For translation just enough must be taken and preserved in order to ward off the charge of noncorrelation, that is, this text here, the translation, does not translate that text there, the original; in order to ward off the hand reaching for the original without keeping the translation in hand. But the hand always reaches, and the translation always correlates in the reach that keeps without keeping. Apotropocalyptic translates apotropaics and apocalyptics always already from no off-scene. Yet so far, this could be said to apply "to originals only," to the original "work of art," not the critical or philosophical essay, in which sense would be transmitted. But the more limiting case for us would be the translation of a translation. What about translations of translations of the original (art work)? Benjamin excludes them: "Translations, on the other hand, prove to be untranslatable not because of the weight, but because of the greater fleetingness [*großen Flüchtigkeit*], with which sense attaches to them."[19] But the apotropaic is also the apocalyptic. The warding off discloses the fleetingness of the original, or the original as the translation of translation, "the divisible dispatch" without destination. According to Mallarmé's *sans* copula syntax, apotropocalyptics, apocalypse without apocalypse, destinerrance.

Destinerrance, the last and the first term to be translated. As you have already surmised, destinerrance is concerned with the divisible dispatch of the apocalypse to be translated, with the apocalypse without assured destination, with the errance of destination, in other words, with the apocalypse without apocalypse, "without truth, without revelation, *dispatches* [des envois] . . . [with] addresses without message and without destination, without sender or decidable addressee, without last judgment."[20] Derrida develops this apocalypse without apocalypse in the reading of the "Come" in John's Apocalypse and Heidegger's call beyond being in "Of an Apocalyptic Tone," and also in an essay on "nuclear criticism" titled "No Apocalypse, Not Now." But destinerrance also occurs in the reading of "Epicurean Stereophonies" in "My Chances / *Mes Chances*" and is suggested but not named in "Living On / Border Lines." In "My Chances" it is the iterability of the mark:

> This iterability is thus that which allows a mark to be used more than once. It is more than one. It multiplies and divides itself internally. This imprints the capacity for diversion within its very movement. In the destination (*Bestimmung*) there is thus a principle of indetermination, chance, luck, or of destinerring. There is no assured destination precisely because of the mark and the proper name; in other words, because of this insignificance.[21]

He adds in a discussion published in *Affranchissement*, the colloquium on his *La carte postale*: "Destinerrance, let's say, or adestination, these are not opposed to destination; the relation is otherwise."[22]

How then write of this relation? In "No Apocalypse, Not Now," Derrida argues against assimilating this relation to undecidable moments in a calculable decision:

> I have often tried, elsewhere, to stress the divisibility and the irreducible dissemination *of* the *envois* (sendings, dispatches), of the acts of sending.

Even what I have called "destinerrance" no longer gives us the assurance of *a* sending of being, of *a* recovery of the sending of being. If the ontico-ontological difference ensures the gathering-up of that sending (*le rassemblement de cet envoi*), the dissemination and the destinerrance I am talking about go so far as to suspend the ontico-ontological difference itself. The dissemination epochalizes the difference in its turn. Of this movement I can only indicate the path. The destinerrance of the *envois* (sendings, missives, so to speak) is connected with a structure in which randomness and incalculability are essential. I am not speaking here of factors of undecidability or incalculability that function as reservations in a calculable decision. I am not speaking of the margin of indeterminacy that is still homogeneous to the order of the decidable and the calculable. . . . it is a question here of an aleatory element that appears in a heterogeneous relation to every possible calculation and every possible decision. . . . the destinerrance of the sendings is precisely what both divides and repeats the first time and the last time alike.[23]

So destinerrance translates the apotropocalyptic, divides and repeats the original apocalypse and apotropaic, re-marks sendings as sendings without destination or message. Translation warrants its own translation and "escape[s] all control, all reassimilation or self-regulation"[24] of any original, which is original only in its division and repetition, allows for no off-scene, the Babel-scene.

The drone of Heidegger on the essence of truth continues, but not now. Destinerrance, the "we are no doubt several," does not play the passacaglia to that drone or to a more elaborate ostinato. Nor is it the *chute* to that drone, *chute* being here, uncontrollably, not the fall of *clinamen* or the case, not the end of a lecture or paragraph, like *envoi,* although the end is near, but the grace note to a fundamental tone. Destinerrance is not even the noise that punctuates the drone in the clacking of the organ, in the hand and the foot playing. Nor is it the silence that the drone and the clacking pierce. Destinerrance—the aleatory division that droning and clacking attempt to translate, apotropize, apocalypticize now in sound, now in language, now in the signature. I sign in my own manner, in my own hand, in my own hands, in an epigraphy, in a series of signatures to the destinerrance of the signature, as an envoy of translation:

from "Télépathie":

tempus enim propre est.[25]

from *La carte postale* (not yet the end, but very near):

23 August 1979. . . . That dossier between two bodies, I mean this, is a
marriage contract. I am always thinking of those contracts that are signed
by just one alone—they are far from being without value, on the contrary. And even when both sign, it is two times by one alone"[26]

from "No Apocalypse, Not Now" (this is the end):

Unless it is the other way around: God and the sons of Shem ["you
know that Shem means 'name' and that they bore the name 'name'"]
having understood that a name wasn't worth it—and this would be absolute knowledge—they preferred to spend a little more time together, the
time of a long colloquy with warriors in love with life, busy writing in all
languages in order to make the conversation last, even if they didn't understand each other too well. One day, a man came, he sent messages to
the seven churches and they called that the Apocalypse. The man had
received the order, "What you see, write in a book and send to the seven
churches." When the man turned around to see what voice was giving
him this order, he saw in the middle of seven golden candlesticks, with
seven stars in his hand, someone from whose mouth "a sharp double-
bladed sword" was emerging, and who told him, among other things: "I
am the first and the last." The name of the man to whom he was speaking, the one who was appointed to send messages, to deliver the seven
messages, was John.[27]

Notes

1. Jacques Derrida, *La carte postale: de Socrate à Freud et au-delà* (Paris: Flammarion, 1980), p. 10. All translations are my own or, if reference is given to an English
translation, modified as desired.

2. William Richardson, *Heidegger: Through Phenomenology to Thought* (The
Hague: Nijhoff, 1967), p. 207. The other two essays are "The Self-Assertion of the
German University" (a "formal address" of May 1933 that "has achieved a renown
beyond its philosophical deserts" [p. 255]) and *An Introduction to Metaphysics* (the
"lecture course of 1935" in which "the problem of thought is made thematic for the
first time" [p. 259]).

3. Martin Heidegger, "On the Essence of Truth," trans. John Sallis, in *Basic
Writings: From "Being and Time" (1927) to "The Task of Thinking" (1964)*, ed. David
Farrell Krell (New York: Harper, 1977), p. 136; "Vom Wesen der Wahrheit," in
Wegmarken (Frankfurt am Main: Klostermann, 1967), p. 195.

4. Richardson, *Heidegger*, p. 223.

5. "On the Essence of Truth," pp. 135–36; "Vom Wesen der Wahrheit," pp.
193–94.

6. "On the Essence of Truth," pp. 136–37; "Vom Wesen der Wahrheit," pp.
194–95.

7. Walter Benjamin, "The Task of the Translator," trans. Harry Zohn, in *Illuminations*, ed. Hannah Arendt (New York: Schocken Books, 1969), p. 78; "Die

Aufgabe des Übersetzers," *Illuminationen: Ausgewählte Schriften* (Frankfurt am Main: Suhrkampf, 1980), p. 59.

8. Walter Benjamin, "La tâche du traducteur," *Œuvres*, vol. 1, *Mythe et violence*, trans. Maurice de Gandillac (Paris: Denoël, 1971), p. 271.

9. *Illuminations*, p. 78; *Illuminationen*, p. 59.

10. Jacques Derrida, "Des Tours de Babel," trans. Joseph F. Graham, in *Difference in Translation*, ed. Joseph F. Graham (Ithaca: Cornell University Press, 1985), p. 206 (translator's note).

11. Ibid., p. 201.

12. The note taken up in part and that also adds a phrase reads: " 'But *what is the stone, the stoniness of the stone? Stone is the phallus. Is that any answer? Is that saying anything if the phallus is in fact the thing's concealing, its stealing? And what if, occupying no center, having no natural place, following *no path of its own*, the phallus has no signification, eludes every sublimating relief (*Aufhebung*), extracts the very movement of signification, the signifier/signified relation, from all *Aufhebung*, in one direction or the other, both types coming down ultimately to the same? And what if the 'assumption' or denial of castration should also, strangely enough, come down to the same, as one can *affirm*? In that case, apotropaics would always have more than one surprise up its sleeve. In this connection, it would be apropos to slate for a rereading Freud and the scene of writing, the march that opens and closes it, the signification of the phallus, the short analysis of *Das Medusenhaupt* . . . and the remain(s) [*reste*]. In lapidary fashion, one could lay out the infinitely opened and turned-back chain of these equivalents: stone-falls (to the tomb)—erect—stiff—dead, etc. Dissemination will always have threatened signification there.' " In Jacques Derrida, *Glas* (Paris: Galilée, 1974), pp. 55ai–56ai, citing *La dissémination* (Paris: Seuil, 1972), pp. 47n–48n; *Glas*, trans. John P. Leavey, Jr., and Richard Rand (Lincoln: University of Nebraska Press, 1986), 45ai–47ai, citing *Dissemination*, trans. Barbara Johnson (Chicago: University of Chicago Press, 1981), pp. 40n–41n.

13. *Glas*, pp. 55a–56a; *Glas*, p. 46a. The translation of *Aufhebung* by *la relève* inscribes the apotropaic as a translation problem. Any translation of *Aufhebung* also completes it, sets this speculative term babbling. Like all conscientious translators, Emmanuel Martineau attempts to anchor this drifting (he rejects *relever* and *sursumer*, proposed respectively by Derrida and Gauthier, for translating *aufheben* and uses *assumer*). See his "Avertissement du traducteur" in Martin Heidegger, *La "Phénoménologie de l'esprit" de Hegel* (Paris: Gallimard, 1984), pp. 13–23.

14. Jacques Derrida, "Of an Apocalyptic Tone Recently Adopted in Philosophy," trans. John P. Leavey, Jr., *Oxford Literary Review* 6, no. 2 (1984): 4.

15. Ibid., p. 3: "In Greek, *apokalupsis* would translate words derived from the Hebrew verb *gala*." And further on, p. 30: "Several times I have been asked (and that is why I shall allow myself a brief galatic ostentation of certain of my writings) why (with a view to what, to what ends, and so on) I had or had *taken on* an apocalyptic tone and put forward apocalyptic themes."

16. Ibid., p. 27.

17. Ibid., pp. 27–28.

18. Ibid., p. 31: ". . . the holocaustic 'burning,' and all the phenomena of *Verstimmung*, of change of tone, of mixing genres, of *destinerrance*, if I can say that, or of *clandestination*, so many signs of more or less bastard apocalyptic filiation."

19. *Illuminations*, p. 81; *Illuminationen*, p. 61.

20. "Of an Apocalyptic Tone," p. 34. Derrida is working here with Blanchot's *sans*, which he explains in a number of texts, for example in "Living On / Border Lines,"

trans. James Hulbert, in Bloom et al., *Deconstruction and Criticism* (New York: Seabury, 1979), pp. 105–6: ". . . this '-less' [*sans,* without] syntax . . . in Blanchot's text so often comes to neutralize (without positing, without negating) a word, a concept, a term (*x*-less *x*): '-less' or 'without' without privation or negativity or lack ('without' without *without, less*-less '-less' [sans *sans "sans"*]), the necessity of which I have attempted to analyze in 'Le "sans" de la coupure pure' and 'Pas.' "

    21. Trans. Irene Harvey and Avital Ronell, in *Taking Chances: Derrida, Psychoanalysis, and Literature,* ed. Joseph H. Smith and William Kerrigan (Baltimore: Johns Hopkins University Press, 1984), p. 16.

    22. Ed. René Major (Paris: Confrontation, 1982), p. 111.

    23. Trans. Catherine Porter and Philip Lewis, *Diacritics* 14, no. 2 (1984):29–30.

    24. Ibid., p. 29.

    25. Jacques Derrida, *Confrontation* 10 (1983): 230.

    26. Pp. 267–68.

    27. P. 31.

Deconstruction and the History of Metaphysics

2

In Stalling Metaphysics: At the Threshold

4

Ruben Berezdivin

Even when he takes that *pas,* step/stop, Pierrot remains, before the doors, the "solitary captive of the threshold."

> Derrida, *Dissemination*

. . . while the daughters of the Sun, hasting to convey me to the light, threw back the veils from off their faces, and left the abode of Night. There are the gates of the ways of Night and Day, fitted above with a lintel and below with a threshold of stone . . . shut by mighty doors, and avenging Dike controls the double bolts.

> Parmenides, *Aletheia*

In the change of the essence of truth from ἀλήθεια to Roman *veritas* . . . truth as certainty changes together with the essence and kind of opposition between truth and untruth. Here there is formed and congealed the self-evident opinion that falsehood is the unique opposite of truth. The *Ausschlag* in this, the essential change of truth, as it dominates the West through the centuries, proffers the *Ereignis* of the *Umschlag* of the essence of truth from Greek ψεῦδος to Roman *falsum.* This *Umschlag* is the presupposition for the modern stamp of the essence of falsehood.

> Heidegger, *Parmenides*[1]

At the Threshold of Metaphysics: Falsehood's Setting

The horizon for the present paper is the Heideggerian reading of the history of metaphysics, if only because that reading redirected philosophical attention to metaphysics as a delimitable epoch with beginning and conclusion. The focus, however, will be upon the setting, place or

placing, position of Plato within metaphysics. A "critical" encounter
with Plato *today* demands taking the Heideggerian reading into account
and summing up its contentions.

In particular, placing Plato as the inaugurator of metaphysics will
be here under interrogation. This will be carried out by examining the
nature of ψεῦδος, deception—Heidegger translates *Täuschung*—or
falsehood, as the case (of translation) may be, within Platonic philosophy, in order to determine to what extent it heralds the transformation
of truth constituting the declining of *Ereignis* for Heidegger. It will
turn out that the issue of the ψεῦδος will entail that of images, and
supplementarily the issuance of theses or hypotheses, positions.

Finally, the "fact" that Plato wrote fictional dialogues, pseudo-
dialogues, will throw some light on what is at stake here, providing the
space for discussing how deconstruction fits in with Plato.

The False Start

In *Metaphysics* Eta 2, entitled by a recent translator "false start on the
analysis" (of οὐσία), a section goes: "A threshold *is*, in that it lies *thus*,
and its being means its lying thus" (1042*b*). The "example" of the
threshold, which the translator suggests is immediately "disavowed"
(title of section 4 of chapter), is brought in to explain the definition of
positionality.[2] A threshold is something which must be pointed to and
out, for its being depends on the arrangement of its constitutive parts as
differentially articulated in relation to a given place, τόπος. Metaphysics, constituted by the separation of a τόπος νοητός of ideal being
from the sensible things and their nonproblematic place, as opened up
by the Χωρισμός, sets up a gap between sensible and intelligible while
postulating truth as the permanence of the ideal, the standard against
which the sensible must be judged, if, in order to be at all, it must share
in the ideal (compare *Timaeus*). Metaphysics comes into place when the
Idea(l)s are posited or postulated, thesis/hypothesis, to be the entities
genuinely designated by dialogue in its search for what things are:

> Because our present λόγος concerns the beautiful itself and the good
> itself . . . no less than the equal; indeed, it is concerned with everything
> on which we set this seal, what it is [αὐτὸ ὃ ἔστι], in the questions we ask
> and the answers we give (*Phaedo* 75*c–d*).

These kernels of sense, which direct dialogue and provide it with
its ultimate purpose, are necessarily postulated by dialogue as a ὑπό-
θεσις allowing dialogue to set out on its way, to follow out its impulse

(ὁρμή: see *Phaedo* 101*d–e*) until it exhausts its explanatory capacity. Dialogue, constituting the dimension of quest(ion)ing after truth, is constrained and contracted, to postulate the essentially permanent being of things as ideal entities beyond what is ordinarily perceived through the senses, in a place beyond. Metaphysics in its Platonic instance consists of the posing of the Idea(l)s instituting the gap between things and their being-ness. Metaphysics is set in place, on its way, by means of a posing in which it constitutes its abiding position as enquiry after and quest for the permanent.

The beginning, ἀρχή, of metaphysics, its ruling principle, stems from that setting which opens up the beyond which allows judging things in regard to their ideality. This distinctive separation is the Platonic ontological difference, installed in the gesture of a postulation within a dialogical requirement presupposed by the possibility of knowledge that is to make sense. That postulation invokes a teleology as to what truth would, in the long run, be found to have been the case, as to what always lies revealed ahead of the present turn of the path of searching. Not only is the placing of metaphysics set into place by a postulation of the ideal as Χωρισμός, separate and allowing for place, it also entails a certain co-positing of the origin in place.

The Ψεῦδος as Deception: Falsehood

At the threshold of meta-physics, at the crossroads of a before and an after, just when about to take the plunge ahead, stalling: Plato, writer and thinker, between writing and thinking. Standing at the start, a place to some degree shared with Aristotle, he shares the Greek background of truth as ἀλήθεια, being as οὐσία as well, but he is already in the process of setting up an interpretation of truth that will predispose it for Roman reappropriation, for conversion into imperial rectitude and justice. Plato, no sooner has he ushered in metaphysics as the gap, than he sends it toward its degeneration, fall, decline, failure: *fallere* or *falsum*.

That event must be read off from what occupies the place of the false within his discourse: not the original λήθη, but ψεῦδος or ἀπάτη. The decline of truth from Greece to Rome can best be foreseen in the wavering of what is counter-essential to truth, falsehood, insofar as its position prepares the consignment of truth within Logos, the encrypting of truth within logic. That takes place concurrently with the assignation of falsehood to λόγος and assertive language. Λόγος as repository of truth *and* falsehood: this is initiated in Plato's thought, concurrently with the start of metaphysics. Metaphysics, from its inception, leans toward its decline, tends to fallibility, begins in decline, as decline. A pseudo-beginning, the stalling of the startled start.

At the threshold of the erection of metaphysics declining, between the arch-origin or *Anfang* and the pseudo-origin or *Beginn,* a certain postulate, pose, position. Hypothesis. This thesis exposes the space of dialogue to the unconcealed by directing a search to what reveals itself as such in its truth. Truth provides the expanse for dialogue, opening it to its sense and direction, sense which is preternaturally, from the first, threatened by deception.

We will translate ψεῦδος as deception instead of as falsehood. Falsehood as the incorrectness of a pro-position can befall λόγος when deceptive, but this reinforces the distinction. Deception distorts (*entstellt*) and displaces the very manifestation of the truth of things by interposing semblance and leading astray, and (we shall see) it is intimately linked with images and their hypnotic wizardry. A few selections from Plato will make this clearer.

The *Theaetetus* suggests the essential perplexity about deception:

Socrates:	Is it still worth while to resume once more about δόξα. . . ?
Theaetetus:	What sort of thing are you talking about?
Socrates:	It's something that in a sense disquiets me now and often at different times has done so, so as to have got me into a great deal of perplexity before myself and before everyone else, when I am unable to say what this affection we have is, and in what manner it comes into being in us.
Theaetetus:	What sort of thing, exactly?
Socrates:	That anyone opines [δοξάζειν] deceptively (187c–d).

The context here is, as always in Plato, essential: right after the first version of what knowledge is, that it is αἴσθησις, has been refuted, following the refutation of the Protagorean and Heraclitean versions of knowledge implying the impossibility of any deception at all. The middle of the dialogue attempts to come to grips with the problem of deception (ψεῦδος), eventually admitting failure. The issue had been dealt with at a different level in the *Republic:*

Socrates:	. . . don't you know . . . that to deceive and to be deceived in the soul about beings, and to be unlearned, and have and hold deception there is what everyone would least of all desire? . . . that what I just talked about would most correctly be called truly deception, the ignorance in the soul of the man who is being deceived? For

> deception in λόγοι is a sort of imitation of that affection
> in the soul, a phantom that comes into being after it, and
> is not quite unadulterated deception (382a–b).

Here, deception is distinguished from falsehood as a quality of a deceptive λόγος, and is described rather, "truly," as what the soul experiences when misled, the state of being of the soul when it is affected by appearances that mislead. Such deception involves being led astray or beguiled, bewitched, and attaches itself to the very appearances as such, their semblance or seeming, that in appearances that might be subtracted from them without reducing their being, their truth or self-manifestation:

> . . . that pleasure and pain both admit of the more and less.

> . . . but what contrivance is there to judge correctly? What and How?—
> . . . whether what our judging wishes in those cases then might not be
> to diagnose for each which in relation to one another is greater or lesser,
> or more intense, to diagnose pain in relation to pleasure or pain with pain
> or pleasure with pleasure?

> —Well then, in the case of sight, to see from near or afar obscures
> [ἀφανίζει] the true size and renders our deemings deceptive. Doesn't the
> same happen with pains and pleasures?

> — . . . But now, due to their being contemplated from near or far, each
> alternatingly, and since they are set down simultaneously by one another,
> the pleasures appear greater and more intense in relation to the pains, and
> contrariwise.

> —Necessarily that happens in such a case because of that.—Then they
> both appear greater than their *ousia* and lesser. If you were to *cut out from
> each their appearance but not their being,* you couldn't say the appearance is
> correct, nor would you dare say that the part of pleasure or pain coming
> into being upon this is either correct or true (*Philebus* 41d–42c, my
> emphasis).

This extended passage shows two things: that the issue of pleasure/pain entails that of relativity and contrast, and hence through the contrast (together with the indeterminacy of the more/less) the possibility of deceptive judgment; and that the semblance generated by the contrast of what is indeterminate by nature intrudes coincidentally super-imprinted on the appearances which would have manifested the thing as it was, hence that semblance is a sort of epi-phenomenon which thought must discount or cut away from the appearances in order to render them as they are (in their true manifestation). The true number measuring the appearing phenomena "disappears" (ἀφανίζει, 42*a*), sets like a declining sun beyond the visible horizon, whenever perspective enters into the picture as essential to judgment, whenever the indeterminacy proper to perspective distorts the vision of theory: and thereby deception intrudes upon the scene, sets up a stage in which what is manifested is concealed in its very appearing, deluding the viewer, himself represented upon the scene:

> . . . all our lives through we are always filled with hopes [ἐλπίς]? . . . what we call hopes are λόγοι made internally, aren't they? . . . And especially painted phantasms [φαντάσματα]; so that often a man appears to himself getting a vast sum of gold, and numberless pleasures in consequence; *and inscribed in the appearance is himself* [ἐνεζωγραφημένον] hugging himself with delight (*Philebus* 39*e*–40*a*).

The encounter with the expectation of pleasure leads to phantasy, which inscribes the desire within a delusive appearance and renders the desirer of delight into a state akin to the bewitched:

> Don't you believe that human beings are unwillingly deprived of good things? . . . or isn't being deceived about the truth bad? . . . don't they suffer this by being robbed, bewitched by wizards, or forced? . . . and further, the bewitched, too . . . are those who change their opinions either because charmed by pleasure or terrified by fear. . . . Yes, he said, that's because everything that deceives seems to bewitch (*Republic* 412*e*–413*e*).

> Therefore, it is not so; but when repose is next to the painful it looks pleasant, and next to the pleasant painful; and there is nothing sound in these appearances . . . only a certain wizardry (584*a*).

The deception due to appearance leads to magical fascination which leads astray, as the *Sophist* intimates:

> To opine and say what is not, this surely is the deception generated by thought and Logos . . . but where there is deception, there one is led

astray [ἀπάτη] . . . and if one is led astray, it is necessary that everything be full of images, semblances, and appearances (261c).

Deception, ψεῦδος, here linked with that intertwining or weave of thought and logos with nonbeing, leads astray, off the track; it deflects the straight shot of thought causing indecision and failure, ἁμαρτία, and may culminate in tragic ἄτη, delusive fate. To be deceived, we suggest, is to fall under the sway of the apparent in the appearing being, to fall in for the generic relativity of the indeterminate, to be affected by the other or the other of the other, by what is necessarily other-than and hence contextual. However, only to the extent that deception is possible can the true, trustworthy logos be safeguarded against sophistry and its ἀντιλογική disputing both truth and deception simultaneously, a dispute which starts from Logos and seeks to refute anti-logistics, the preliminary common essence of the sophist, just when the *Sophist* is about to veer into the ontological section momentarily paralyzed by the puzzle of saying what is not, and hence unable to start, startled, on the definition of images and deception (*Soph.* 232E). The sophists belong to the class of imitators and know-alls and wizards of deception, skilled in the conjuring of illusive scenes, a trick they perform by means of Logos, thus unsettling the terrain in which philosophy as dialogical search for the ideal seeks to establish itself.

The possibility of images, their being able to be, coincides with the scattering of the rigid version of Parmenidean being, permeating the tissue or web of being. Such dissemination, dispersal of being (διεσπαρμένον in the *Sophist* [260B], a scattering through Parmenides thus decapitated) as otherness, allows not only for the truth of Logos but inevitably also for the complication of semblance, appearance, deception and nonbeing as well. Images, both natural and artificial, are required within the web of being by the very conditions allowing the distinction of a true from a false judgment, a thought or simply a being-affected by the truth.

The prototypically philosophical gesture by which the being of λόγος is saved in the συμπλοκή of being the same and the other generates not only truth but multiplicity, hierarchy, and order, thus requiring disorder as presupposition. If truth is to be henceforth guarded against pseudo-truth and a critical distinction is to be made, it must comprehend deception by allowing it a *marginal* place within the hierarchy, a sort of wild reserve in which it may be cautiously bound off, supervised.

Two tentative suggestions emerge from the above dis-course.

First, the hermeneutic reconstruction of genuine Platonism must traverse the Heideggerian interpretation of the ψεῦδος as deceptive appearance, ontological error and not epistemological error, deception declining towards falsehood, always already falling towards its own failure, a transition whose consummation heralds the advent of genuine λήθη, a true incipient latency of being becoming destined.

Second, that the location of the sophistry of deception, unachievable and interminable for analysis, leaves a certain margin for the deceptive play of images within the text of philosophy in the process or trial of inaugurating metaphysics, a sort of evil augury, and that metaphysics *as such* must, on pain of stalling, allow for this play-room while attempting to fence it in and enclose it by corralling it in a mesh or net, as the *Sophist* suggests. The place of deception as pseudo-falsehood is (remains) indeterminate.

Deception would then lie at the threshold of the start of metaphysics, at the instant when, startled by the inaugural incipience of the latent, it comes to stall and thereby becomes installed, set up, constituted in its very hesitance. Deception would be what befalls the soul swayed by appearances; its only antidote would be the skill of measurement, logistics. Whoever plays upon the apparent and contrives through it delusion, is an imitator and wizard, affecting that in the soul subject to the hypnosis of appearances and their semblance, exposed to appearances as such: what, in the discourse on the divided line, is called εἰκασία, which (following Blanchot) I translate as *fascination*. The sophist, the arch-deceiver, fascinates, insofar as he is himself fascinated by images, by the semblance or phantomatic duplicity of appearances. That fascination leads astray from dialogic, ideal truth, and hence from virtue and philosophy, away into the pathless errant course of unceasing recurrent power. What fascinates sophistry is the very nonbeing of the image, its peculiar wavering between appearing and not being, its constantly shifting perspectival illusionism, generating the alternation of pleasure and pain, allowing for the deception of fantasy as the inscription in the soul of the hope for boundless pleasures within the fascinating mirror-image of what is boundlessly desired.

The whole set (which allows of additions, of course) of motifs herein examined—appareance/truth, semblance, image, phantom, imitation or copy, deception, wizadry, pleasure/pain—all go together to make up what the "esoteric" Plato called Two, one of the two primary principles or beginnings postulated by Plato along with the One and its cohort of Ideas, out of which the harmony of the Cosmos is made, the Two being the indeterminate power of duplication, mimicry, splitting images, doubleness, a set without apparent hold or position as such.

Dreaming, Duplicity, Fiction: Stalling

The One and the Two, then, represent ultimate ἀρχαί in Platonic metaphysics. The Two can only be partially bounded by the One, otherwise there would be no multiplicity and manifoldness of beings and appearances and, therefore, no retrospectively postulated truth. The Two is not a number as indeterminate dyad, Aristotle makes clear, but becomes 2 when delimited by the One, which itself becomes 1 through that bounding. This place-less Two, ἄ-τοπος, generates the remainder of the numbers through its power of duplicating and splitting, though the precise unfolding of the number series remains unclear from the doxographic accounts. The Two was—that is agreed by all—the generative principle of beings, a sort of interstitial void in analogy with the Pythagorean κενόν:

> The Pythagoreans, too, claimed the void to be, and that from the boundless Pneuma itself the void enters into the heavens itself as if it were inhaled, demarcating the natures of things, being a sort of separating and distinguishing gap [κενοῦ] among things in series [τὸν ἐφεξῆς]; and this happens primarily among numbers, for indeed the gap/void demarcates their nature (Aristotle, *Physics* Delta 6).[3]

The similarity between that voiding gap and the other of being should not escape notice: the Two wavers between an indeterminate combination and the number 2, which it is not but which, through its capacity for demarcation and distinction, differentiality, it generates, along with the number series. Deception and images, introduced along with this primordial duplicity, inhaled by the heavens from the "boundless" (ἄπειρον), allow for the original One-ness to be imaged forth, reproduced, multi-plied, disseminated, whence the place-less (dis)location of the Other in the gap of the χωρισμός, between the ideal and the things which the ideals haunt, akin to that χῶρα which in the *Timaeus* is said to nurse and generate everything that comes into being.

As a ruling principle in the κόσμος the Two is not altogether controlled by the One and its ideality; its two-folded-ness is needed (τὸ χρέον, *es braucht*) in order that the ab-original One may be split open and apart, so that beings may scatter far and wide throughout the whole order of things, so that beings may wander astray, strayed and inevitably straying, because of the scattering power of that self-replicating and other-duplicating Two, the other of being, other than itself, not-self-same. The Two as other is the articulate jointure separating the aesthetic from the noetic, which as the *tertium non datur* is given as *not* being.

The strange thing is that to displace duality as requiring images is to allow the multiplicity of beings to emerge into the exposure of an expanse of disclosure, openness; it is to allow and grant room for existence, standing-out from full concealment, being. The place of the image which originates deception as indeterminate dyad or duality remains undecided between 1 and 2, neither original nor mere copy because original copy or copying originality, a twofold implicated in all generation and change, constantly reduplicating. Hence, if the postulation opening up the metaphysical articulation as gap sets it underway only by interweaving ideality with sameness and otherness, it must have spacing, void, difference as actively generating separation, differance, taking place as the dual displacing, disposition, of deceptive imaging, implacable and irreversible when beings are to be. The space, gap, or void of the image allows for the commencement of things, their always already having begun. But it itself cannot be determinately located; it disposes of all settings, unsettling any thesis seeking to set things ultimately in order as a whole, generating unfinalizable dis-course.

Up to a point, of(f) course. The weave of dissemination is, within the instance of truth and its regime of philosophic teleology, supervised and meant to serve the dialogical search for ultimates, at least within the threshold of metaphysics as Platonic. This threshold turns or hinges upon the articulation of duplicity, both inside and out, neither inside nor out. It constitutes as gap of differance the hinge of the doors of Night and Day while metaphysics "lies thusly," at once opened up, disclosed, and enclosed, ushered in and issued hence, within that threshold, which it seeks to reappropriate by positing it from within, reinscribing it, as one of the two principles of being.

At the threshold inscribed in the articulated stricture of its hinged gap lies the deception of the issuance of metaphysics mirroring itself in the duplicity of its own projected image: trans-scribed, beyond.

Which veers the present trajectory into an expected, albeit profound, turnabout. While the Platonic dialogues cross and cross out, reconstruct and deconstruct, at once, that threshold, upon which truth *literally* hinges, weaving truth as superinscribed within the space of fiction thus articulated as a recounted dialogue, a narration becomes possible because of the essential deception generated by the fascinating play of the images which λόγος cannot help but re-count without altogether accounting for; Truth as such gets deposited, written down and out, set forth, posited and posed, within the setting of a dialogical framework, a *Gestell*, an in-stalling, itself fictive and imaginal, eikastic, iconic, a setting which dialogue can but remark upon while attempting to erase it in an impossible sum without remainder. The fiction of the re-counted dialogue amounts to having the dream which tells of a dream in which a dialogue is recounted. It is paradoxically the weave of the fictive textual framework of the dialogues that sets truth at work, into motion, trying to capitalize the telic energy of sense, allowing for a movement of displacement wherein truth and untruth inevitably get inextricably interweaved, awaiting the final instance of the impossible contextual divisive cut, the decision or κρίσις, which the deed of a present discourse or Logos would finally bring about, fulfill.

Thus: live discourse present to its own finality and energy is defined as what contextually replaces deception by cutting the thread of the text and its interminably duplicitous undecidability, by counterposing to the fascination of indeterminate dreaming the self-identical referentiality of an ideally terminable dialogue, postulated along with ideality itself as the eschatological παρουσία of the truth of whatever is in question, in itself and as such.

Which provokes two further supplementary remarks on my part. First, at all the relevant points in the dialogues, this may be verified: where the question of deception intrudes, the exemplary instances produced for inspection in their very enigmatic density are dreams and madness. A case in point from the *Theaetetus* (where the context completes the demonstration):

> what token could one give to demonstrate *at the present moment* whether we're asleep or dreaming? . . . That's it, Socrates [Theaetetus answers], it is most perplexing . . . for all the same things follow in parallel and like the strophe and counter-strophe of a chorus. For just as there's nothing to prevent what we're now conversing about be also dreamt as a conversation with one another during sleep, so whenever in a dream what we dream we are recounting is itself a dream, the similarity of that to this conversation is strange (158*b–c*).

This problem draws the attention of Aristotle under similar circumstances in the fourth book of his *Metaphysics* and provokes the retort that such a question simply betrays the educational ineptitude of the questioner who thinks out such strange and useless problems, for an infinite regress cannot be stopped unless some principle be posited to begin with (*Met.* 4.6.1011*a*). Dreams can perfectly well mirror what is supposed actual, and their images naturally deceive because within a dream the distinction image/original is not operative (hence their exemplary value for εἰκασία, as I intend to show elsewhere). The only way to destroy the hypnosis of dreaming is by a sudden shift to the mode of wakefulness, but the truth of dialogue as dialectically mediated must be such that it would hold even under the condition that a dialogue be itself dreamt: dialogue must forsake the hold of the sensible present and its actuality and attach itself to the repetitive pattern of a postulated ideality, so that the ensuing truth may reappear whether the dialogue be dreamt, narrated, or fictionally recounted: capable of surviving within a foreign, fictive, imagistic, other context.

Metaphysical dialogue must discount in advance the duplicitous power of deceptive sophistry by reinscribing the space of fiction within a doubly guarded, framed, enframed, reposing, dialogical space in a fictional dialogue supervised by the instance of truth, a counter-fictional, counterfeit dialogue: fiction versus fiction, φάρμακον or drug against φάρμακον. But that requires the re-inscription of dialogue within fiction and the interiorization or internalization, representation, or repression of fiction within its own space, now occupied from within by the antagonistic instance of truth organized as dialogue attempting to representatively reappropriate the jointure articulating and setting off metaphysics.

This rearticulation, representation, or setting (out, forth, up, upon) of fiction allows for the repositioning of dialogue as telic and ruling instance and generates appearance as captive and to be captured, recapitulated, capitalized, within a critical dialogic discourse, always ready, awaiting, to cut the knot of a given context in the present, as present, and to apply the vigilance of dialogue as deed in the opportune moment, the καιρός (see *Phaedrus*). Philosophy must cut the web of fiction, but only after it has helped thread and rethread it. Hence its formidable powers of closure, the illusory fold of the topology of metaphysics in its Platonic moment.

If, then, fiction takes place, displaced, within the metaphysical space, and allows for the placing or spacing, opening up the transversal of intervals, and articulating the hinge of the threshold between what makes metaphysics possible and its recaptured "other," it follows that the place of the beginning or start, the startled placing, the postulation of the beyond as ideal, must itself be quasi- or pseudo-fictive, a mirage generated by the very decision allowing for the illusion of a present deed referred to by the dialogical fictional writing, referring and transferring truth to a lived presence determining the sense or situation of a given context, rupturing the plait making λόγος itself possible. Which must be replaced by the deed, the work, the achievement, the performance of what the utterance could only allude to and evoke without quite rendering present.

The impossibility of reading the (metaphysical) text is programmed in the Platonic corpus under the disguise of dialogic writing inscribed as fiction. And that generates the illusion of a start, a beginning for metaphysics as the event of the operation of the gap, at the threshold, stalling between the deception of dialogical truth fictionally propounded and the imagistics of the installed place where something like a principled beginning of a series can take place in order: metaphysics, installed in the very place of stalling, if it begins, impossibly and fictively, with Plato, begins at the threshold, in the threshold, between the image of beings and the necessary deception generated by such an image, stalled and disseminated already and yet recaptured spectacularly within the space of a posed ideality.

There would only remain to distinguish between ideality and the repetitive and re-presentative power of displacement latent in pseudo-fiction, in the falling of deception away from latency into the falsehood of λογος. Which will always already have befallen metaphysics as such, so as to set it underway, astray, searching for signs to mark out the proper from the improper pathways, choose the fork in the crossroads, the Two in the One or the 1 in the 2.

Tentatively: Plato's other disperses the Parmenidean One disseminating deception, effectively deconstructing the traversal of the divine gates, turning their hinges around, making the metaphysical voyage appear to be more than a mere illusion of an adventure, setting it forth as a genuine path. Only then is Platonic metaphysics start(l)ed, possible, installed, stalled, *gestellt,* but precisely under those conditions it is fore-stalled, paralyzed, unable to cross the threshold and get things underway for the voyage of discovery beyond. Frozen at the threshold, metaphysics stands like the wanderer in Trakl's famous poem commented on by Heidegger, paralyzed: no table is set for it with bread and wine, however.

Set you that down.

Notes

1. Heidegger, *Parmenides, Gesamtausgabe,* vol. 54 (Frankfurt a.M.: Vittorio Klostermann, 1982), p. 84.
2. I refer to Aristotle, *Metaphysics,* bks. VII–X, trans. Montgomery Furth (Indianapolis: Hackett, 1985).
3. Compare Kirk and Raven, *The Presocratic Philosophers* (Cambridge: Cambridge University Press, 1957), p. 252.

Doubling the Space of Existence: Exemplarity in Derrida— the Case of Rousseau

5

Irene E. Harvey

In his "Introduction to the 'Age of Rousseau'" in *Of Grammatology* Derrida asks the following questions:

> Why accord an *"exemplary value"* to the "age of Rousseau"? What *privileged place* does Jean-Jacques Rousseau occupy in the history of logocentrism? What is meant by that proper name?[1]

His answer to these questions is by his own admission only "the beginning of an answer" and "perhaps only the beginning of an elaboration, limited to the preliminary organization of the question."[2] It is these issues—Derrida's answers, his questions, and those questions concerning this *problem of exemplarity* that Derrida does not ask—to which we shall be addressing ourselves here.

We will briefly summarize: (1) Derrida's justification of his "choice" of Rousseau as *the good example* who, as he says, nevertheless *"occupies a singular position"* in the history of metaphysics; (2) Paul de Man's initial response to Derrida's reading as an attempt to reclaim Rousseau's intentions;[3] (3) our own attempt to show that there is yet another Rousseau whom neither Derrida nor de Man make reference to and who proposes yet another theory of writing in his *Reveries;* and (4) our position that the *structure of exemplarity* used by both de Man and Derrida is itself questionable with respect to that same metaphysical tradition which neither thinker wishes to be reduced to. Finally we will suggest that there is a further complicity between Derrida's notion of differance and what we will call the *structure of exemplarity*. The nature of this complicity as it relates to metaphysics will only be alluded to here since it is the subject of a much longer and more detailed study.

60

Derrida's Choice

Far from aiming to reveal Derrida to be deluded or mistaken concerning his relation to metaphysics, we wish here only to begin with the open admissions he makes concerning the difficulty of justifying (according to him) his choice of Rousseau as the particularly *good example*. It is clear that Derrida is fully aware of the problem of exemplarity as a metaphysical problem—perhaps even as *the* metaphysical problem par excellance. But let us begin with the given reasons for this privileged example. Rousseau, Derrida claims, "is undoubtedly *the only one* or *the first one* to make a theme or a system of the *reduction of writing* profoundly implied by the entire age (between Descartes and Hegel)." Further, "he [Rousseau] *repeats* the inaugural movement of the *Phaedrus* and *De Interpretatione* but starts from a new model of presence: the subject's self-presence within consciousness or feeling."[4]

Thus, Rousseau is a good example and indeed the *best* example for at least two reasons: (1) he *repeats* the tradition (which began with Plato and Aristotle) and reduces, denounces, and devalues writing; and yet also, (2) he inaugurates something *new* in this tradition by locating the privileged place or the "other" of writing in the feeling or consciousness of the subject. Hence, we find *exemplarity* here already entails a twofold structure. On the one hand, *the good example* is just another instance, a repetition, a confirmation, a revindication, and here situated *inside* the tradition, yet on the other hand, our *good example* is *outside* that same tradition. Rousseau is a *good example* because he does something *new*, and indeed Derrida also claims that Rousseau occupies a *singular* position—unique and *un*precedented. We shall return to this duplicity, but for the moment let us consider Derrida's justification and admissions of the limits of justifiability.

Rousseau is a *good* example, in particular, of an illustration or demonstration of the logic of the supplement, the play of differance, or as Derrida synonymously calls it, the economy of difference. Rousseau's texts exhibit a twofold structure which Derrida will claim is *lawbound*. Indeed it is this lawfulness that Derrida's analysis to Rousseau, later known as the deconstruction of the same, sought to reveal. As Derrida explains:

> as the first and primordial phase, in fact and in principle, of the development of this problematic consists in questioning *the internal structure of the texts* [Rousseau's] *as symptoms,* as that is the only condition for determining these symptoms themselves in the totality of their metaphysical

appurtenance; *I draw my argument* from them in order *to isolate* in Rousseau and Rousseauism, *the theory of writing*.[5]

This theory of writing is essentially equivocal for Derrida, as is well known, and involves at least three possible translations: (1) Rousseau's theory of writing; (2) the theory of writing in general, as script literally speaking; and of course, what Derrida will later transfer to (3) the non-theory of arche-writing or differance.

More specifically, Rousseau is a *good example* for Derrida in the following respect. Rousseau's texts, in their overt, explicit denunciations of writing and privileging of the voice, the subject, and immediacy in general, also have a covert, unintended, implicit side or aspect (performative side) which does not *cohere* with or support the overt side. These two aspects of the text Derrida refers to as the *declared* (thematized) and the described, undeclared and unthematized. Together they exhibit a peculiar "logic," a peculiar law of textuality which Rousseau as a singular proper name merely exhibits in a more profound way than others but which is in no way peculiar to Rousseau's writing alone. This is one of the paradoxes of exemplarity, to be sure. Rousseau is chosen then because his texts display something (differance) more clearly, more easily, more evidently than others, yet what is therein displayed is in fact and in principle a much more general and generalizable phenomenon. Thus Rousseau is a *mere example* on the one hand, a *superfluous addition* and in principle could have been replaced or substituted by anyone else in such a demonstration, yet on the other hand is a particularly *good example*—a crucial and critical choice, a unique individual, non-substitutable, and offering an *essential addition* in order to fill a void. In passing we should recall that Rousseau is both a mere example and a particularly good example of supplementarity which in itself has this same double foundation—a mere addition to something already full and constituted in itself, and also, at the same time, an essential addition which fills a gap and makes the whole what it is.[6] We will return to this also but now let us turn to Paul de Man who claimed that Derrida's reading of Rousseau was itself *exemplary*.

De Man's Choice

Consistent with Derrida's position concerning the "surprises" for the author in textuality, de Man claimed that Derrida's analysis of Rousseau is *exemplary* in at least two ways. First, it is exemplary in the sense of being a *model* of textual analysis.[7] Derrida's work in this sense forms an *Exemplar* for de Man. On the other hand, it is also, and this is more ironic, an *example* of *traditional* readings of Rousseau—or misreadings, as de Man renamed them. The first level or phase of Derrida's deconstruction of Rousseau—where Rousseau's explicit, thematic, and intended claims are elucidated—was for de Man a *repetition* of the traditional interpretations of Rousseau.[8] What was dramatically *new* in Derrida however, was how he went beyond this tradition and found new news in Rousseau—albeit as the unintended aspect. Hence, Derrida is also a *mere example* on the one hand, and *the example* par excellance in his uniqueness on the other, from de Man's perspective.

De Man's version of Rousseau, however, also turns the latter into a particularly *good* and hence *unique example*. Rousseau's true uniqueness and strength, de Man claimed, comes from the fact that he not only knew what he was doing but also indeed exhibited (with both eyes open) the *undecidability* that characterizes textuality in general. The discrepancy between the *rhetorical mode* and the *theoretical mode,* as de Man would later call these levels, was what allowed for Rousseau's text to be, as all texts are for de Man, "an allegory of its own misreading."[9] It tells us how and why it will be misread, and yet this commentary or foreconceptive structure does not prevent such a misreading. In short, then, Rousseau for de Man also plays the role of a privileged example but contrary to Derrida, what Rousseau exemplifies is not the tradition of metaphysics on the one hand, and a new theory of writing on the other, but rather a general theory of textuality as an irreducible relation between the figurative and the literal as de Man initially divided the two disjunctive levels, or the rhetorical and the theoretical, as he would later come to rename this duplicity.[10] For our purposes, the transformation of Rousseau into *an example,* by both de Man and Derrida (as well as de Man's interpretation of Derrida as an example) itself repeats and represents a singular or identifiable and identical structure—albeit of duplicity. This duplicity—of the mere example and the privileged case—is what we call the *structure of exemplarity.*

Let us now turn once again to Rousseau himself—as mediated no doubt infinitely behind and beyond our own awareness but consciously mediated by this problem of exemplarity as it "presents itself" in de Man's and Derrida's orientation to Rousseau. In addition, we shall consider the problem of writing in Rousseau in order to narrow the focus to a manageable limit and also to parallel the evident concerns of our two predecessors in this matter.

Rousseau's Reveries on Writing

Unlike Derrida and de Man, Rousseau does not use overtly or covertly the structure of exemplarity to which we have drawn attention here.

Rather, he is concerned, overtly and covertly, to "give a faithful account" of his experiences, of his thoughts and feelings, daydreams, and, as he calls them, *reveries*.[11] It is a phenomenological account therefore that he claims, at least, to offer us in the *Reveries of a Solitary Walker*. As Rousseau says:

> My enterprise is like Montaigne's but my motive is entirely different, for he wrote his essays only for others to read, whereas I am *writing* down my reveries *for myself alone*. If, as I hope, I retain the same disposition of mind in my extreme old age, when the time of my departure draws near, I shall *recall* in *reading them* the *pleasure I have in writing* them and thus by reviving times past I shall as it were *double the space of my existence*. In spite of men I shall enjoy the charms of company, and in my decrepitude *I shall live with my earlier self* as I might with a younger friend.[12]

On the face of things it would seem that Derrida's reading, notably of texts other than this one in particular of Rousseau's, is confirmed also by this passage. Writing, it would seem, is for Rousseau merely a means to supplement the present and make the past experiences present again, to restore a lost presence, and thus can be used as an aid to memory—as mentioned in Plato's *Phaedrus*.[13] On the other hand, it seems to be a means of copying or supplementing the full presence of Rousseau's *now* (or current) experiences. It is his *means* of copying, or representing his reveries, or thought and hence radically external to them and non-productive or constitutive in itself, as Aristotle had claimed in *De interpretatione*.[14] Further, as Derrida had suggested, writing for Rousseau is situated now for the first time in relation to consciousness and feeling and hence, as Rousseau says above, in reading his own "faithful account" of his own reveries he will recall the pleasure he had in writing them.

Despite the apparent adequacy of a Derridean reading here we wish to supplement the supplement with an additional aspect of Rousseau's position that Derrida seems not to account for. We wish also to supplement de Man's reading of Rousseau but will address that issue later.

Rousseau also adds that *writing* will, as it were, serve to "double the space of his existence." It will also create for him a "younger friend" that he can turn to as compensation, indeed as a supplement or substitute, for the "company of men" who now despise him.

This claim is not reducible to either the metaphysics of presence or the structure of supplementarity or differance, we suggest. Rather, Rousseau has discovered that *writing is productive*, differs essentially from its source, or author, carries within itself an *inflation of affect* from the original situation, and expands one's existence at least by a factor of two. Rousseau can aim to return to his own reveries via his writings only with an eye to the radical difference thus instantiated—from his earlier self at the time of writing to his current self at the time of reading. In addition, there is thus no concept of a unified or unifiable consciousness for Rousseau here but rather a displacing, differing/deferring and transformational notion that has no center. His former self is as different now as another person. In short, writing is the medium of otherness on the one hand and inflation of affect of the other.

Concerning the notion of a writer being *surprised (sur prise)*[15] by one's own writing, or overtaken as Derrida suggests, we would agree with de Man in a sense that Rousseau was fully aware of this process but not that he was fully aware of "what he was doing" in his own text. Rather, the awareness that Rousseau documents in the *Reveries* is precisely of the *slippage* that Derrida has pointed to in textuality in general between the "in control" and "out-of-control" aspects of the text and specifically in the "language used by the author." Let us turn now to Rousseau for more on this as a problem.

That language went ahead of his thoughts Rousseau has often claimed throughout his work and has offered us confessions enough which witness the shame he brought upon himself. This was true of *spoken* language as well as *written* for Rousseau as he says:

> never have I lied to my own advantage; but I have often lied out of shame, to avoid embarrassment in trivial affairs or affairs that concerned only me, as when in order to keep a conversation going I have been *forced* by the slowness of my ideas and my lack of small talk to have *recourse* to *fiction* for something to say. When I am obliged to talk, and interesting truths do not spring to mind readily enough, I invent stories rather than keep quiet[16] [emphasis added].

Further:

> I should naturally prefer to put a moral truth in the place of a factual truth . . . but it would call for *greater presence of mind* and a readier tongue than mine to be able to make such instructive use of idle chatter.
>
> The *talk runs on more quickly than my ideas* and forces me to *speak before thinking* so that I have often been led into foolish and inept statements which my *reason had condemned* and my *heart disowned before I had finished speaking,* but which had forestalled my judgment and thus escaped its censure[17] [emphasis added].

This is a crucial passage with reference to Rousseau's own awareness of being surprised or overtaken by language and discourse themselves. Far from being an Aristotelian position whereby language would simply be an extended representation of a pre-thought and formulated idea, language for Rousseau always already runs ahead of his thinking and to his surprise he finds himself always already (or at least, often already) saying things he neither intends to say, wishes to say, or can justify having said.

Let us turn to the Platonic connection and add a small supplement there as well. Rousseau at times, it is true, refers to writing in the *Reveries* as giving an account, making a faithful record of events, thoughts, and feelings which have *already* occurred. But he also considers writing to have *formative* and *informative* powers beyond the original.

At times, Rousseau admits, when he was *writing from memory* (not using writing as simply an aid to memory) his memory of the true and actual events or thoughts failed him. In such circumstances he allowed or was permitted by the process of writing itself to "fill in the gaps" with "details that he dreamed up to complete his memories but which never contradicted them."[18] In addition, he claimed, as Derrida is fully aware, that writing itself gave him enormous pleasure.[19] Indeed it is this *pleasure of writing* that led him to go *beyond* or even to abandon the faithful records and "to embellish reality with ornaments of his invention."[20] Writing, as he often says in his *Reveries,* thus is not simply an aid to memory which would allow him to relive the past, or rather a lost presence, but rather it outstrips memories. When he is *writing from memory* (this is not reducible to *remembering from writing*), and when memory fails him, the free associations which arise as he writes "fill in the gaps of his failing memory."[21] Writing is, thus, not an aid to memory for Rousseau in the sense that Plato considered it to be (although Plato also considered it a *threat* for precisely this reason). Rather, for Rousseau, writing is inherently beyond authorial intention, beyond the mere mapping of events, and beyond the conscious control of the author or writer. Indeed one is swept along in the process of writing (and even more so in arche-writing, if we understand Rousseau here within Derrida's terms) and one finds oneself always already *displaced* essentially from oneself.

Thus de Man's case for Rousseau's awareness seems to stand, yet it is not a question here of illustrating that Rousseau knew what he was doing. On the contrary, he was, shall we say, *well aware* that he did not know what he was doing in writing, and that his will was essentially situated within a larger process over which he had no control. The slippage which allows for or is perhaps the condition of the possibility of deconstruction is what Rousseau was well aware of but certainly not the master of, as de Man's reading seems to imply.

The issue, however, arises that for Derrida, Rousseau is a particularly good example, not only of this slippage between control and non-control (as if conscious and non-conscious) but of an internal network of effects which characterize the tradition of Western metaphysics as such. In this sense, Rousseau's texts exemplify what we might call a historical unconscious.[22] The nature of this traditional netting, however, is the connection of Rousseau's assumptions, orientation, and presuppositions concerning writing with, specifically, Plato's and Aristotle's articulation of the same. In particular, as Derrida says, the denunciation and reduction of writing. This participation by Rousseau is not questioned as such by us here and we do not disagree with Derrida's claim; we do however suggest that there is *more to Rousseau* than this with respect to his understanding—conscious or not—of the powers of writing, as we have shown.

We wish now to return to the issue of exemplarity as such, as it organizes Derrida's relation to Rousseau and perhaps authorizes the former to reduce the latter's position to that of a mere example on the one hand and a particularly good example on the other.

Examples and Signs

It is clear that to take something *as* an example involves a transformation of the relation to that thing. The thing no longer is what it is (even if it ever was self-identical) and becomes an *example of something else*. In short, the transformation of something into an example entails the same structure as the making of that thing into a *sign* for something else. It is no secret that Derrida's early work focused on the problem of the traditional understanding of the sign as a *sign for* something else that is not a sign and that he aimed to deconstruct this framework. Using Saussure initially, Derrida invoked the sense of a sign as that which is an indissociable connection between signifier and signified as well as that which is necessarily situated within a system of signs which thereby gives the particular sign its function or meaning. Now if we consider the role of exemplarity in Derrida's analysis of Rousseau, it is clear that he takes Rousseau to be a *sign for* a number of things such as (1) the age of Rousseau (from Descartes to Hegel); (2) the tradition of Western metaphysics from Plato to Hegel; (3) the traditional understanding of the nature of writing and its reduction by that tradition in favor of immediacy, presence, and the like; and (4) the first and only thinker to thematize this reduction. What consequences can we draw from Derrida's transformation of Rousseau into such a sign and what kind of structure does Derrida need in order to keep Rousseau *at a distance* from what he signifies and yet also internally related to that same system? First, Derrida needs the particularity and uniqueness of Rousseau's position to sustain the distance; second, he needs the *repetition* of the traditional positions by Rousseau to sustain the internal connection; third, he needs a *sign system* in which the meaning of Rousseau's position is determined. The first two requirements, however, have been brought in question by our supplement here, we suggest. Rousseau's position with respect to the reduction of writing, profoundly implied by the entire age, is not identical to or reducible to that of Plato and Aristotle nor is his position concerning consciousness and self-identity coherent with that of Hegel and Descartes. Rousseau neither starts nor ends with the self's immediate relation to itself but quite the contrary, at least in the *Reveries*.

The larger issue here is perhaps *why* Derrida (and de Man too) needs to transform Rousseau into a *sign* or into an *example* of something that Rousseau both *is* and *is not*. What type of violence and what loss or gain does such a transformation entail, and on what grounds can it be legitimated or authorized? Regardless of the conscious/ unconscious or intended/unintended dilemma of traditional hermeneutics, the issue here is how can one thinker, or one text, be made to stand for another text or thinker? How is the tradition of metaphysics possible as a structure rather than (or at least as much as) a history (as Derrida claims)?[23]

In short, is it not a metaphysical gesture par excellence to transform the "given particular" (whatever it may be) into an *example* of a non-given generality? Is it not the transformation of the *ontic* into the *ontological* (or shall we call it translation?) that is at stake here, and hence the *conditions of the possibility* of such a translation that must be addressed?

Heidegger, as we know, abandoned the early project of aiming to do just this, but the structure of exemplarity as a metaphysical gesture lives on in the work of Derrida and de Man and certainly many others. The point here is not to point out the obvious—that Derrida and de Man use metaphysics (as they know and we know)—but rather to question a strategy that organizes the foundations of such powerful thinkers and which seems in itself to be a questionable procedure. Finally, let us say that Rousseau's *Reveries* is, for us, not only a good example, nor a mere example, yet it is, of necessity, both of these. The structure of argumentation itself transforms what is intended as specific, particular, and unique into the general, universal, and replaceable in the *Augenblick* that unfortunately is still in need of deconstruction.

Notes

The following abbreviations are used in references in the text and the notes:

> BI   Paul de Man, *Blindness and Insight;* see note 3.
> OG   Jacques Derrida, *Of Grammatology;* see note 1.
> R   Jean-Jacques Rousseau, *Reveries of a Solitary Walker;* see note 11.

1. Jacques Derrida, *Of Grammatology,* trans. Gayatri Spivak (Baltimore: Johns Hopkins University Press, 1974), p. 97. Henceforth *OG.*

2. *OG* 97.

3. I am referring here to the essay entitled "The Rhetoric of Blindness" in Paul de Man's early book, *Blindness and Insight* (Minneapolis: University of Minnesota Press, 1971); henceforth *BI.* His later work on this subject is not as pertinent to the issue of exemplarity which is my primary concern here. See de Man's *Allegories of Reading* (New Haven: Yale University Press, 1979) for more on the relation between Derrida and Rousseau from his later viewpoint.

4. *OG* 98.

5. *OG* 99.

6. For more on supplementarity in Derrida's thinking see his *OG,* pp. 269–316.

7. For instance, de Man claimed (*BI* 111): "His [Derrida's] commentary on Rousseau can be used as an exemplary case of the interaction between critical blindness and critical insight, no longer in the guise of a semiconscious duplicity but as a necessity dictated and controlled by the very nature of all critical language." It is this interaction between blindness and insight that de Man claimed was lawbound and that Derrida's strategy of deconstruction exhibited in an exemplary fashion. There is also a glorification of the "rigor and intellectual integrity" of Derrida's work as exemplary in this same sense of being a model for others and for de Man himself.

8. As de Man says: "Derrida starts out from the current view in Rousseau interpretation and then proceeds to show how Rousseau's own text undermines his declared philosophical allegiances" (*BI* 123).

9. De Man claims that "the text also postulates the necessity of its own misreading. It knows and asserts that it will be misunderstood. It tells the story, the allegory of its own misunderstanding" (*BI* 136). The "text" here for de Man means Rousseau's in particular, but also Rousseau's text *as* an example of all textuality.

10. For more on this distinction see *Allegories of Reading,* in particular the essay "Semiology and Rhetoric," pp. 3–19.

11. Rousseau repeats this intention in a number of places in the *Reveries of a Solitary Walker* (*R*), trans. Peter France (New York: Penguin Classics, 1979); p. 33: ". . . my true aim which is to give an account of the successive variations of my soul." Further, he says (p. 35): "Having therefore decided to describe my habitual state of mind in this . . . I could think of no simpler or surer way of carrying out my plan than to keep a faithful record of my solitary walks and the reveries that occupy them, when I give free rein to my thoughts and let my ideas follow their natural course, unrestricted and unconfined."

12. *R* 33.

13. In the *Phaedrus,* Socrates denounces writing as dangerous to memory on the one hand but also as merely an aid to memory on the other. The latter claim runs as follows (275 *c-d*): "Then anyone who leaves behind him a written manual, and likewise anyone who takes it over from him, on the supposition that such writing will provide something reliable and permanent, must be exceedingly simple-minded; he must really be ignorant of Ammon's utterance, if he imagines that written words can do anything more than remind one who knows that which the writing is concerned with" (*Collected Dialogues of Plato,* ed. Edith Hamilton and Huntington Cairns [Princeton: Princeton University Press, 1961], p. 521).

14. Aristotle claims (*De interpretatione* 16*a*): "Spoken words are the symbols of mental experience and written words are the symbols of spoken words" (*Basic Works of Aristotle,* ed. Richard McKeon [New York: Random House, 1941], p. 40).

15. In *OG,* p. 158, Derrida speaks of this textual disjunction as sur-prise in the following way: "This question is therefore not only of Rousseau's writing but also of our own reading. We should begin by taking rigorous account of this *being held within* (*prise*) or this *surprise:* the writer writes in a language and in a logic whose proper system, laws and life his discourse by definition cannot dominate absolutely. He uses them only by letting himself, after a fashion and up to a point be governed by the system."

16. *R* 73.

17. *R* 74.

18. *R* 76.

19. For more on this as it relates to onanism see Derrida's *OG,* pp. 141–64.

20. *R* 76.

21. *R* 76.

22. Derrida refers to the history of metaphysics as a structure as much as a history, and it is this in particular to which we are referring here. It is the hidden yet presupposed tradition of metaphysics that we suggest might be called, for the Western world at least, its historical unconscious.

23. *OG* 3–5.

Regulations: Kant and Derrida at the End of Metaphysics

6

Stephen Watson

> Vladimir: . . . We could start all over again perhaps.
> Estragon: That should be easy.
> Vladimir: It's the start that's difficult.
> Estragon: You can start from anything.
> Vladimir: Yes, but you have to decide.
> Estragon: True.
> > *Silence*
>
> —*Godot*[1]

I

"Human reason has a natural tendency to transgress"[2] (A642/B671), Kant concluded, "a compulsion . . . to disobey certain rules" (A709/ B737). It was a problem that was part and parcel of a critical tribunal into Reason. Indeed the fact that litigation began at all was in one sense a symptom that something had radically gone wrong. Kant was specific about what invoked the need for diagnosis—metaphysics had been, perhaps always already been, a matrix, an architectonic, for a *controversia perennis*. Reason was inevitably *"subreptive."* The *Inaugural Dissertation* elaborated it simply as a fallacy involving the permutation of things sensible with things intellectual.[3] That was not simply the case, however, with the first *Critique*'s resolution of transcendental dialectic, that logic of *Schein* which is the τέλος of transcendental logic. Here Kant was quick to add that the fact that Reason never reached its goal, never reached perfection, "complete purposive unity" (A694/B722), was not to be blamed upon the nature of Reason itself. The failure to reach theoretical "completeness" (A728/B756) was to be ascribed rather to *judgment*. "All errors of subreption are to be ascribed to a defect of judgment, never to understanding or to reason" (A643/B671). While the force of Kant's account differs little here, its formulation alters, appealing to an argument that is archaic. The finite should not quarrel with its faculties, should not blame its origins for its straying. Error is not an attribute which adheres to these faculties by nature, but rather is to be attributed to our *use* of them.

It is an old argument, an old *metaphysical* argument. And it is surprising that, after all those pages which denied the validity of such arguments, Kant should wax nostalgic. Perhaps especially at this point. When he had just faced the failure of foundations in dealing with the Transcendental Ideal, the ultimate failure of Reason to provide grounds for its rational practices, to provide justification for its sensible engagements, it is surprising that Kant's arguments would seek out ultimate views about nature in universal quantifiers:

> Everything that has its basis in the nature of our powers must be appropriate to and consistent with their right employment. . . . We are entitled, therefore, to suppose that transcendental ideas have their own good, proper and therefore *immanent* use. (A642–43/B670–71)

It was a view of nature as old as the metaphysical hills that would continue to evoke Kant's awe in the third *Critique*. Since nature is ordered, measured to a proper end (and thus rational), all of our powers must be so as well. By nature they are in themselves *good* and therefore, within this proper goodness, "valid," recalling that "immanent" for Kant just meant standing "within the limits of possible experience." Even the last section of the first *Critique* would have little problem then invoking the sublime here: Kant referred without blinking to "the magnificent equipment of our human nature" (A827/B855). It provided in fact, he claimed, sufficient ground for the doctrinal belief (which is *not* to say knowledge) in the immortality of the soul, just because in this world "the shortness of life [is] so ill-suited to the full exercise of our powers" (ibid.). And in this it doubtless provoked (or perhaps was provoked by) a certain moral *analogy* with the postulates of practical reason, an "affinity" (A122), to engage a Kantian trope, which was perhaps overdetermined without ever being capable of becoming *determinate*.

II

Nonetheless, the immanence in question is *not* natural. On the contrary, it is an immanence constituted on nature's lack, on what withdraws from the grasp of the concept. While occurring in relation to the presence of sensation, an entity's affecting the faculty of receptivity, all that was properly human mitigated against a *natural* immanence. The entity in question ultimately withdrew from all that was in fact most properly human, a finite mode of intuition. In human knowing instead, the nature in question would always be constituted, *un*-natural, at best the mirror-image of nature, that is, reflected; its re-presentation by a kind of deferral which is *de facto* categorical.

The immanence in question departs then from all other forms of transcendental immanence: classically taken (that is, metaphysically taken) truth, goodness, unity, and beauty. The last two, even within this other, constituted, transcendental would remain even for Kant problematic, tied to an essential unity which had been denied in the abyss of the Transcendental Ideal: that Being which would unify all beings in such a way that we could claim with respect to each that there were one ground through which one of every pair of possible predicates became determinate (A573/B601). But this ground is just what he could never provide. In this regard, as Gadamer has rightly claimed, Kant is the "All-shatterer" of rationality.[4] The shattering remained nonetheless a fortuitous one for Kant himself, since it was precisely this lacuna which provided possible room for faith against the nihilistic onslaught the determinist principles of the Analytic had underwritten.

Still, granted the difference which intervenes, what would be the other of this proper *Ordo* the *Critique* institutes? Kant leaves this, for the most part, unthought. But in one sense it is precisely that which made possible "room" for faith: *heterogeneity:*

> For with what right can reason, in its logical employment, call upon us to treat the multiplicity of powers exhibited in nature as simply a disguised unity, and to derive this unity, so far as may be possible, from a fundamental power—how can reason do this if it be free to admit as likewise possible that all powers may be heterogeneous and that such systematic unity of derivation may not be in conformity with nature? (A651/B679)

For Kant the possibility of heterogeneity here would involve a chaos in which our rational practices would undergo an essential and uncontrollable dispersion. And yet how was this risk to be denied? What could license Reason against the counterfactual—that all that Reason called "nature" and constituted as such in the transcendental object may not *not* be in accord with this other *Nature* to which Kant makes allusion in this section and with which, against all that he had claimed in barring access to the *Ding-an-sich,* Reason is now supposed to be in possible "conformity"? What guarantees, then, that the heterogeneity that the Transcendental Deduction overcame, "the rhapsody of perceptions . . . ungovernable by rules" (A156/B195), cannot ensue by a kind of subreption more fundamental than any of Reason's own doing? What guarantees, in short, that the difference between this constituted "nature" and the Nature to which Kant appeals here is not unencompassable, dispersing itself in the quarrel between the faculties? What if that were "true" in some sense unavailable to Kant's usage of the term? In face of all this, Kant's nostalgia would not quit:

> Reason would then run counter to its own vocation, proposing as its aim an idea quite inconsistent with the constitution of nature. (A651/B679)

But "nature" within Kant's text appears always within the tissue of a certain dehiscence. If, on the one hand, this is the "nature" of the Analytic for which the understanding is the lawgiver (A126), then it is difficult to understand how the problem of Reason's non-conformity and the transgression of nature could arise in the first place, since this other Nature, the one before which heterogeneity may be insurmountable, has nothing overtly to do with it. And if, on the other hand, the constitution in question is one concerning the *nature* of Reason (after all, the dehiscence is one of Reason's genitives), then the metaphysical claim licensing such an assertion would be in jeopardy, inaccessible *de juris*. In either case (in accord with the results of the Paralogisms) the question of nature and reason's vocation remains oblique.

   Now in the third *Critique,* for example, Kant proceeded otherwise. There he refers to the spontaneous productions of productive imagination as "creating *another* nature . . . in accordance with analogical laws."[5] But is Kant to be taken seriously then? Is the "nature" of the Analytic and its determinate laws merely an ἀνάλογον? Does "nature" ever really appear within the Kantian text, a *Ding-an-sich* too far removed to be made present, a pseudo-spontaneity whose spontaneity will never in fact be entirely "natural"? Did Kant ever intend the image of "lawgiver," refracted analogue of perfect spontaneity, *intuitus originarius,* to be taken seriously?

III

Still, if the problem of nature becomes overdetermined in Kant's exit from his ἀγών with metaphysics. it is not the case perhaps that he provides no more answers, indeed more straightforward ones in line with the transcendental forms which underlie the *Critique:*

> The law of reason which requires us to seek for this unity is a necessary law, since without it, we should have no reason at all, and without reason, no coherent employment of the understanding, and in the absence of this, no sufficient criterion of empirical truth. In order, therefore, to secure an empirical criterion, we have no option save to presuppose the systematic unity of nature as objectively valid and necessary. (A651/B679)

The appeal at bottom, Kant finally writes, would derive from the law of reason itself. The possibility of heterogeneity would bring the critical tribunal itself to a standstill. In the absence of such unity, we would be, Kant is absolutely convinced, "without reason." Mad, the *Anthropology* will relate, since to be without reason involves itself a positive but hopelessly irrational form. And, in this light the Dialectic shows in the inevitability of transgression, in fact, an inevitable flirtation with madness in a *specific* positive form. In "vesania" (*Aberwitz*) Kant states, "The patient flies completely beyond the guidance of experience, snatches at principles that can be altogether exempt from its touchstone."[6] In the above passage he states minimally and yet with a straightforwardness which identifies the critical project in general: "without reason no criterion of empirical truth." In order to save the latter, the principle of the systematic unity of nature becomes necessary.

Kant speaks then variously of unity, that of the manifold (homogeneity), the variety of lower species (specification), and a systematic unity by which these species would be interrelated (continuity). Still, this unity again is never given, these being "ideas which reason follows only as it were asymptotically" (A663/B691). No transcendental deduction can be given of them since the nature(s) which they portend (as a totality) can never be given. Nonetheless, in line with the logic of *Schein* which underwrites the Dialectic itself, Kant claims that "they seem [*scheinen*] to be transcendental," schemata of Reason, almost. But since Reason can have no transcendental schemata, they too are at best ἀνάλογα, ones whose indeterminacy becomes concretized in the infinite *Als ob* which, Kant claims, is a matter of Reason's *interest,* a transcending which occurs by a kind of legitimate self-deception, a fictitious subjunctive which occurs for the sake of the literal. And yet one which is not supposed to get in its way.

IV

Reason's transcending is nonetheless a *natural* transgression. The *Religionslehre* would put it similarly: man by nature strays; transgresses.

And yet within the moral realm the nature involved (i.e., human nature) does not "stray" as a matter of *natural* necessity. Man is stricken by a certain frailty (*fragilitas*), having both an innate inclination towards the good, a predisposition, and at the same time an inclination (which "ought not to be represented as innate")[7] towards evil, a propensity. The latter occurs then in relation to the former by a "certain perversion within the human heart." Still, this perversion cannot be seen as naturally compelling, since "despite a corrupted heart . . . there remains hope of a return to the good from which he has strayed."[8] That is, human frailty may be overcome; freedom remains a possibility underlying moral choice. There can be, as Kant puts it, a "revolution" against the frailty which afflicts us.[9]

Kant could hold out no such hope in the epistemic realm, however. Kantian transcendental schematics would brook no miracles. All references to Copernicus aside, the "revolution" here is also, in a sense, decisively Newtonian. The ἀνάλογον of practical reason cannot return upon pure reason. Transcendental reason undergoes, on the contrary, a transgression which is as necessary as it is natural.

> There is something very strange [*Merkwürdiges*] in the fact that once we assume something to exist we cannot avoid inferring that something exists necessarily. . . . [W]e cannot avoid the transcendental subreption by which this formal principle is represented as constitutive, and by which this unity is hypostatized. (A615/B643; A619/B647)

Here, unlike in the moral realm, the problem in question is not simply anthropological—not simply a matter of the nature of human frailty, or the constitution of *homo criticus*. Nor is it a question even of a transcendental causality, carried out in accord with the categories of relation's demand. The categories are merely the *modus operandi* of the extension. The transcendental subreption in question, rather, stems from a problem of grounds of a different sort. Kant's discussion of regulative employment is based upon what he calls "the logical principle of reason" which "calls upon us to bring about such unity as completely as possible" (A649/B677). In this regard, it is the call of Reason itself which is the call to transgress, to turn metaphysical, to institute *metaphysica naturalis*. The strangeness to which Kant makes appeal is a *logical* strangeness: the ground calls forth a ground. The strangeness is not psychological, and the fallacies in question are not genetic, but ones, rather, which find their origin directly in the nature of rationality. Reason itself invokes the problem of subsumption and foundation, the search for the condition of the condition. That is, syllogistic is inher-

ently *ratiocinatio polysyllogistica,* "a series of inferences which can be pro-
longed indefinitely" (A331/B387). Little wonder then that at the end
of his discussion of mental illness in the *Anthropology* Kant felt a special
need to include random remarks warning against a certain miring in
texts which he calls *textomania* (*Schrifttoll*).[10] Reason in principle is essentially textomanic. And while the young require, Kant said, "spurs
rather than reins" for reasoning, he believed quite the opposite was true
of scholars whose spurs had gone far enough, leading them once more
to a "perversion" and even a "bad taste" which transcended sound understanding and the "touchstone" of experience.[11]

But the point is that such extension, the spur to polysyllogistic, is
invidious, unavoidable, and most properly *natural:* one involving, consequently, a natural and inevitable illusion.

> There exists, then, a natural and unavoidable dialectic of pure reason—
> not one in which a bungler [*Stumper*] might entangle himself through
> lack of knowledge, or one which some sophist has artificially invented to
> confuse thinking people, but one inseparable from human reason, and
> which, even after its deceptiveness has been exposed, will not cease to
> play tricks and continually entrap it into momentary aberrations and
> again call for correction. (A298/B354)

Before this necessity, this inevitability which is inextricable, each of us is
a *Stumper* even at the height of our powers. It involved an entanglement,
a delusion, a loss, perhaps even a destiny (*Geschick*) that modernism from
its inception had feared fundamentally and foundationally. Still, buttressed by that other Nature (as well as an archive concerning it), whereby the faculties have an appropriate and proper employment, that is,
buttressed by the argument from *Design,* that argument for which he
continued to maintain a certain favor even after pure reason's purge,[12]
Kant refuses once more to claim that Reason itself is deceptive.

> The ideas of pure reason can never be dialectical in themselves; any de-
> ceptive illusion to which they give occasion must be due solely to their
> misemployment. For they arise from the very nature of reason; and it is
> impossible that the highest tribunal of all the rights and claims of specula-
> tion should itself be the source of deception and illusion. (A669/B697)

One might wonder. In any case, as has been seen, the nature of
their misemployment arises precisely from the call of Reason itself:
judgment's *need* for foundation. And, granted Reason's penchant as
well as need to tell tall tales (*meta-récits*) to found syllogistic, one might

wonder whether the critical tribunal itself did not remain stricken by the same unconquerable necessity to wax metaphysical, suffering from the same infatuation to put to rest the underdetermination against which polysyllogistic weighs: the necessity, the compulsion, to find a ground for all other grounds; to find, if nothing else, the ground for final and univocal adjudication and decidability.

Kant could escape, of course, only if he found a ground without need of further grounding, an *epistemic consequentia immediata* (A303/B360), one without a third and its third. He tells us without little ado (and in lieu of an argument) that such a consequence he would prefer to entitle an "inference of the understanding." In fact, it was necessarily just such an "inference" which underwrote the empirical criterion of the Analytic, the axioms of Kant's account of *Sinn und Bedeutung*—that the senses are such pure takings as to *present* validity conditions for a finite intellect. It arrived in full dress with the *Kritik*'s first line: "In whatever manner and by whatsoever means [*Mittel*] a mode of knowledge may relate to objects, *intuition* is that through which it is in immediate relation to them" (A19/B33). It was the myth of the given, the philosophy of presence in full regalia. With it, in any case, Kant could face the polysyllogistic unrequited, textomania in rein, without completeness and without care—and without the thought that every theory must contain its own sign-theorem, and thereby its own metaphysics of the sign, perhaps.

V

Kant's solution for the natural illusion into which Reason inevitably fell involved a regulative heuristics. By it, and against all that it *knows,* Reason is to act as though it were what he calls a "self-subsistent" reason:

> This I do by representing all connections as if they were the ordinances of a supreme reason, of which our reason is but a faint copy. (A678/B706)

But the illusion of reason's μίμησις here, the illusion of ontotheological completeness (A632/B660) and consequently the "divine man within us" (A569/B597), as has become clear, is as much one of reason's constitution as of its constituting. Nonetheless, the illusion is taken to be one in Reason's self-interest, involving a necessity that is equally "necessary" for the sake of the greatest possible extension:

> Nevertheless, this illusion (which need not, however, be allowed to deceive us) is indispensibly necessary if we are to direct the understanding

beyond every given experience (as part of the sum of possible experience), and thereby to secure its greatest possible extension, as in the case of mirror vision, the illusion is indispensibly necessary, if beside the objects which lies before our eyes, we are also to see those which lie at a distance behind our back. (A644–45/B672–73)

Reason's call inevitably became then the invocation of a play of images and projections, ideas and grounds, none of which, Kant hastens to parenthesize, "need" deceive us. Nonetheless, the delusion, he has said time and again, is unavoidable, necessary, inextricable, entangling, and natural. And yet, how can it be that we "need not" be deceived, if all this is true in a sense that would not allow, logically "could not" involve, a retrieval in the moral sense, unless that delusion was one perhaps more archaic than Kant thought—a delusion, a dogma, which quite possibly struck reason blind from the beginning (and not just one of its variants), that there could be a *consequentia immediata,* that a simple inventory could be made (A xx), that, in short, there could be an analysis which did not presuppose synthesis (cf. B130)? How could Kant insure then that all forms of transcendental Reason were not blind from the start, dependent upon a synthesis which did not contain the propriety of a preordained and transparent *Ratio,* but one for which it could not account and from which it could not recuperate? Rather than the *foci imaginarii* which were to be the heuristic delusions of Reason's own self-interest, filling in the background extended behind Reason's back, what guaranteed that Reason's speculum was not itself in play upon a "reason" more "cunning" than it, which involved (Hegel would repeat again and again, without ever overcoming it) a play which might take place even "behind the back of consciousness," a contingency which no necessity would overtake?

VI

The failure of transcendental ideas, the failure of transcendentalism, is overdetermined, a failure to access a foundation for a being which is by nature not its own foundation. It was a failure regarding *Ursprungen,* as much as the totalities of its projections, a failure that was as much *natura naturans* as *natura naturata*—a failure to confront, consequently, what remains always already partial, manifold, dispersed. Jacques Derrida has throughout, in this regard, traced out the logic of such a transgression, tracing the site of what had, to Kant, shone like transcendental subreption. In one sense it was a logic which remained still transcendental in Kantian terms, a logic which would "treat of the origin, of the modes" by which objects appear (A55–56/B80). Yet, more primordially, it was a logic of synthesis, of an *"arche-synthesis,"* as Derrida put it in *Grammatology,*[13] the common root (*racine commune*)[14] for which no "transcendental" synthesis might account, the synthesis of the appearing (and consequently, by nature, the withdrawal) of what, by the condition of any and all transcendental *possibility* might remain absent. The "untamed genesis"[15] that ensued marked then the failure of that *actus,* of that ἐνέργεια, which could by necessity bring the manifold to a unity, a bringing-together of the elements of knowledge. And, as this *Elementlehre,* it was the destruction of the synthesis of system, of the *de-founding* of Being's irruption in a λόγος that could by necessity combine Being and Certainty. The Knower as *"Kosmotheoros,"* as Kant put it in the *Opus Postumum,*[16] underwritten by that textomanic dream through which, grounded by an essential identity, "the subject would become his own author."[17]

Kant's *Als ob* was to provide the fiction by which transcendental illusion could remain validly effective. Reinvoking the infinite task of Being's emanation, its "self-gathering," as Plotinus had already dreamed, the *Als ob* could provide hypotheses, "weapons of war" (A777/B805), in the philosopher's confrontation with metaphysical ἀγών. It would provide the infinity by which Being in its inexhaustible transcendence could remain nonetheless infinitely, *almost* transcendentally, *present*—by a deferral which was never simply denial, but itself *potentia,* potency and force. And yet a *potentia* which could never in fact be capable of becoming, of being *ens actualitas.* An absence, in short, which could never *become* present. On the contrary, such an *Augenblick* and its *Erfüllung* would constitute the simple denial, the death of that infinity: Reason's demise. *Nature morte.*

Derrida put the paradox of the legitimation concerning Kant's regulations quite clearly:

> [T]he *Idea in the Kantian sense* designates the infinite overflowing of a horizon which, by reason of an absolute and essential necessity which itself is absolutely principled and irreducible, *never* can become an object itself, or be completed, equaled, by the intuition of an object.[19]

What was this Idea, the delusion of this *focus imaginarius,* if not the impossibility of grounds, the ultimately impossible ground, infinitely deferred beyond "the hope of a return to the good" of *Sinn und Bedeutung,* and yet still Kant's Godot—waiting "in anticipation of some tangible return?"[18] It provided a mask whose semblance would not interfere with the equally supposed immediacy of the faculty of receptivity's *Mittel,* regulated by a strategy of nonintervention in the *Kampfplatz* of metaphysics, divided *in indefinitum* between the literal and the fictional, and granted, thereby, an "apparently transcendental" exception which was, if nothing else, absolutely exceptional to the transcendental project—if for no reason other than it depended on it. It was, after all, a strategy by which the critical tribunal awarded a stay of execution in its own interest. And yet, it still threatened by reason of its own (enlightened) "soaring" to turn the Platonic μῦθος to which Kant appealed still in its construction into a mere "novel," as Derrida put it—or to put it in Kantian terms, to transform *cognitio ex principiis* into mere narration (*Erzählung;* A835/B864), and thereby, the products of Reason into mere *monograms* (A570/B598). As such it marked the introduction of a contingency at the heart of the transcendental text, a danger and its risk which no reason and no rational "extension"—theoretical or practical—could surmount.

VII

It was in a sense the *"argument derridien,"* if that could continue to make any sense,[20] and it could not be taken as a *methodos,* an organon, or a critique, all of which it bars. The invocation of this idea, its regulation and its failure, would appear implicitly and explicitly time and again in the texts of Jacques Derrida—in his own dealing with economimesis in Kant,[21] but, as well, when he is dealing with the question of the principle of principles in Husserl,[22] the undermining of classical hermeneutic theory,[23] the *recherche pour les réquisites* in Austin,[24] the transcendental of transcendence in Levinas,[25] the breath of Artaud,[26] etc. And he made it, refusing all the while to simply abandon the critical for the sake of the precritical, to abandon "the transcendental moment" and its ἀρχή for the sake of a simple objectivism, or to simply abandon the descriptive for the sake of the structural or the functional.[27] And he made it, even when accused of invoking transcendental logic in texts which seemed precisely to be devoid of it. But that was Derrida's point about transcendental ideas and transcendentalism in the end. There is "always a short of and a beyond of transcendental criticism,"[28] as he put it. "Always already," it might be supplemented, a transcendentality and a transcendence which undercut one another, a totality and its de-totalization, to wax Sartrean, a statement and its semiotic loss, its "contextualization,"if that did not imply a renewed analytic totalization and a metaphysical relation between parts and wholes which Kant himself was perhaps the first to challenge in bringing the questions of determination (*Bestimmung*) and completeness together.[29]

Veri-similitude, the *Scheinung* of truth invidious to its claim—
and its performative—and the possibility which escapes both—is inherent to "textuality," a difference which divides assertion from within,
a function of the sign's distance from the signified, of the *Schein* from
the *Erscheinung,* of the withdrawal of the *noumenon,* of the episyllogisms
and prosyllogisms which lead apparently to everywhere and yet to nowhere.[30] Confronted with its contingency, there is *de juris* no safe in-
duction, no safe first principles from which to make deduction, no
Wesensschau without threat of *phänomenologischer Streit.* Transcendental
arguments then can neither be grounded *nor* escaped, "at sea" upon a
"structural possibility," as he reminded John Searle,[31] that always already escaped reason's bungling.

Kant asserted that "transcendental questions demand transcendental answers" (A637/B6650). But in what sense are there questions
which are *not* ultimately transcendental—that is, without transcendental implication, standing in need of ultimate grounds? Kant, nonetheless, thought one could ask questions without asking more—*as if* one
could exit this polysyllogistic once having entered it, *as if* it did not
enforce a certain "provisionalness"[32] upon assertion and a kind of undecidability which was insurpassable. *As if,* one could alleviate, then,
what a classical phenomenologist called "the Kantian fear of transcendental chance"[33] and the contingency which haunts all possible worlds.
The only question is whether such provisionalness and its risk marks the
demise of Reason and rationality or not—if it remains true, equally,
that apart from this risk, to perform a Kantian graft, there could be no
reason at all.[34]

It is at least clear that before this risk, in any case, one can no
longer be confident of assertions without remainder. There will always
be Kant's "wide abyss" between the contingent and the necessary in
need of "bridging," (A628/B656), a *lapsus judicii* (A146/B174)[35]
which allows no metaphysical return. Against it, rather, stands the necessity of a different sort: not the respect (*Achtung*) for the law, but for
what escapes law, or the law of what escapes: the universality which
withdraws from the "universality" of the concept, for what remains
Other to the Same. Another *Achtung* which blocks Reason's advance.

But that is precisely what Kant and transcendentalism, and perhaps philosophy in general must deny in order to stand their ground,
refusing in principle to face this risk. The risk of the finite—or at least
that which allows the difference between the finite and the infinite to be
meted out. The critical tribunal is, in fact, nothing else but a tribunal
which not only obliterates that risk through a profound forgetfulness,

but in the last analysis destroys it: paradoxically, perhaps unveiling the nature on which Kant depended, dreamed about, and finally, invoked.

> The root of these disturbances, which lies deep in the nature of human reason, must be removed [*ausgerottet*]. But how can we do so unless we give it freedom, nay nourishment to send out shoots so that it may discover itself to our eyes, and that it may then be entirely destroyed? (A777–8/B805–6)[36]

Notes

1. Samuel Beckett, *Waiting for Godot* (New York: Grove Press, 1954), p. 41.

2. Immanuel Kant, *Critique of Pure Reason,* trans. Norman Kemp Smith (New York: Macmillan, 1929). All references to this text will be made according to the usual practice of providing references to Kant's first and second editions.

3. Immanuel Kant, *Selected Pre-Critical Writings,* trans. G. B. Gerferd and D. E. Walford (New York: Barnes & Noble, 1968), p. 82.

4. Hans-George Gadamer, "Historical Transformations of Reason," in *Rationality Today,* ed. Theodore F. Geraets (Ottawa: University of Ottawa Press, 1979), p. 7.

5. Immanuel Kant, *Critique of Judgement,* trans. J. H. Bernard (New York: Hafner, 1968), p. 157.

6. Immanuel Kant, *Anthropology from a Pragmatic Point of View,* trans. Mary J. Gregor (The Hague: Nijhoff, 1974), p. 85.

7. Immanuel Kant, *Religion within the Limits of Reason Alone,* trans. T. M. Green and H. H. Hudson (New York: Harper & Row, 1960), p. 24.

8. Ibid., p. 39.

9. Ibid., p. 42.

10. *Anthropology,* p. 87.

11. Ibid.

12. "The physico-theological proof as combining speculation and intuition, might therefore perhaps give additional weight to other proofs (if such there be); but taken alone, it serves only to prepare the understanding for theological knowledge, and to give it a natural leaning in this direction, not to complete the work in and by itself" (A637/B666).

13. Jacques Derrida, *Of Grammatology,* trans. Gayatri Spivak (Baltimore: Johns Hopkins University Press, 1976), p. 60.

14. Ibid., p. 52.

15. Jacques Derrida, "Genesis and Structure" in *Writing and Difference,* trans. Alan Bass (Chicago: University of Chicago Press, 1978), p. 157.

16. Immanuel Kant, *Gesammelte Schriften,* vol. 21, *Opus Postumum* (Berlin: Walter de Gruyter & Co., 1938), p. 31.

17. Ibid., p. 78.

18. Beckett, *Godot,* p. 51.

19. Jacques Derrida, "Violence and Metaphysics," in *Writing and Difference,* p. 120.

20. An "argument" which questions the univocal decidability of argumentation obviously places itself in scare quotes. It remains, in this sense, a thought "beyond philosophy" as Derrida has said recently:

> Now reason is only one species of thought—which does not mean that thought is "irrational." . . . I insisted . . . on stressing the dimension in this context I am calling "thought"—a dimension that is not reducible to technique, nor to science, nor philosophy. ("The Principle of Reason: The University in the Eyes of Its Pupils," *Diacritics* 13, no. 3 [Fall 1983], p. 16)

21. See Jacques Derrida, "Economimesis," trans. R. Klein, *Diacritics,* June 1981, p. 9.
22. See *Edmund Husserl's "Origin of Geometry": An Introduction,* trans. John P. Leavey, Jr. (Stony Brook, N.Y.: Nicolas Hays, 1978), pp. 137ff.
23. See Jacques Derrida, *Spurs: Nietzsche's Styles,* trans. Barbara Harlow (Chicago: University of Chicago Press, 1979), p. 113.
24. See Jacques Derrida, "Signature Event Context," trans. Samuel Weber and Jeffrey Mehlman, *Glyph 1* (Baltimore: Johns Hopkins University Press, 1977), p. 174.
25. See "Violence and Metaphysics" in *Writing and Difference,* p. 120f.
26. See "The Theater of Cruelty," ibid., p. 249.
27. *Of Grammatology,* p. 61.
28. Ibid.
29. Compare Immanuel Kant, *Logic,* trans. Robert Hartman and Wolfgang Schwarz (Indianapolis: Bobbs-Merrill, 1974), p. 105: "Since only single things or individuals are of an all-sided determination, there can be cognition of an all-sided determination only as intuitions, not, however, as concepts; in respect of the latter, logical determination can never be considered complete."
30. Compare Kant's statement in the *Critique* concerning the paradox of transcendental reason:

> Appearances demand explanation only so far as the conditions of their explanation are given in perception; but all that may ever be given in this way, when taken together in an *absolute whole,* is not itself a perception. Yet it is just the explanation of this very whole that is demanded in the transcendental problem of reason. (A483–84/B511–12)

It is precisely this paradox concerning explanation (*Erklärung*) which underlies the failure of transcendental reason in Kant's Dialectic, a failure (one which concerns an insurmountable *heterogeneity*) regarding the relation between the conditions and the conditioned, part and whole, perception and horizon, and ultimately assertion and its conditions (*Erklärungsbedingungen*), its "assertibility conditions"—or its "contextual saturation," as Derrida has put it in his reading of Austin and the research program underlying linguistic analysis, a reading which once more reflects his "deconstruction" of the logic of transcendental regulation:

> (A)re the conditions [*les réquisites*] of a context ever absolutely determinable? That is, fundamentally, the most general question that I shall endeavor to elaborate. Is there a rigorous and scientific notion of *context*? Or does the notion of context not conceal behind it a certain confusion, philosophical presuppositions of a very determinate nature? Stating it in the most summary manner possible, I

shall try to demonstrate why a context is never absolutely determinable, or rather, why its determination can never be entirely saturated. ("Signature Event Context" p. 174)

Ultimately here, too, Derrida will rediscover risk, a risk inherent within all speech acts: "Austin does not ponder the consequences issuing from the fact that a possibility—a possible risk—is always possible, and is in some sense a necessary possibility" (189).

31. Jacques Derrida, "Limited Inc. a b c . . . ," *Glyph 2,* trans. Samuel Weber (Baltimore: Johns Hopkins University Press, 1978), p. 194.

32. See Martin Heidegger, *On Time and Being,* trans. Joan Stambaugh (New York: Harper & Row, 1972), p. 35.

33. Max Scheler, *Formalism in Ethics and Non-Formal Ethics of Values,* trans. Manfred S. Frings and Roger L. Funk (Evanston: Northwestern University Press, 1973), p. 376.

34. The exposition of concepts then is at best, Kant admitted, "probable" and "never apodeictically certain" (A729/B757), haunted by a risk which affects all "verisimilitude" without simply nihilating it—as Gadamer (among others) has noted regarding the latter:

> The eikos, the verisimile [*das verisimile*], the "probable" *Wahr-Scheinliche,* literally true shining, the "clear" [*Einleuchtend,* literally "shining in"], belong in a series that defends its own rightness against the truth and certainty of what is proved and known. . . . The thing itself compels us to speak of an event and of an activity of the thing. . . . The idea is always that what is clear is not proved and not absolutely certain, but it asserts itself by reason of its own merit within the area of the possible and the probable. (Hans-Georg Gadamer, *Truth and Method,* trans. Garret Barden and John Cumming [New York: Seabury, 1975], pp. 441–42)

Nonetheless, if Gadamer perhaps rightly retrieves a notion of truth, of "truth-taking" (*Wahr-nehmung*), which points to the insurpassability of verisimilitude, this does not mean that interpretation ever overcomes the re-move which its risk institutes, nor that all that may be rightly retrieved for the sake of the phenomena does not undergo a certain phenomenalization—notwithstanding what he often states to the contrary. See my "Between Truth and Method: Gadamer and the Problem of Justification in Interpretative Practices," forthcoming.

35. See Jean-Luc Nancy, "Lapsus judicii," *Communications,* vol. 26, 1977.

36. There is, then, perhaps a third figure within the models or typology of nature contained in the Kantian text, one which provides an essential confrontation for the other two. Beyond, that is, the "Newtonian" object of the principles, and the "Aristotelian" horizon of teleological judgment, a third appears which is perhaps best described as "Hobbesian" with all its juridical overtones, a state of nature, that is, which stands in need of overcoming by institutional intervention. As Kant states in "The Discipline of Pure Reason":

> In the absence of this critique reason is, as it were, in the state of nature, and can establish and secure its assertions only through war. (A751/B779)

Still, there can be little doubt that the play of images here contains again its own ἀγών, one perhaps still where "the parties beat the air, and wrestle with their own shadows"

(A756/B784). *Inter alia,* liberal models for the institution of political contract necessarily contained a certain scepticism concerning political authority. But this is precisely what Kant's account concerning the foundations of rationality must deny. The institution of the critical tribunal, on the contrary, presents an authority which is indisputable:

> The critique, on the other hand, arriving at all its decisions in the light of fundamental principles of its own institution [*Einsetzung*], *the authority of which no one can question,* secures to us the peace of a legal order, in which our disputes have to be conducted solely by the recognized methods of legal action. (A752/B780; I have stressed the text.)

Derrida's challenge to the authoritative account of rationality Kant has provided, as stated, the model of a certain "legal positivism" that *indisputably* founds Reason, obviously departs from such unchallengeable foundations—which is *not* to say, as is too often thought, that it simply gives up the problem of justification:

> (O)ne can justify [*justifier*] one's language, and one's choice of terms, only within a topic [*à l intérieur d'une topique*] and an historical strategy. The justification can therefore never be absolute and definitive. It corresponds to a condition of forces and translates an historical calculation. (*Of Grammatology,* p. 70)

A Point of Almost Absolute Proximity to Hegel

7

John Llewelyn

eine Wahrheit kann durch Aufschreiben nicht verlieren; ebensowenig
dadurch, dass wir sie aufbewahren.

Hegel, *Phänomenologie des Geistes*

Why almost? Why is the point of proximity between Derridian differance with an *a* and Hegelian difference with an *e* also a point of
rupture? (*Pos* 60/44).[1] Because the conflict of forces that goes by the
pseudonym differance, as opposed to the conflict of positions in dialectical contradiction, refuses incorporation (strange word) into the encyclopaedia and is refuse for the phenomenology of spirit. That is to
say, differance and dialectical difference are not dialectically opposed.
They are not opposed as one diction is to another. They are opposed in
the way that a contradiction is to the unconscious scription that makes
contradiction possible as semantic effect but impossible as a means toward some transcendentally signified *Resultat*. Results of speech acts of
denial and of other abnegating activities (*Tätigkeiten*) are to be reread as
effects of affirmative forces. So, too, are the so-called primal words
embodying opposite senses listed in the paper by Karl Abel that Freud
reviews and later adverts to in his own paper "Das Unheimliche."
Unheimlich itself, assuming it is an itself, is such an antithetical word
according to Freud because it is opposed to *heimlich* yet at the same
time subsumed under it on account of the fact that *heimlich* can mean
both that which is homely, familiar and within our ken and, on the
other hand, that which is hidden, dangerous, uncanny, and unconscious. Freud says, incidentally illustrating what he calls elsewhere the
effect of *déjà raconté,* that it was reading Abel's paper that enabled him
to understand ten years *après coup* what he had himself written in *The
Interpretation of Dreams* about the uncanny way in which the dream-

work finds it difficult to say no. Difficult because it seems not to know the word no, with the consequence that there is no easy way by which the analyst can know whether an element that admits (of) an opposite is to be taken as having a positive or negative force. No easy way, says Freud. No way, says Derrida, "in the last analysis," for the so-called last analysis is the psychoanalysis of the unconscious of a certain familiar psychoanalysis. The temporary undecidability is the effect of a pre-originary undecidability that cannot be talked away. This anasemic undecidability of differance that is the condition of the ambivalent concepts to which Freud refers is also the condition of the *Gegensinnigkeit* of the *Aufhebung* (its being both cancellation and preservation) that gives the movement of Hegel's dialectic its direction (*Sinn*) from the unconsciousness of the in-itself toward the self-consciousness of the in-itself-for-itself. Differance is not a condition in the manner of a category, a formal concept of concepts or their phenomenological ground. It is a condition paradoxically in the concept, re-citing and re-siting it (Fors 48/96). Something like a transcendental, except that what the Scholastics called transcendentals (e.g., being and unity) belong to every genus and are common to every concept, whereas differance "is" the degeneration of genus that prevents the genus being authentically self-possessed in absolute proximity to itself and foments disunity in the concept.

In the Concept.

How close does Hegel come to recognizing this transcendental, transphenomenal differance in *Differenz* that turns the latter inside out? Some way, Derrida suggests, pursuing a remark of Koyré's, when in the Jena Logic Hegel replaces his usual word for difference, *Unterschied,* by the phrase *absolut differente Besiehung,* where *differente* is the active infinitive opposed to itself, maintenance losing a grip on itself, the decompresence of the *Gegen-wart* (M 14–15/13–14). And in the *Encyclopaedia,* Derrida says,

> Hegel recognizes, in passing, certainly, but quite clearly, [that] there is not and there cannot be a purely phonetic writing. The alphabetic system as we practice it is not and cannot be purely phonetic. A script never permits itself to be saturated through and through by the voice. The nonphonetic functions, the operative silences, if one may so put it, of alphabetic writing are not matters of accidental fact or waste products that one could hope to reduce (punctuation, figure [*chiffre*], spacing). The *fact* of which we have just spoken is not just an empirical fact; it is the example of an essential law that irreducibly limits the fulfillment of a

teleological ideal. In effect, Hegel concedes this in a parenthesis that he closes very quickly and [that] deserves to be underlined. (*M* 111–12/95–96)

Derrida then reproduces the following words of the *Encyclopaedia:*

> Leibniz allowed himself to be misled by his understanding (*Verstand*) in considering that it would be highly desirable for communication between people of different nationalities, especially scholars, if we had a perfect written language constructed after the style of hieroglyphics, which already obtains in some measure with [*bei*] alphabetic writing (as in our signs for numbers, planets, chemical substances and suchlike). (*Enc.* § 459)

Is Derrida being over- (or under-)generous to Hegel in seeing in Hegel's parenthetical remark recognition of more than the empirical fact that we sometimes use figures *alongside* words? Is Hegel recognizing that there cannot be a purely phonetic writing? Is he acknowledging the necessary permeation of the phonetic by the graphic, its transfiguration? Perhaps we should note [*entre crochets*] that Derrida may be alluding less to the words between the parentheses than to the brackets themselves which, like commas and other punctuation marks, have, most remarkably in German, a grammatical function that cannot be bracketed away. In any case, it is not obvious what counts as a recognition, particularly a recognition "in passing." Are Spaniards recognizing the necessary graphematicity of the phoneme when they call names *nombres?*

Strangely intestinal to the cunning of reason is the uncanniness of differance. Foreignly *heimlich,* somewhat like the circumferential ducts, wastepipes, elevators, moving staircases, and other processional inwards of the Centre Pompidou. No more than somewhat. At most almost. For while the *pompe funèbre* of the phenomenology of spirit is the self-deconstruction of an eternally self-consuming and self-consummating ring, differance "does not pass *around* a circular field, but works it *otherwise*" (Ja 118). Differance is an absolute exterior that no longer permits itself to be internalized (*M* 339/285). An inside-out *restance* that is the non-negatively improductive force without which there would be no restlessly *sich aufhebende Ursprung.* The *sourdre de la source,* the surgeance of the *zugegrabenen Brunnen* (*M* 353/297), the spir(i)t of the *unheimlich* spring.

Scription Auf-hebung *à relire.*

We shall never be finished with the reading or rereading of the Hegelian text, and, in a certain way, I do nothing but try to explain myself on this point. In effect I believe that Hegel's text is necessarily fissured; that it is something more and other than the circular closure of its representation. It is not reduced to a content of philosophemes, it also necessarily produces a powerful writing operation, a remainder [*reste*] of writing of which one must re-examine the strange relationship it entertains with the philosophical content, the movement by which the latter exceeds its meaning, allows itself to be turned away, turned back, repeated outside its self-identity. (*Pos* 103–4/77–78)

This question of the outside of the Hegelian text is picked up again in the sixty-seven prefatory pages of the unbook entitled *La Dissémination.* "Ceci (donc) n'aura pas été un livre," Derrida tells us in the first line of this plurally prefatory part to which he gives the title "Hors livre." This *hors livre* is Derrida's *Differenzschrift* on the philosophical systems of Hegel and Feuerbach, notwithstanding that mention of the latter is limited to a footnote, which may seem a sad irony in view of the fact that this note cites the following statement from Feuerbach's "Preliminary Theses on the Reformation of Philosophy": "The philosopher must introduce into the *text* of philosophy that side of man that does *not* philosophize, that is rather *against* philosophy, opposes abstract thinking, that therefore which in Hegel is relegated to a *note.*"[2] Philosophy must begin with nonphilosophy, Feuerbach goes on to say in a sentence that would provoke Derrida to ask whether we are clear about this opposition of philosophy and nonphilosophy. Does not Feuerbach himself refer to nonphilosophy as the "*Prinzip* des Sensual*ismus*"? And can the text of philosophy be so simply distinguished from the *Anmerkung?* Are not the remarks already introduced, *aufgenommen,* into the text? Or are they introduced only into the introduction, or into the preface, the pretextual endpapers? According to Hegel, random remarks about the empirical circumstances attending the genesis of a philosophical system and anticipatory observations about its structure should be restricted to the *hors livre.* But, as Derrida observes in "Hors livre," Hegel's philosophical system is omnivorous. In the end it digests its own empty shell. The foreword is no less an afterword, the hors d'oeuvre a suite, *die Sachertorte selbst,* the *Resultat* of the *Tat,* the real McCoy. What Hegel identifies as extraneous to philosophy, the formal, empirical, and methodological comments of his predecessors and contemporaries, what is allegedly foreign to philosophy is a moment that melts into its *for intérieur,* subliminated into the Concept itself (*Diss* 26/18). Lost so that it shall have been saved.

Thus, willy nilly, Hegel recognizes that there is only the text. And there is that much proximity between him and Derrida. But the textuality of the text according to Hegel is conservative. It is a restricted, thrifty economy of absolute knowing in which the end is at the beginning and the beginning is at the end, in which the not yet is already there and the ἀρχή and the τέλος are intestinally intersusceptive, the snake that swallows its tail—though not to the point at which it has turned itself inside-out. In the cycle of dialectical speculation Hegel's pre-text is a Monsieur Teste "*étant, et me voyant*" ("*debout avec la colonne d'or de l'Opéra,*" "*étayá par la grosse colonne*"), so strongheadedly *en-tête* that it penetrates and vanishes into the semantics of the text. Hegel is the last philosopher of the book, but because he is the first *thinker* of writing (*Gr* 41/26), he is both as near and as far as possible from Derrida's ancient and modern description of writing and the text. For with Hegel, since he thinks writing, the prefatory is fated to be raised up to the text. With Derrida "there is" a general pretext that loses its head, does not know what heading to take (*Diss* 27/20), has no sense of direction. No sense. In the book, says Hegel, for *ça, das Diese,* read *Sa, Savoir absolu.* For *Sa,* says Derrida, read *ça,* "*la-chose-qui-n'est-pas*" (Ja 121), and, because the book is strangely, *unheimlich,* inscribed within an appended part, for *Phenomenology of Spirit* read *PS.*

PS

How can one read without thinking? *Was hisst Denken?* What jacks thinking up, jacks it off, puts it out of play and puts it into *play*? What hoists thinking with its own petard? What is the force that through the green fuse drives it to dehisce? How can the general economy of a spendthrift text dispense with and deconstruct a thrifty economy of thought that makes full compensation? This is the sixty-four-thousand-dollar question, a question that may beg the question *jusqu'à un certain point* (*M* 126/107), at any rate if it is cast in the form Why? What is this? or What does this mean? Derrida gives us a metaphor to help us on our way, the metaphor of "a machine defined in its pure functioning, and not in its final utility, its meaning, its return, its work" (*M*126/ 107). Defined? Only if the limit laid down by the definition is also delimited. And only if this delimitation is an in-finitizing that amounts neither to what is a bad infinite nor to what is a good infinite according to Hegel, but, beyond good and evil, "exceeds the always-already-constitutedness of meaning and truth in the theo-logico-encyclopaedic space of self-fecundation without limen" (*Diss* 61/53).

What is of special interest to us here is this "up to a certain point" of Derrida's writing, the way its path passes through a point of almost absolute proximity to Hegel and explains why he says that he is doing no more than a repeated rehearsal of Hegel's lines. Indeed, his machine metaphor is based on the lines in which Hegel insists that calculation is an unthinking, mechanical business, and that only speculative logic can save mathematics by infusing into its forms *Berechtigung, Sinn und Wert*, justification, meaning and value (*Science of Logic* vol. 1, bk. 1, sect. 2, ch. 2, remark 2). Could there be a machine, a calculating machine, that would be safe from that salvation, would succeed in Zarathustra's mission to "*sauver le hasard*" (Blanchot), without risking the reassurance of being "outside at all costs"(*Diss* 42/36) as does the author of a concluding unscientific postscript whose path, although, like Derrida's, indirect, may pass through a point so close to the path of the *Phenomenology of Spirit* that it coalesces with its Unhappy Consciousness? This machine cannot be conceived. But can it be contrived? Can such a machine be improvised (Ja 99), machinated? And can it be got to go, *marcher*, without having to be driven by the travail of contradictory negation? Not simply by negating that negation or attempting to put the dialectic in reverse. Nor by consigning the project to silence, contenting ourselves with the thought "*Wovon man nicht sprechen kann, darüber muss man schweigen.*" We bricolate a contraption and see if it works. Such a contraption as *Glas*.

The *glas* is about to be tolled. There are too few minutes left to tell of minutiae. No time to chronicle the particular questions into which *Glas* shatters its overriding question, "*Que reste-t-il du savoir absolu?*" What remains over of and from absolute knowing? Questions like: (1) As we make the last step in the *Phenomenology of Spirit* over the threshold from revealed religion to its absolute philosophical truth, how can we read *encore*, still and again, and *pas encore*, not yet? Is this a step out of time, to the concept from the concept that is there? Can the temporal adverb be read according to the absolute concept? Or without it? In the former case it loses its temporal sense. In the latter case it sacrifices its absolute conceptuality and prohibits comprehension. In neither case is it read. "In both cases it is read provided that it is not read" (*Gl* 254L/ 318L). The strange word "read," λέγειν, has been read both as semantic plenitude and as semantic void. For dialectical contradiction read dyslectic double-bind. (2) Is the bastard conceivable in the dialectic of *Aufhebung*? (*Gl* 12L/8L) (3) Is the orphan? (*Gl* 186L/231L) (4) Is the sister, the sister of Polynices? (*Gl* 170L/210L) (5) Is repression? (*Gl* 214L/266L) (6) Is murder or suicide, murder which is suicide, where the line between life and death is so thinly drawn that no dialectical concept seems able to grasp its inexistence? (*Gl* 158L/195L) Each of these apparently undecidable questions which are catalogued in the column of *Glas* in which Derrida takes stock of Hegel's phylo-phallo-genealogy turns out to be only *almost* undecidable, "*presque* indécidable" (*Gl* 159L/196L)—like Freud's problems over whether a bipolar element in a dream is to be interpreted negatively or positively. With difficulty, but a difficulty that facilitates their resolution, all these questions and problems can be resolved or dissolved, *aufgelöst*, by being *aufgehoben*. Unless . . .

Unless *Aufhebung* is upheaved.

Such an upheaval is activated in *Glas*. *Glas* takes a rise out of *Aufhebung*, repeating it as rhyzomatic relay, less lift than nomadic laterality, but without reducing it to subjective unilaterality (En 16/313) or to unmotivated free play. Its recto and rectal column may be read as an attempt to show that from the system examined in its left column there is something that it is a relief to leave behind. Someunthing, an almost nothing (*rien, presque* [Mal 376]), the residual subsubstantial *je ne sais quoi* of which Plato could not decide whether it had a Form, the dropping of a Swabo-Prussian eagle, "*le vomi du système*," "neither solid nor liquid, neither out nor in" (*Gl* 84L/100L; 183L/227L), the orally-anally disgusting *Ekel* of which Kant treats in the *Anthropology* (Ec 91–93), the innominable *dégueulassenheit*, neither one thing nor the other, of which (*duquel? de laquelle? donc dont*) *gl* is the obscene cloackroom trace ("*cloca:* horseman's cape named from its bell shape [clock]" *Concise Oxford Dictionary*).

A declination of Hegel's indeterminate sphinx, an unmentionable sphincter, *gl* is that *ersatz* glottis in the Cointreau bottles on sale duty-free at international airports nowadays that so infuriates us, especially scholars, *insbesondere die Gelehrten*, whatever our language, because it hoists the tongue but lets it fall back again (*Gl* 263R/329R), because it is the indefinite dyad that announces the *spasme, final, de la glotte* (Mal 379), the *glas* of classification, of binary opposition and of the syllogistic Trinity (*eglan* OE, *agljan* f. *egle* troublesome [Goth. *aglus*]). Troublesome (simple inversion won't make it go glug-glug; try solicitation), yet what no home should be without. Perhaps it is what Bradley was needing in order to glue terms to the relations that glue terms to the relations that glue. . . . Hume and Wittgenstein kept a tube of it handy. This agglutinative "principle of all principles" of differentiation is what the an(a)thematic, prothetic, galactic, Genet-ic column of *Glas* applies to its thematically genealogical partner as the condition that makes Hegel's dialectical synthesis an effect produced by a *nécessité hasardeuse* (Diss 56/48). "*L'infini sort du hasard*" (Mallarmé, *Igitur*). Hence, *gl* is the cadence that syncopates ascendence, the *ruiner* concealed, without being cancelled, in the almost absolutely anagrammatical *réunir,* the protocol of Hegel's prefaces and of his and our PS.

PPS

Save that if we have said what it is, it is not what we have said. We shall have read *Glas* as a Moebius strip. We shall have misconceived it, because we shall have conceived it. We shall have annulled the remainder by annulation. Whereas a remainder remains in the space between. Between the columns and between the pages where what remains on the left is what is incorporated by being assimilated and by living on, while what remains on the right is incorporated as an eliminated foreign body (Fors 18/72, Ja 93), the nonlinguistic *corps impropre* of writing (EC 112), Limited Ink. The *glas,* which is the *glas* of classification and the *glas* of *classification* (strange word, *of*), swings between in the space that Kant's schema attempted to fill and remained unfilled by Hegel's *Aufhebung.*

The unbook *Glas,* like a *porte à brisures,* a folding partition which is open when it is closed and vice versa, would machinate a non-Euclidean geometry in which the Hegelian circle is squared and the Hegelian triangle is forcibly opened up to a rectangular stage (*carrefour, theatrum* [*Diss* 386/347]), "(almost) pure spacing, going on forever and not in expectation of any Messianic fulfillment" (*Diss* 383/345), the *mise en (s)cène* of nothing more nor less than a *deus ex machina.*

PPPS

This impotence of nature sets limits to philosophy, and it is quite improper to expect the Concept to comprehend these contingent products of nature—and, as it is put, construct . . . them.

. . . Nature everywhere blurs the essential limits of species and genera by intermediate and defective forms, which continually furnish counter examples to every fixed distinction; this even occurs within a specific genus, that of man, for example, where monstrous births, on the one hand, must be considered as belonging to the genus, while on the other hand, they lack certain essential determinations characteristic of the genus. In order to be able to consider such forms as defective, imperfect and deformed, one must presuppose a fixed, invariable type. This type, however, cannot be furnished by experience, for it is experience which also presents these so-called monstrosities. . . . (Hegel, *Enc.* § 250, Note)[3]

Notes

1. The references in the text to the writings of Derrida are:

Diss   *La Dissémination* (Paris: Seuil, 1972); *Dissemination,* trans. Barbara Johnson (Chicago: University of Chicago Press, 1981; London: Athlone, 1981).

Ec   "Economimesis," in Sylviane Agacinski et al., *Mimesis des articulations* (Paris: Aubier-Flammarion, 1975).

EC   "Entre crochets," *Digraphe* 8 (1976): 97–114.

En   "Envoi," Actes du 18e Congrès des Sociétés de Philosophie de Langue Française, Strasbourg (Paris: Vrin, 1980), 6–30; "Sending: On Representation," trans. Peter and Mary Ann Caws, *Social Research* 49 (1982): 294–326.

Fors   "Fors: les mots anglés de Nicolas Abraham et Maria Torok," introduction to Nicolas Abraham and Maria Torok, *Cryptonymie: le Verbier de l'homme aux loups* (Paris: Aubier-Flammarion, 1976), 7–73; trans. Barbara Johnson, *The Georgia Review* 31 (1977): 64–116.

Gl   *Glas* (Paris: Galilée, 1974; Paris: Denoël/Gonthier, 1981).

Gr   *De la grammatologie* (Paris: Minuit, 1967); *Of Grammatology,* trans. Gayatri Chakravorty Spivak (Baltimore and London: Johns Hopkins University Press, 1974, 1976).

Ja   "Ja, ou le faux-bond," *Digraphe* 11 (1977): 83–121.

M   *Marges de la philosophie* (Paris: Minuit, 1972); *Margins of Philosophy,* trans. Alan Bass (Chicago: University of Chicago Press, 1982; Brighton: Harvester, 1982).

Mal   "Mallarmé," in *Tableau de la littérature française: De Madame de Staël à Rimbaud* (Paris: Gallimard, 1974), 368–79.

Pos   *Positions* (Paris: Minuit, 1972); *Positions,* trans. Alan Bass (Chicago: University of Chicago Press, 1981; London: Athlone, 1981).

The passages cited from Hegel's *Encyclopaedia* are adapted from the translations by W. Wallace and A. V. Miller (Oxford: Oxford University Press, 1971–1975).

2. Ludwig Feuerbach, *Gesammelte Werke, Kleinere Schriften,* vol. 2 (Berlin: Akademie Verlag, 1970), 254. See *Diss* 36/30.

3. I am grateful to Dr. Stephen Houlgate for discussions we had while I was preparing this paper. There is further treatment of some of the questions raised in it in my *Derrida on the Threshold of Sense* (London: Macmillan, 1986; New York: St. Martins, 1986), especially chapter 1.

Deconstruction
and Phenomenology

3

The Economy of Signs in Husserl and Derrida: From Uselessness to Full Employment

8

John D. Caputo

In the *First Investigation* (§ 15) Husserl gives two examples of non-sense—"Green is or" (*Grün ist oder*) and "Abracadabra."[1] These are dangerous expressions for Husserl, indeed not expressions at all, but examples of a wild grammar which defy the rules of pure logic. Husserl wants to banish them, to escort them to the edge of the city, to exile them from the πόλις of meaning and sense, of λόγος and language. Derrida, ever alert to the rights of those who are excluded and denied privilege, comes to their rescue. For these signifiers are illustrative indeed, not of non-sense, but of the deeper work which signifiers do, the deeper formality of the signifier, a structural formality which Husserl both recognizes and represses. By means of this blatant agrammaticality, Derrida thinks, we gain access to the freedom of signs, their liberation from intuition. Their banishment by a priori grammar is in fact a liberation from an oppressive regime.

But Derrida is interested not only in the liberation of signifiers, here represented by these jarring examples, but in finding them a job. He is interested, not only in battling for their freedom, but in defending their right to work. For even the signifiers which Husserl admits into the πόλις, those which bear a meaning and a possible relation to intuition, are declared useless, *Zwecklos*, without purpose. They are "unproductive" members of society; they make no contribution. So Derrida's task is to show what they can do, the work of which they are capable, the contribution they can make.

My task in this paper then will be to follow the case study of "green is or" and "abracadabra," to see if they have been denied their rights, to see how Derrida comes to their defense and what sort of work he finds for them to do. I will proceed in three steps. (1) In the first section, I examine Derrida's arguments against the "uselessness of signs" in Husserl's *First Investigation,* which is the central deconstructive thread in *Speech and Phenomena*. (2) In the second, "the freedom of signs," I pursue the liberation of "green is or" and "abracadabra," which results in what Derrida calls the "freedom of language, the candor of speech" (*VPh* 100/89).[2] And it is here, I will argue, that the impact of Derrida, the pointed tip of his stylus, can best be felt. (3) In the final and concluding section, entitled "the productivity of signs and the economy of full employment," I try to show that the very productivity and indefatigability of signs, the full employment which Derrida gains for them, produces a phenomenogical result which goes against Derrida's intentions, even as his contention that presence is a constituted effect produces a deconstructive result which goes against Husserl's intentions. Here I consider the question of *die Sache selbst, la même chose*.

The Uselessness of Signs

Husserl has two arguments against allowing indicative signs to play a role in solitary life. First, any such interior dialogue of the self with the self is purely pretended and imaginary—there is no genuine, effective, real communication of anything to the self by the self. Second, signs are ultimately without purpose (*Zwecklos*) in the monological sphere. In soliloquy, in the life of the ego with itself, Husserl thinks, the instrumentality and mediation of indicative signs would be quite useless (". . . *solchen Anzeigen hier ganz zwecklos wäre*" [§ 8]).

Derrida argues each point in turn. Against the first, he delimits the claim of real communication to be real and effective—inasmuch as it must rely upon the representative power of indicative signs to produce its effect. That is to say, there can be no naked contact, no immediate presence of mind to mind, in actual communication, but only a work of mediation carried out by signs and representations. Against the second, he shows that signs are not useless, that there would be a role for them to play were they allowed back into the city, and that it is precisely Husserl himself who establishes this role. It is with this second argument that I concern myself here.

With the momentous discovery of the reduction, Husserl isolates an operation which is at once the fundamental gesture of philosophy and the undoing of the classical role of philosophy to provide foundations and assured presence. The reduction is the name of philosophy's critical power, its impulse to get beyond naiveté and already constituted products. Derrida does not quarrel about the reduction, does not question its possibility, does not want to short-circuit its critical operation. He only wants to see that it is carried out far enough, that the work of critique is not subverted in advance by a teleology of presence and ful-fillment. He wants thus to carry out what Husserl set in motion, to extend the work of reduction, but to do so ruthlessly, without pity, with the hardness of heart of Zarathustra. For in Husserl himself the reductive impulse is cut short. Phenomenological vigilance is not enough. It is satisfied with presence, intuition, self-showing—when that is precisely what needs to be questioned. The teleology of fulfill-ment obscures Husserl's achievement and causes us to lose sight of Husserl's discovery of the genuine reduction, let us call it here, the semiotic or semiological reduction.

Signs are useless in solitary life, according to Husserl, because there can be no need to indicate mental acts to oneself. This is because "the acts in question are themselves experienced by us at that very mo-ment" (§ 8). *Im selben Augenblick:* there is not the blink of an eye be-tween the ego which speaks and the ego which hears itself speak. Nothing intervenes in this diaphanous medium of pure, inner voice. There is no opacity, no thickness to divide the ego from itself.[3] Yet that is a view which has been effectively undermined by Husserl's own ac-count of inner time-consciousness. For the now is not altogether now, is not all together, is not self-identity, pure and simple. Instead, in vir-tue of his own doctrine of retention, Husserl insists that now must be continuously compounded with now (*VPh* 72/64), presence with non-presence, in order to make up (constitute), to make up for (supple-ment), the present in the wider, more pregnant sense, which is a pro-tential-retentional synthesis. That means that the present depends upon the function of representation, of retentional making present again. If retention is a representational modification of the now (which is the present in the strict, narrow sense), nonetheless the genuine and living present (in the wide, pregnant sense) is an effect, a product, of the work of retention. In the living present, now is woven together with now to produce a more complex fabric/text. Here representation makes pres-ence possible; presence is the effect of representation. The metaphysical prejudice that representation is a modification of presence is rooted out.

Husserl realizes the disruptive potential of this admission and hence takes great pains to contain it by insisting on the distinction be-tween retention and reproduction. Phenomenologically, there is an es-sential distinction between the tones which have just lapsed in the melody which is still sounding, or the syllables which have just lapsed in the multisyllabic word which is still being uttered, and, let us say, a melody we heard yesterday, or words spoken an hour ago. Different sequences of *Erlebnisse* have intervened in the meantime, the intentional stream has been inhabited by different objects. Yet what is the difference *in principle,* Derrida asks, between what is just lapsed and what has been lapsed for some time now? What is the difference in principle if—and this is a constraint which Husserl imposes upon himself—one demands absolute self-presence, perfect immediacy, *im selben Augenblick?* A moment cannot be qualified as just a little bit past, just a little lapsed. The present in the pregnant sense cannot be just a little bit pregnant! That is not a difference in principle. Retention and reproduction are but variant degrees of representation, different only in virtue of the extent to which they are distanced from the simple now-impression.

But if retention is necessary, signs are *not* useless:

> The fact that nonpresence and otherness are internal to presence strikes at the very root of the argument for the uselessness of signs in the self-relation. (*VPh* 74/66)

There *is* a role for signs to play. For the work of protention and retention is a work of *tenere,* tenancy, place-holding, a work which is facilitated by the φάρμακον of signs, the remedy which will provide a supplement for memory. Indeed would it be "humanistic" and "anthropomorphic" to compare what Husserl calls *animalia,* which have no recourse to signs, with the tremendously enhanced powers of the beings whose conscious stream is supplemented by signs, which aid it in the work of compounding now with now, of holding together presence with non-presence, strengthening it with the tenaciousness of retention and protention?[4] Signs are not useless. They make consciousness stronger, more tenacious. Indeed they make consciousness in the pregnant sense (*con-scire*) possible.

Husserl takes consciousness to be a diaphanous life which operates by means of the pure voice. The voice is not spatial and mundane. The voice is heard and understood as soon as it speaks, in "absolute proximity" to the speaking subject, in perfect auto-affection:

> My words are "alive" because they seem not to leave me: not to fall outside me, outside my breath, at a visible distance. (*VPh* 85/76)

The worldly body of the voice fades away at the very moment it is produced. That at least is how it *seems.* For Husserl's phenomenology operates in a naiveté generated by the invisibility of the voice and the phonetic sign, even as it is the task of the semiotic reduction to make signs conspicuous. Husserl's reduction is waylaid by a natural attitude, not about language, but about the transparency of sound which leads him to think that language is not productive, that it merely reproduces the pre-expressive stratum. Husserl carries out a reduction *of* phonetic signifiers, not a reduction *to* them. His transcendental phenomenology operates in a naive belief in the works which have been wrought by the phonetic signifier. But this reduction of language is never quite complete, the subjugation of the reduction to this phonological metaphysics never quite succeeds. An uneasiness pervades his text:

> because an underlying motif was disturbing and contesting the security of these traditional distinctions from within and because the possibility of writing dwelt within speech, which was itself at work in the inwardness of thought. (*VPh* 92/82)

The analysis of internal time-consciousness betrays the realization that presence is infiltrated with non-presence, that presence is a constituted effect, that the primordial comes to be under the hand of the trace. The production of presence is the work of retention. But how can the work of retention be carried out without the labor of signs? ("Doubless Husserl would refuse to assimilate the necessity of retention and the necessity of signs. . ." [VPh 74/66].)

With that, the role of signs is made conspicuous. The opacity of writing infiltrates the pure medium of the voice. The *cogito* is thick with time, as Merleau-Ponty said, differentiated and extended in a temporal continuum. And just so it is also thick with writing, whose work it is to weave the stream of *Erlebnisse*, of *tenere*, tenancy, into the unity of a text, *texere*, textuality. A lingering naiveté is rooted out. The reduction is radicalized, transformed into a semiotic reduction which discovers the work of the signifier and its anonymous productivity.

The Freedom of Signs

Now I want to turn to Derrida's strategy for liberating "green is or" and "abracadabra," these two refugees from pure grammar. Even if signs are necessary to the work of retention, why must that implicate us in such non-sensical signs? Why does Derrida insist on keeping such unsavory company?

When Husserl identified the structural capacity of the sign to operate in the absence of its object he isolated the essence of the sign as such. The sign is *für etwas*. It plays the role of *tenere*, tenancy, standing in and holding the place for something, just when what is present, *für sich,* is not to be had. More importantly, and this is the essential point for Derrida, for it is the more treacherous situation, the sign stands in for and holds the place for something *even when it is to be had, even when it is present*. The sign, on Husserl's own accounting, implies non-plenitude, the power to function without fulfillment. And this is structurally necessary to it as a sign. Derrida writes:

> The whole originality of this conception lies in the fact that its ultimate subjection to intuitionism does not oppress what might be called the freedom of language, the candor of speech, even if it is false and contradictory. One can speak without knowing. And against the whole philosophical tradition Husserl shows that in that case speech is still genuinely speech, provided it obeys certain rules which do not immediately figure as rules for knowledge. (*VPh* 100/89–90)

Speech is still good speech when its object is absent, when it is true but not fulfilled—as when I speak of Madrid, the capital of Spain, even though I have never been there. It is still good speech when it can only be fulfilled imaginatively (the golden mountain). It is good speech even when it cannot be fulfilled at all, because it is false or even because it is contradictory (the circle is square). Even the *Widersinn* is not an *Unsinn*. Speech is not impaired when it has neither object nor consistent meaning.

But here the series of reductions breaks off. Despite the "boldness" of pure logical grammar, Husserl loses his nerve. He senses that he is skirting dangerously close to the edge of the city, risking exile, and so he takes care. The wandering signifier must be contained. He calls upon the police to establish law and order. Rules of a priori grammar, combinatorial rules governing the forms of meanings, are put into effect, limiting where one may travel.[5] He takes measures to contain wild grammar—"green is or"—and wild articulate sounds—"abracadabra." But why are these signifiers wild and dangerous? Because they declare their absolute independence of all possible intuition. Unlike "the circle is square," they are not even of a *form* such that, were one to replace them by other signifiers of the same form, intuition could result. They are absolutely defiant; they practice absolute civil disobedience.

Yet Husserl himself has shown that it belongs to the very structure of the sign to operate without fulfillment, in the absence of its object. That is Husserl's own view. But on that accounting "green is or" and "abracadabra" represent the isolation of this structure and hence a welcome *liberation* from the rule of intuitionism, a liberation which is in fact made possible by the reduction of the rules of a priori grammar. Pure logical grammar, because it measures meaning in terms of intuitability, is not formal enough to resist the semiotic reduction, to survive as a semiotic residuum. This reduction—the one which is in place when we write "green is or" and "abracadabra"—*liberates* the signifier from the oppressive regime of intuitionism and its unfair demand that every signifier lead to Being, presence, objectivity, even when such demands cannot be met. Intuitionism exacts a tax which no one can pay.

"Green is or," "abracadabra" are thus the first utterances of free speech, wondrous examples of the "freedom of language, the candor of speech" (*VPh* 100/89), of "the emancipation of speech as non-knowing" (*VPh* 109/97). "Green is or" is free and licit sign-making, no less than anything of the form "S is P," indeed more so. It represents the weaving together of a text, an interweaving of signifiers which produces an effect, an odd, obscure effect which tantalizes us, but an effect nonetheless, one we could spend some time pondering and unraveling. There is sign-making here even where there is what metaphysics regards as *Unsinn,* where there is no possible relation to an obejct. Indeed Derrida even suggests that there is a *Sinn* here, a *Sinn* which has been rewritten in a wider nonmetaphysical sense, which does not promise knowledge, truth, or objectivity, for the latter are so many unjust restrictions of the civil rights of *Sinn,* so many attempts at intuitionistic conscription.

Thus, by means of "green is or" and "abracadabra," we are able to isolate the pure form of the signifier, the formal system of signifiers, the repeatable code. We liberate the form of writing, not writing in the narrow sense, but arche-writing, differance. We make reduction *of* a logico-grammatical form, which is still heavy with the matter of metaphysics, in order to make reduction *to* the pure power of signs to produce their effects, to generate their products.

But Derrida warns us not to conflate the two examples, that they are different:

> (and Husserl links up these last two examples somewhat hastily; he is perhaps not attentive enough to their difference). . . . (*VPh* 110/98)

What is the difference? What difference can there be between two examples of non-sense? Does non-sense come in degrees? Are they not both equally non-sensical? In fact, "abracadabra" is not non-sense.[6] In the first place, it serves as an example of non-sense, and hence, as Derrida points out in "Signature Event Context,"[7] performs a meaningful, repeatable function which is to be found in any respectable dictionary. Furthermore, "abracadabra" is an old name, an old cabalistic word: *abra, cad,* and then again *abra,* and hence structured around a form of repetition.

Meant to be written in triangular form—*abra* at the right and left hand angles, *cad* at the apex—it functions as an invocation of the Holy Trinity (for which it is likely an acronym) in order to drive out a malaria-like disease.[8] "Abracadabra" is an incantation, a power of producing effects with the aid of signs alone. One need only utter the words, to invoke the signifier (under certain circumstances, the village Austinian would insist), and the effect is produced. "Abracadabra" thus is a performative utterance, while "green is or," is constative, or tries to be.

But on my reading "abracadabra" is not just an exotic example of a performative utterance; it is the very form (albeit a formless form) of any utterance, indeed of any signifier at all. It is a way of signaling the productive power of signs *as such*. It is not so much a signifier as a way that the very act of sign-ing is itself signaled, signified. Its preeminence is not semiotically "ontic," if we may say so, not to be a particular signifier, but "ontological," because it awakens us to the productive power of the semiotic system as a whole. "Abracadabra" is an old name which points to the power and productivity of signs, impresses upon us that signs are not useless but magical performatives, which, like all magic, know how to hide behind their effects, so that you see only the effects, the products.

What else is magic than to have command of occult powers, to be able to produce mysterious effects? How can the trace—let us prescind from its substance, let it be phonic or graphic—do such things? How can signifiers name things which are not there? How can the word "I" function when he/she is not there, continue to produce effects when I am dead? Is this not necromancy and black art? How can signifiers operate in the absence of things? How can these signifiers walk on water like this? Signifiers work like magic. They are powerful forces which produce extraordinary effects—and this by uttering a formula. They have the power to traffic with things which are not present, to produce results with signs. For it is the very function of the sign, its structural necessity, to be able to operate in the absence of its object. The semiotic reduction *releases* the power of signifiers to work their magic, lets them be what they are, magical performatives.

Consider the first example, "green is or." Against Husserl's intentions, this produces an effect, in German or English, no less than in French where, when spoken, it sounds like a question about where (*où/ou*) we are to look for the green, or for the glass (*vert/verre*) (*Marges* 381/320). Indeed this example produces exactly the opposite result of the one Husserl intends, for it shows that signifiers *retain* their powers even in the absolute absence of intuition, and that it is impossible ever to deploy them in such a way as to produce *no* effect. "Green is or" illustrates the "abracadabra." The agrammatical example points to a power which we cannot repress, extinguish, one capable of producing grammar itself. Husserl's example—against his intentions—defies us to create a string of signifiers which has no product, which leaves no comet's tail trailing behind it. It belongs to the very magical power of signifiers to produce effects. The Husserlian-Derridean reduction lets a genie out of the bottle whom we cannot master and control.

Signifiers are magical performatives which produce a staggering array of amazing results: science, art, outright fictions, graffiti, metaphysical systems, ethical exhortations, mythologies, scriptures, insults, commands, baptisms, poems, political constitutions, public prohibitions, curricula, colloquia, soliloquies, logical systems, normal and abnormal discourses of all sorts, and on and on. We can liken this productivity to the power of the "imagination" in German Idealism. For here, too, we have to do with *Ein-bildungs-kraft:* with an inexhaustible power to engender form, to produce formed effects. This is not to say that the power of differance is a subjective faculty. The energy in question is not the energy of a subject but the power of the differential system to generate new effects indefinitely.

Indeed Husserl himself had a glimpse into this abyssal power of productivity, albeit one which was couched in the language of transcendental subjectivity and transcendental freedom. He describes this for us in §§ 47–49 of *Ideas I* in terms of "the annihilation of the world," in a discussion aimed at showing the "constitution" of the world. The world around us is radically contingent, he says. The actual world is but a special case of a multitude of different, possible worlds. Things take shape for us as the correlate of a factual sequence of experiences, and we can imagine that these sequences would be different, would change. We can imagine that clouds would turn into monstrous animals and sweep down upon us in a wave of anger, that the seas could begin to boil, that all sorts of Kafkaesque transformations would transpire. There is a radical contingency in the make-up of things, for consciousness has the resources to constitute the world in a multitude of alternate ways, and even to survive the total breakdown of all meaningful configuration, so that it would be left to rule alone over a Dionysian flux.

Now what is the upshot of all this? What has Derrida wrought by this defense of "green is or" and "abracadabra"? That is embedded in the rhetoric of "liberation" which I have employed throughout this essay. The story of the "liberation" of "green is or" and "abracadabra"—about their banishment from the polis of good grammar, about the police work of a priori grammar—all of this is an allegory about liberation at large. Liberation is what I think Derrida is all about, the impact his work has, the point of his writing, the tip of his pointed stylus. He is interested in a long list of liberations. "Green is or" and "abracadabra" are only the first beneficiaries, which includes the liberation of literature and of every kind of discourse: scientific, political, ethical, institutional, religious, discourse within and discourse without the university, *intra muros* and *extra muros*.

What Derrida has done above everything else, in my mind, is to expose the primal and unsettling contingency which lies not far beneath the surface of our creations. He alerts us to the danger of falling into subjugation by created things, contingent unities of meaning.[9] He keeps his transcendental-semiotic reduction in place so as to keep everything open, to show the revisability, contingency, reformability, rewritability of whatever has achieved hoary prestige and the look of irreformability. He interrogates entrenched authority, the established powers that be, which pretend to be, which pretend to be present. He solicits the people of substance, *ousia*. Such authorities, as he likes to say, have not dropped from the sky; they are contingent formations, constituted products. He gives the critique of metaphysics—hitherto understood only in terms of *Gelassenheit*—a socio-political cutting edge, pointing it in the direction of a politics of liberation.[10] He is interested in producing a Socratic effect.

The Productivity of Signs and the Economy of Full Employment

I want now, if I may say so, to philosophize a bit with this critique of Husserl, and in so doing to see if phenomenology does not reemerge under the hand of Derrida's critique, rewritten, reproduced, repeated, this time under the sign of the sign.

Derrida knows that it is not enough just to liberate signs. For if we do not find them gainful employment, give them honest work to do, they will roam the streets aimlessly and risk confinement and incarceration. But this produces a curious result. In defending the right of signs to useful work—against Husserl's intentions—Derrida likewise defends the rights of the things themselves—against his own intentions. He concludes this essay—which is essentially an essay on retention—by writing that the thing itself always steals away: *la même chose se dérobe toujours*. But by the very terms of his own analysis of Husserl, that can hardly be. For signs are not useless; he has himself put signs to work in the indefatigable labor of saving things from such a fate. That is part of their magic, part of what results when one insists that they are not useless. The thing itself always sticks around! Though, doubtless, Derrida would resist this assimilation of the necessity of signs to the necessity of the things themselves.

Presence is, he argues—against Husserl's intentions—a constituted effect. For signifiers have work to do, not only in the absence of their object, but even when the object is present. Here, too, the signifier intervenes, producing the effect of presence as something constituted, compounded with absence, dependent upon signs, structured and textualized. Derrida warns us against the seductive "effect" of presence and the cleverness of signs which, by making themselves transparent, lead us to believe that they are not productive, that they are useless. But Derrida has found gainful employment for them, which is the labor they expend in the production of presence. The work of signs is to produce presence in the pregnant sense, where presence is impregnated with absence, presence in the supplemented sense, where presence is supplemented by signs, sustained, maintained (*maintenant*) by protention and retention. Presence is not fallen from the sky; it is generated by constitution, engendered by repetition. It is a work wrought by signs which produce the effect of the things themselves: *die Sache selbst, la même chose*.

Yet Derrida has written, has meant to say, the thing itself always steals away:

> And contrary to what phenomenology—which is always phenomenology of perception—has tried to make us believe, contrary to what our desire cannot fail to be tempted into believing, the thing itself always steals away. (*VPh* 117/104)

La même chose se dérobe toujours? But how is that possible? Are signs useless? Can they not do an honest day's work? Have we not given them a job? Can they not make themselves useful? Indeed. That is what Derrida has shown. They have been hired to do the work of retention, *tenere*, employed because of their tenaciousness, to hold on to the thing itself before it slips too far, before it sinks away (*herabsinken*) altogether. Derrida has shown, not that there is no retention, but that retention is the work of signs, which stand for, hold the place for, what is sinking away. That is why signs are productive, not useless. That is the work which Derrida finds for them to do, how he gets them off the unemployment line.

The thing itself steals away. But what is the thing itself for Husserl? It is not some absolute being, for it is only the conscious flux—and not Being in the sense of existence of reality—which is absolute for

Husserl. It is not some thing in itself, absolutely independent of conscious life, for that, too, is a phenomenological error (*Ideas I*, § 43), the Husserlian equivalent of the "transcendental signified." That steals away indeed. And good riddance.

Rather, the thing itself is the φαινομένον, which is to say, precisely that which has been released by the reduction from the conditions of absolute presence and absence, from the constraints of real being, which is free to be the compound product of presence and absence, or even to be hallucinatory. It is precisely because the living present is a fabric of presence and absence that Husserl finds it necessary to withdraw the authority of real being, of absolute presence, by means of the reduction. The thing itself is *phenomenal* being, a structure of *appearance*, which Derrida has shown to be, not an illusion, but dependent upon the work of signs. If signs are not useless, then what phenomenology regards as the thing itself, the phenomenal living present, does not sink away, but is, rather, shown to be a textured product, a woven fabric which is always and already brought forth by the play of signifiers. For Husserl, the thing itself is a phenomenal *system*, a systematic interconnectedness of νοήματα, and Derrida has shown that such a system cannot be woven together without the work of signifiers, of *texere*.

The productivity of signifiers is the power of weaving together the noematic system, the protentional, retentional system of phenomenal being. Derrida, thus, not only finds employment for signs, but he has them working night and day, in the absence and the presence of objects, around the clock of internal time-consciousness, in a top-security job at the heart of the phenomenological industry. The one form of plenitude that Derrida does not object to is the economy of full employment for signifiers, whose right to work full-time he always defends.

But if that is so, then the final sentiment of *Vois et la Phénomène—la même chose se dérobe toujours*—must be held in tandem with, must be supplemented with, another more phenomenological principle, one which Heidegger borrows from Stefan George: *Kein Ding sei wo das Wort gebricht:* no thing may be where the word breaks off. That is to say, failing the intervention of the signifier, the thing itself slips away. The magic of signs is also the magic of the goddess in George's poem who saves things from loss by the word.

> She sought for long and tidings told:
> "No like of this these depths enfold."

> And straight it vanished from my hand
> The treasure never graced my land. . . .[11]

The work of signifiers is retentional, preservative; they keep the world from vanishing altogether. The task of thinking is to learn to think these two sentiments about the things themselves *together*, to learn to say them, if not at the same time, *im selben Augenblick,* at least in rapid succession. In this way alone can we gain access to the work of differance in all its productivity.

The productivity of the pure signifier, its power to produce effects, prodigious and irrepressible, draws near to the power of ποίησις in the sense described by Heidegger. This Derridean-Husserlian reduction liberates the power of world-making, the magic of *creation*. It makes contact with what Heidegger and Husserl alike call *Stiftung,* institutive creating, a making which gives origin to. The productive power of the signifier is the power of *Stiften* which, in "The Origin of the Work of Art," Heidegger associates with *Dichten* and *Dichtung*.[12] It is the primal poetic power of words, the ποίησις, the power to create, to weave worlds out of signs, the magic, the incantation. There is no way to suppress the ongoing *institution* of the world.

Indeed, that is hardly the problem. The danger is not that we will run wild in creativity, in rewriting and rereading. The danger is the scales on the dragon, thousands of years old. And that, as we said above, is what Derrida is after, to slay the dragon with his magic, to rid us of idolatry before graven images, to remind us of the radical contingency and reformability of things, the gravenness, the createdness, of whatever is brought forth, produced, constituted, un-concealed. And that is at the same time to recall us to the power of ποίησις, of making anew, of bringing forth anew thing and world.

The thing itself always steals away.

Where the word fails no thing may be.

The thing itself steals away if signs are useless.

Where the word fails the thing itself steals away.

The power of the signifier, the work it does, its ultimate art and magic,[13] its ultimate economy of full employment and triumph over uselessness, is the ποίησις, the *Stiften,* which brings forth the things themselves.[14] The things themselves are woven products, brought forth, engendered by the work of signs.[15] That is the matter for thought, *die Sache des Denkens.* Is the thing itself, *das Ding,* Heidegger's jug, half-empty or half-filled?

Abracadabra. Ἀ-λήθεια.

Notes

1. All reference to the *First Investigation* will be to the appropriate section and enclosed in parentheses in the text. See Husserl, *Logische Untersuchungen*, vol. 2, pt. 1, 5th ed. (Tübingen: Niemeyer, 1968); *Logical Investigations*, trans. J. N. Findlay, 2 vols. (New York: Humanities Press, 1970).

2. *VPh: Le voix et le phénomène* (Paris: PUF, 1967). The pages following the slash are of the English translation *Speech and Phenomena*, trans. David Allison (Evanston: Northwestern University Press, 1972).

3. J. N. Mohanty suggests ("On Husserl's Theory of Meaning," *Southwestern Journal of Philosophy* 5 [1974]: 240), that Derrida's argument fails because it neglects Husserl's theory of reference and focuses entirely on the theory of meaning. But nothing is changed by switching from sense to reference. For in referring, consciousness would still, on Husserl's account, claim to know that it refers and what it is referring to, and to know it in the self-same moment of referring; it would still claim to carry out the act of referring prelinguistically, self-presentially. It is not solipsism that Derrida objects to, but the theory of prelinguistic self-presence. See also Mohanty, *Edmund Husserl's Theory of Meaning* (The Hague: Nijhoff, 1969), chapter 2. For a defense of Mohanty's position see Susan Ruth Carlton's dissertation at the University of Michigan, "On Authors, Readers, and Phenomenology: Husserlian Intentionality in the Literary Theories of E. D. Hirsch and Jacques Derrida" (1984), chapter 3.

4. Derrida regards this attempt to set humanity off as something higher than animals as a hallmark of metaphysics. Yet he will certainly agree that the human use of signs is vastly superior to that of animals. His point is that this superiority is a difference in degree rather than a neat, categorical difference, without overlap or partial convergence.

5. This is the point of the *Fourth Investigation*, on the idea of a pure grammar. For more on the relationship between Derrida and Husserl which takes its point of departure from the theory of pure grammar, see the writings of Rodolphe Gasché, in particular his contribution to the present volume and "Deconstruction as Criticism," *Glyph 6* (Baltimore: Johns Hopkins University Press, 1979), pp. 177–215. It is interesting too that Heidegger's habilitation dissertation dealt with the *Fourth Investigation*. See my "Phenomenology, Mysticism and the 'Grammatica Speculativa': A Study of Heidegger's 'Habilitationsschrift,'" *Journal of the British Society for Phenomenology* 5 (1974): 101–17.

6. That is why Mohanty modifies the example to "abcaderaf" (*Edmund Husserl's Theory of Meaning*, p. 36).

7. In *Marges de la philosophie* (Paris: Minuit, 1972), pp. 365–93; *Margins of Philosophy*, trans. Alan Bass (Chicago: University of Chicago Press, 1982), pp. 307–30.

8. See the entry "abracadabra" in the *Oxford English Dictionary*.

9. I do not mean that Derrida criticizes only the contingent and not the necessary, but that he shows the contingency of this very distinction, that it is a produced effect; "contingency" is thus another case of Derridean paleonymy for me.

10. In discussions from the floor Derrida resisted this suggestion only to the extent that it implied optimism, utopianism, some kind of metaphysics of the future in which all will be free. I do not mean anything of the sort by liberation, but only a kind of local strategy to be put into place wherever possible.

11. *Unterwegs zur Sprache* (Pfullingen: Neske, 1965), p. 220; *On the Way to Language*, trans. P. Hertz (New York: Harper & Row, 1971), p. 140. Heidegger also emphasizes that it is the *Wort* which holds and sustains (*hält*) the thing in Being

(appearance); the *Wort* gives things their *Unterhaltung:* sus-tenance, main-tenance; see *Unterwegs,* pp. 176–77, 187–88; *On the Way,* pp. 73, 82. Thus the *Wort* in Heidegger plays the role of "tenancy" isolated by Husserl—in accord with the Derridean demand for a role for signs to play.

12. *Gesamtausgabe,* vol. 5, *Holzwege* (Frankfurt am Main: Klostermann, 1977), pp. 58–66; "The Origin of the Work of Art," in *Poetry, Language, Thought,* trans. A. Hofstadter (New York: Harper & Row, 1971), pp. 71–78.

13. There is something of this same magic of productivity in this passage from Merleau-Ponty: "It [language] appears as mere sign only once it has provided itself with a meaning, and the coming to awareness, if it is to be complete, must rediscover the expressive unity in which both signs and meaning appear in the first place. When a child cannot speak, or cannot yet speak the adult's language, the linguistic ritual which unfolds around him has no hold on him, he is near us in the same way as is a spectator with a poor seat at the theatre; he sees clearly enough that we are laughing and gesticulating, he hears the nasal tune being played, but there is nothing at the end of those gestures or behind those words, nothing *happens* for him. A story is told in a children's book of the disappointment of a small boy who put on his grandmother's spectacles and took up her book in the expectation of being able himself to find in it the stories which she used to tell him. The tale ends with these words: 'Well, what a fraud! Where's the story? I see nothing but black and white.' For the child the 'story' and the thing expressed are not 'ideas' or 'meanings,' nor are speaking or reading 'intellectual operations.' The story is a world which there must be some way of magically calling up by putting on spectacles and leaning over a book. The power possessed by language of bringing the thing expressed into existence, of opening up to thought new ways, new dimensions and new landscapes, is, in the last analysis, as obscure for the adult as for the child. In every successful work, the significance carried into the reader's mind exceeds language and thought as already constituted and is magically thrown into relief during the linguistic incantation, just as the story used to emerge from the grandmother's book" (*Phenomenology of Perception,* trans. Colin Smith [Atlantic Highlands: Humanities Press, 1962], p. 401).

14. For a delimitation of the Husserlian notion of the "things themselves" from Derrida's point of view, see John Sallis, "The Identities of the Things Themselves," *Research in Phenomenology* 12 (1982): 113–26. See also the contribution of Rudolph Bernet in the same issue devoted to "Husserl and Contemporary Thought."

15. Since completing this paper, I have come upon a comparable reading of Derrida which I recommend: Joseph O'Leary, *Questioning Back: The Overcoming of Metaphysics in Christian Tradition* (Minneapolis: Winston, 1985), pp. 36–48.

The Perfect Future: A Note on Heidegger and Derrida

9

David Farrell Krell

Some of you have been worried about the future. Do not worry about the future. The future is perfect.

I will not say a word during these twenty-five minutes about an entire array af questions and topics evoked by the names *Heidegger* and *Derrida*. Not a word about the end of metaphysics as closure or eschatology of Being, not a word about the metaphysics of presence; not a word about the essence of truth, whether as correctness or unveiling or historic unfolding; not a word about representation and the destiny or sending of Being; nor about metaphor and metaphysics, *Ereignis* and abyss, proximity and un-distancing, not even to ask whether we are at all understanding the relation of questioner and questioned when we take it as one of proximity rather than distance and evasion. Not a word about two of the three topics this paper was originally to have introduced—nothing about either the vaunted neutrality of the "who?" of Dasein or the troublesome distinction between *Eigentlichkeit* and *Uneigentlichkeit* in *Being and Time*.

Not a word about these things? Well, then, what?

A few remarks concerning Heidegger's analysis of ecstatic temporality and the finitude of time—an analysis deconstruction dare not continue to avoid as though it had all the time in the world. For Heidegger's ecstatic analysis makes all the difference to deconstruction. However much in Heidegger's own view the ecstatic analysis of temporality may have failed, that analysis is perfect. Or at least *of* the perfect.

In section 18 of *Being and Time* Heidegger writes that in our everyday concerns we have always already let things have their application or involvement (*Bewandtnis*) in the world. The fact that we always have already done so characterizes the perdurant manner of being of Dasein itself. We always have already let something go, released it and

114

let it become involved (*bewenden lassen*), with a view to the whole of
our involvements in the world. Heidegger writes:

> Das auf Bewandtnis hin freigebende Je-schon-haben-bewenden-lassen ist
> ein *apriorisches Perfekt,* das die Seinsart des Daseins selbst charakterisiert.

> Always-already-having-let-something-be-involved, which liberates a
> thing for its involvements, is an *apriori perfect* that characterizes the man-
> ner of being of Dasein itself. (*SZ,* section 18, p. 85)[1]

The crucial words with respect to the *apriori perfect* are the prepo-
sitions *auf* and *hin:* Heidegger aims to define the *Woraufhin,* "that
upon which" every involvement is projected. In the 1925 lectures on
time, the 1927 *Basic Problems of Phenomenology,* and the 1928 logic
course, Heidegger designates the *Woraufhin* as "presence," *Praesenz.* (A
highly complex *Praesenz,* it must be said, one that is ostensibly non-
ecstatic and yet in some bewildering way includes *Absenz.*) Strikingly,
in *Being and Time* Heidegger does not at all identify the upon-which of
liberation as "presence," nor does he employ the phenomenological vocabulary of "horizon." Here the *Woraufhin* is called simply "world."
One must sympathize with Heidegger's reluctance to invoke *Praesenz.*
For what would it mean for an existential analysis of Dasein, committed
as it is to the primacy of the *future,* to assert that the *apriori perfect* is
presence? It would at least imply that the relationship of Divisions 1 and
2 of *Being and Time* is not merely one of recovery or repetition; it might
even suggest that the preparatory analysis of everydayness (of beings
that are either handy or at hand, where *presence* prevails) does not and
cannot prepare the way for the analysis of Dasein proper (where the
future is said to be the ecstasis from which the others spring).

I am not at all certain that the *apriori perfect* corresponds to what
in Division 2 is called *Gewesenheit,* "having-been." I will not repeat here
what I have tried to say elsewhere in some detail about ecstatic temporality,[2] but will merely note that for the project of fundamental ontology everything depends on the question of whether the ecstases of
time (future, having-been, and present) are "equally original," *gleichur-
sprünglich,* or whether they are structured by some order of implication,
priority, or ontological founding. Heidegger is by no means embar-
rassed by the notion of "equal originality." Indeed, he criticizes the
"unbridled tendency" of traditional ontologies to seek for every element a "simple 'primal ground,'" *einen einfachen "Urgrund"* (*SZ* 131).
He does not so much surrender the notion of equiprimordiality—by
which future, having-been, and present would stem from one another

in a ringdance of changes and exchanges—as vacillate on the question of the locus, site, or horizon of temporalization as such. Because traditional ontologies understand Being as presence and beings as *Vorhandenheit,* Heidegger will stress the primacy of the *future* in Dasein as possibility-being. Yet the following quotations from *Being and Time* indicate that no particular ecstasis, not even the future, can claim any sort of primacy over the others:

> The phenomena of the *toward* . . . , *back onto* . . . , and *by* . . . , reveal temporality as the ἐϰστατιϰόν as such. *Temporality is the original "outside itself" in and for itself.* We therefore call the designated phenomena of future, having-been, and present the ecstases of temporality. Temporality is not, prior to that, a being that merely steps outside of *itself;* rather, its essence is temporalization in the unity of the *ecstases. (SZ* 329)

Later *(SZ* 350) Heidegger writes, and italicizes, as follows:

> *Temporality temporalizes completely in each ecstasis. That is to say, the totality of the structural whole of existence, facticity, and falling*—and thus *the unity of the structure of care*—is grounded in the ecstatic unity of any given full temporalization of temporality.

For the first account it is the *unity* of the three ecstases, their shared and encompassing *horizon,* that serves as the ground; for the second it is each ecstasis "in itself," as it were, that embraces the whole. The Marburg lectures of 1927 and 1928 remain on the lookout for the "in and for itself" of the original "outside itself," the ἐϰστατιϰόν. Heidegger's most telling depiction of the site of temporalization is captured in the word "rapture," *raptus, Entrückung.* The transports or raptures of time, including the μεταβολή that Aristotle saw at the heart of the "now," are discussed in *Being and Time* and, much more fully, in the subsequent lecture courses. In both cases they are taken to be the proper site of the *finitude* of time. Yet ecstatic displacement, the sudden transports or raptures of temporality, the very metabolism of time, provide nothing like a fundament. They prove to be far more destructive of fundamental ontology than any *Destruktion* Heidegger may have envisaged for traditional ontology. The gathering of the ecstases into a unity, ground, or order of implication—having-been springing from the future and releasing the present—is frustrated. While Heidegger retains the word *Entrückung* in his later writings, it is no longer in service to the ecstatic analysis of temporality. As early as 1928 he concedes the following:

> The totality of the *Entrückungen* is not, as it were, centered in something that itself would be raptureless, nonecstatically at hand as a collective center for the instauration of and point of departure for the ecstases. Rather, the unity of the ecstases is itself ecstatic.[3]

Was Heidegger correct in saying in 1961 that his earlier, abandoned analysis of ecstatic temporality was unable to reach what was most proper to time, *das Eigenste der Zeit,* albeit correct in a way he himself may never have grasped? For if the unity of the ecstases or of any given ecstasis is "itself" ecstatic, hence radically displaced to the point of dispersion, what is left of Dilthey's concatenation of life (*Zusammenhang des Lebens*), of the "substance" of "existence," of the stability (*Ständigkeit*) of Dasein, stretched between birth and death? What is left of the *Augenblick,* the moment of vision, the blink of an eye that a resolutely open and appropriate Dasein would presumably carry with itself into a perfect future? What is left of the self of selfhood, the Da of Dasein, the clearing and truth of Being "itself"? Did the ecstatic analysis fail, or did it succeed smashingly well?

If ecstatic displacement—*raptus, Entrückung,* μεταβολή—is a movement of excess and dehiscence, you will hardly be surprised to hear me echo now certain phrases from another discourse, phrases such as *la possibilité de la trace, le jeu du monde, différance, l'archi-synthèse irréductible, le passé absolu* (as a) *toujours-déjà-là* (which is just perfect), and finally, *le temps mort* (which is somewhat less than perfect).[4] Nor will it surprise you that I wish to insert the Heideggerian analysis of ecstatic temporality into the *Grammatologie,* precisely between pages 95 and 96. These pages conclude the section on the outside/inside and open that hinged wound entitled *la brisure.* They appear recto-verso on a single sheet, however, so that I will have to slit that sheet from margin to spine in order to make the graft. But why go to all that trouble? Why the violation? Because deconstruction of the Husserlian "living present" will not of itself—not even with the help of the Freudian economy of life/death—suffice to rescue deconstruction from its transcendental archi-limbo.

Can Heidegger's ecstatic analysis do what no other *Destruktion* can do for deconstruction? Is it privileged? Perhaps it is, precisely because it succeeds beyond Heidegger's own expectations, by some strange sort of dissemination subverting the very fundament of fundamental ontology. Perhaps we should try to *recover* Heidegger's analysis? Not now, to be sure, but in the future?

Some of you have been worried about the future. Do not worry about the future. The future has always already been perfect.

A brief remark therefore on the "later" Heidegger, for whom what-has-been, *das Gewesene,* became increasingly significant, increasingly Heidegger's own future. One example among the many possible. Commenting on the final line of Georg Trakl's poem "Jahr" (Year), in which something is said of *das Ende* (the end), Heidegger wrote:

> Here the end is not what follows inception; it is not evanescence of the inception. The end, precisely as the end of the decomposing race [*Geschlecht*], precedes the inception of the unborn race. However, as the earlier dawn, inception has already outstripped the end.[5]

"Outstripped" translates the word *überholt.* In *Being and Time* Heidegger defines the death of Dasein in terms of its never being outstripped: essential to the existential conception of death is *die Un-überholbarkeit des Todes.* Now it seems as though something is going to be outstripped. What is it?

> This dawn preserves the still veiled original unfolding [*das Wesen*] of time. . . . Yet true time is advent of what has been [*Ankunft des Gewesenen*]. The latter is not the bygone but the gathering of what essentially unfolds, a gathering that precedes all advent. For the advent, as such gathering, always safeguards within itself what is earlier.

Ge-wesen: "true time" as the gathering and safeguarding of the earlier, the gathering of essence. What can that mean? Will all passage, transiency, and even death itself be outstripped? It sounds as though Heidegger were trying to provide some sort of solace, as though to say, "Some of you have been worried about the future. Do not worry about the future. The future will always already in each case have been being perfect."

Yet essence as gathered, *Ge-wesen* (presuming that the *Ge-* is to gather all the variants of *Wesen* in the way *Ge-birg* gathers the solitary mountain crags), is haunted by another kind of *Wesen: Ver-wesen,* the *ver-* of what is ineluctably bygone, *ver-gangen. Ver-wesen* invokes the disessence of decay, decomposition, and wasting away. Which early in the history of metaphysics was called φθορά.

I am moving far too quickly, I know, and toward an uncertain future. Looking forward to the hand of man according to Heidegger, remembering the radical displacements and dispersions of ecstasis, dwelling still on *Entrückung* or rapture as the finitude of time, I want to read some lines by Georg Trakl in which this troubling word *Verwesen* appears. First, from the later version of *De Profundis:*

> Turning homeward
> The shepherds found the sweet body
> Wasted in the brier.

> Bei der Heimkehr
> Fanden die Hirten den süssen Leib
> Verwest im Dornenbusch.[6]

And now, from "Dream and Delusion," *Traum und Umnachtung,* section 1:

> . . . he gazed on . . . the corpses, the green marks of decay on their beautiful hands.

> . . . er besah . . . die Leichen, die grünen Flecken der Verwesung auf ihren schönen Händen.[7]

If *Ge-wesen* be the all-gathering hand, *ver-sammelnd,* how will that hand gather the wastage, *die Ver-wesung,* that lays waste to it? Surely no manipulation will suffice, not even the machinations of perfected representation, not even *Ge-stell.* By sheer force of will, perhaps, will as will to power?

Zarathustra calls revenge "the will's ill will toward time and its 'It was.'" In the lecture "Who Is Nietzsche's Zarathustra?" Heidegger insists that the *Es war,* the *imperfect,* far from being superfluous to time, is nothing less than "the fundamental trait of time in its proper and entire unfolding as time," *der Grundzug der Zeit in ihrem ganzen und eigentlichen Zeitwesen.*[8] *Ganz* and *eigentlich,* the two watchwords of the second division of *Being and Time,* here apply to time *as* such *as* imperfect:

> Yet how do matters stand with time "as such" [*mit* der *Zeit*]? They stand in this way: time goes. And it goes by passing [*sie geht, indem sie vergeht*]. Whatever of time is to come never comes to stay but only to go. Where to? Into passing [*Ins Vergehen*].

If the essential unfolding of time "itself" and "as such" is *Vergehen,* passing, "transiency," my own reflections on the apriori perfect and the perfect future should in the end become—not apocalyptic, and not apoplectic—but ecstatically somber. Not without a certain anxiety, not without risk of violence, the following extracts from section 3 of that same prose-poem, *Traum und Umnachtung*. Allow me to read first a translation, in order that we can hear the words "race," "generation," "curse," "dispersion," and "hand," and then the German text, in which each of these words tolls a knell. By the time the knell fades I will have ended, if I have not already done so.

> O of the accursed race! When in maculate rooms every destiny is consum-
> mated, death steps into the house with musty footfall. . . . O, the vernal
> twilight paths of one in revery. . . . Freely the brook flows where his
> silvery foot strays, and a tree speaks, rustling above his benighted head.
> And he lifts with a fragile hand the snake, and in molten tears his heart
> melted away. . . . O the beaming angels that the wind of purple night
> dispersed. . . . Woe the stooped forms of the women. Fruits and imple-
> ments fell from the rigid hands of a race in terror. . . . O languor of
> death. O you children of a darkling generation. . . . O, of the night; O,
> of the accursed.

> O des verfluchten Geschlechts! Wenn in befleckten Zimmern jegliches
> Schicksal vollendet ist, tritt mit mordenden Schritten der Tod in das
> Haus. . . . O, die dämmernden Frühlingswege des Sinnenden. . . . Frei
> ergrünt der Bach, wo silbern wandelt sein Fuss, und ein sagender Baum
> rauscht über dem umnachteten Haupt ihm. Also hebt er mit schmäch-
> tiger Hand die Schlange, und in feurigen Tränen schmolz ihm das Herz
> hin. . . . O die strahlenden Engel, die der purpurne Nachtwind
> zerstreute. . . . Weh der gebeugten Erscheinung der Frauen. Unter
> erstarrten Händen verfielen Frucht und Gerät dem entsetzten Ge-
> schlecht. . . . O die Wollust des Todes. O ihr Kinder eines dunklen
> Geschlechts. . . . O, der Nächtlichen; o, der Verfluchten.[9]

Some of you have been worried about the future. Do not worry about the future. The future was perfect.

Notes

1. I cite the 12th edition of *Sein und Zeit* (Tübingen: Niemeyer, 1972) through-out, as *SZ* with page number. The *Gesamtausgabe* edition of *SZ* adduces the following "marginal note" after the word "perfect":

> In the same paragraph there is mention of an "anterior liberation" ['*vorgängigen
> Freigabe*']—namely (stated in a general way), of Being, for the possible openness

[*Offenbarkeit*] of beings. "Anterior" in this ontological sense means the Latin *a priori*, the Greek *proteron tēi physei* (Aristotle, *Physics* A 1; even more strikingly in *Metaphysics* E 1025*b*–29: *to ti ēn einai*, "that which already was—being," "that which in each case already ahead of time unfolds essentially" [*das jeweils schon voraus Wesende*], the has-been [*das Gewesen*], the perfect). The Greek verb *einai* knows no perfect form; it is designated here in the *ēn einai*. Not some bygone ontic thing [*ein ontisch Vergangenes*], but that which in each case is earlier, that *back* to which we are directed with the question concerning beings as such; instead of a priori perfect it could also say ontological or transcendental perfect (cf. Kant's doctrine of the Schematism).

Spacious margin—for it contains the history of metaphysics up to and including *SZ*.

2. In chapters 2 and 3 of *Intimations of Mortality: Time, Truth, and Finitude in Heidegger's Thinking of Being* (University Park: Pennsylvania State University Press, 1986).

3. Martin Heidegger, *Metaphysische Anfangsgründe der Logik im Ausgang von Leibniz* (Frankfurt am Main: Klostermann, 1978), p. 268.

4. Jacques Derrida, *De la grammatologie* (Paris: Minuit, 1967), pp. 69, 73, 77, 88, 97, and 99, respectively.

5. Martin Heidegger, *Unterwegs zur Sprache* (Pfullingen: Neske, 1959), p. 57 for this and the following quotation.

6. Georg Trakl, *Dichtungen und Briefe,* edited by Walther Killy and Hans Szklenar (Salzburg: Otto Müller, 1969), p. 26.

7. Trakl, p. 80.

8. Martin Heidegger, *Vorträge und Aufsätze* (Pfullingen: Neske, 1954), p. 116 for this and the following quotation. For the English translation, see *Nietzsche,* vol. II: *The Eternal Recurrence of the Same,* trans. David Farrell Krell (New York: Harper & Row, 1984), p. 224.

9. Trakl, p. 82.

Deconstruction and the Possibility of Ethics

10

Robert Bernasconi

It seems that the demand now on everyone's lips is that Derrida give us an ethics, or at least that he make manifest an ethical significance to deconstruction. And yet in the face of this situation we might be forgiven for suffering from a sense of *déjà vu*. Heidegger had similarly been faced with the demand for an ethics. In the "Letter on Humanism," he remembers how, soon after the publication of *Being and Time,* a young friend had asked him when he was going to write an ethics.[1] Is the response rehearsed by Heidegger in 1946 equally appropriate to Derrida now? Will what was said then of the relation of ethics to the destruction or overcoming of philosophy serve now when we prefer to talk of its deconstruction?

Whatever Heidegger's reply may have been to his young friend at the time, in the "Letter on Humanism" the story is repeated within a philosophical context. The "Letter on Humanism" was, as is well known, a revised version of a letter written in response to certain questions put to him by Jean Beaufret. Heidegger quotes Beaufret as saying that he has for a long time been trying "to determine precisely the relation of ontology to a possible ethics." Beaufret's sentence has an almost studied cautiousness about it which Heidegger instantly penetrates (perhaps on the basis of other comments in Beaufret's letter, still unpublished). Heidegger assimilates Beaufret's position to that which insists that " 'ontology' be supplemented (*ergänzt*) by 'ethics.' " And it is at that point that Heidegger remembers the incident almost twenty years earlier of the young friend demanding an ethics. Heidegger's reply to Beaufret focuses on the relation of ethics and ontology, but no longer as two philosophical disciplines. "Ethics" is referred to the basic meaning of the Greek word ἦθος: " 'ethics' ponders the abode of man." In consequence "original ethics" is a "thinking which thinks the truth of Being as the primordial element of man, as one who eksists" (*W*

187/235). "Ontology" as "fundamental ontology" is likewise referred to the "truth of Being." Ethics and ontology are in this way brought together, but so withdrawn from our conventional understanding of them that it is not easy to tell what their conjunction amounts to. And so long as we take this to be the thrust of Heidegger's reply, the story of the young friend is a digression. Like the anecdote about Heraclitus's encounter with some strangers over the kitchen stove, which Heidegger retells a page or two later. These apparent digressions lend credence to the common view that, since it had its source in a private correspondence, the "Letter on Humanism" is less rigorous than other of Heidegger's essays.

But to return to the two questioners, the unnamed young friend and Jean Beaufret, the former was to be disappointed. Heidegger did not write an ethics, but wrote the "Letter on Humanism" instead. It might seem that Beaufret, the original recipient of the letter, was also refused by Heidegger. Heidegger wrote that the very question of supplementing ontology with an ethics "no longer has any basis in this sphere" of the truth of Being (*W* 188/236). And yet Beaufret's question, understood not as a question about ethics as the production of rules, but "thought in a more original way, retains a meaning and an essential importance" (*W* 188/236). And what is most important for human beings, according to Heidegger, is coming to abide in the truth of Being (*W* 191/239). Understood in its traditional sense, ontology thinks the truth of Being no more than ethics does. But it seems to Heidegger that we could as readily call the thinking which attempts to think the truth of Being "original ethics" as call it "fundamental ontology," which is the title given to the thinking to be found in *Being and Time* (*W* 187/235). Whatever we call it, the task is not to dismiss ethics and ontology as human invention, but to attain to the realm from which they arise. Insofar as *Being and Time* was indeed "fundamental ontology"—in the sense Heidegger gives to the phrase in the "Letter on Humanism"—*Being and Time* was already original ethics.[2]

That does not mean that we should be trying somehow to reread *Being and Time* in the expectation of finding that it prescribes laws and ethical directives of its own. Laws and ethical directives are assigned according to the dispensation or sending of Being, which conditions, determines, and makes ethics possible. There is an original sense of law, as there is of ethics and ontology.

Νόμος is not only law but more originally the assignment contained in the dispensation of Being. Only the assignment is capable of dispatching man into Being. Only such dispatching is capable of supporting and obligating. Otherwise all law remains merely something fabricated by human reason (*W* 191/238–39).

Heidegger thus refers ethical rules back to the destiny of Being as that which rules them; and it is more essential to belong to that destiny than it is to follow these rules or to devote oneself to questions about ethics and ontology.

It might, therefore, seem to be appropriate for a thinking informed by Heidegger to respond to the demand for an ethics by subjecting the notion of "ethics" to examination, indicating its different senses as both a specific set of directives and a specific philosophical discipline. It would trace them back to a more "original" sense, one governed by the notion of "sending" or destiny. In this way the demand for an ethics undergoes instruction. It is informed that the demand betrays traditional presuppositions about ethical systems. Ethics is not impossible. It is a possibility which can in principle be realized. Yet an ethics cannot simply be produced to order. Nor is it what is most pressing or most essential. It is as if the thinker *qua* thinker must remain deaf to demands which come to him or her from elsewhere in order to concentrate on coming to abide in the destiny of Being. The thinker cannot do more than this without coming up against the boundaries set by the truth of Being (*W* 182/230).

In "Violence and Metaphysics," Derrida's essay on Levinas, Heideggerian considerations of this kind are prominent. To ask this essay, which predates Derrida's adoption of the word *deconstruction,* to bear the weight of determining the relation of deconstruction to the possibility of ethics is no doubt to ask too much. But "Violence and Metaphysics" warrants most careful consideration, not least because it is a key document both in Derrida's development of deconstruction and in the reception of Levinas's own ethical thinking. Indeed Derrida has in "Violence and Metaphysics" given us a reading of Levinas which in large measure has determined the reception of Levinas ever since—notwithstanding the fact that the essay has not been read carefully, as is clear from the fact that it is almost invariably referred to as Derrida's *critique* of Levinas. I shall suggest that the essay would better merit its influence, if it were better understood.[3]

Derrida draws heavily on the "Letter on Humanism" in "Violence and Metaphysics." He does so not simply to question Levinas's interpretation of Heidegger, though this proves a major preoccupation of the second half of the essay. In its opening pages Derrida uses the "Letter on Humanism" in order to situate his own inquiry within "the impossible." And "the impossible has *already* occurred" (*ED* 118/80).

In raising the impossible question of the death of philosophy, the question of the relation of philosophy and nonphilosophy, Derrida announces an injunction: "The question must be maintained." Or one might say (in recollection of the word which is associated with the English translation of Heidegger) "preserved." And, asking about the meaning of this injunction, Derrida writes that "if this commandment has an ethical meaning, it is not in that it belongs to the *domain* of the ethical, but in that it ultimately authorizes every ethical law in general" (*ED* 119/80). The implicit reference to the distinction introduced in the "Letter on Humanism" is clear. The domain of the ethical corresponds to ethics as a discipline; the authorization of every ethical law is equivalent to what Heidegger calls law as the assignment of the dispensation of Being. This question, which Derrida in the second version of the essay redefines as "the question of the relations between belonging and opening, the question of closure" (*ED* 163/110), is imposed on us by an injunction, an imposition perhaps similar to that which Heidegger refers to as the dispensation of Being.

Thus Derrida in "Violence and Metaphysics" follows Heidegger's treatment of ethics in the "Letter on Humanism." In particular, Derrida at one point offers a sustained attempt to measure how Levinas fares according to the standard Heidegger established.

> It is true that Ethics, in Levinas's sense, is an Ethics without law and without concept, which maintains its non-violent purity only before being determined as concepts and laws. This is not an objection: let us not forget that Levinas does not seek to propose laws or moral rules, does not seek to determine *a* morality, but rather the essence of the ethical relation in general. But as this determination does not offer itself as a *theory* of Ethics, in question, then, is an Ethics of Ethics. In this case, it is perhaps serious that this Ethics of Ethics can occasion neither a determined ethics nor determined laws without negating and forgetting itself. Moreover, is this Ethics of Ethics beyond all laws? Is it not the Law of laws? A coherence which breaks down the coherence of the discourse against coherence—the infinite concept, hidden within the protest against the concept. (*ED* 164/111)[4]

Leaving aside for the moment the question as to how we should read these remarks about coherence, Derrida seems here to bring Levinas into correspondence with the Heidegger of the "Letter on Humanism."[5] What is the "Law of laws" except "the assignment contained in the dispensation of Being"? That is why Derrida is at such pains to show that what Levinas says of ontology does not hold for Heidegger's thinking of Being and that Heidegger's attempt to separate them in the "Letter on Humanism" is to be accepted. On this interpretation, what Levinas has to say can be reconciled with Heidegger. Of course, this will run quite contrary to the whole rhetoric of Levinas's discussion of Heidegger from the moment in *Existence and Existents* when Levinas, declaring his debt to Heidegger's thinking, also announces his "profound need to leave the climate of that philosophy."[6] Such a reassimilation of Levinas to Heidegger would no doubt be attractive to all those who have already pledged their allegiance to Heidegger but who cannot overlook his relative silence, after the discussion of *Mitsein* in *Being and Time,* about our fellow human beings. What matter that Levinas on every page protests his distance from Heidegger when we now know better than to be bound by authorial intentions?

Certain remarks in Derrida's more recent essay on Levinas, "At this very moment in this work here I am," are germane to this reassimilation. In one of the strands of his many-sided essay, Derrida investigates the curious structure of the ethical relation as explicated by Levinas.[7] He recalls that for Levinas gratitude can serve to compromise the generosity of the Self which in work goes towards the Other. To give thanks in return is to destroy transcendence and return an apparently gratuitous act to the order of the same. Levinas puts it this way: "Work fundamentally considered . . . demands an ingratitude from the Other. Gratitude would be precisely the return of the movement to its origin."[8] It would seem to follow that to preserve the ethical relation of the giver I am obliged to show no gratitude. That is a strange ethical requirement whereby in order to let the Other be as Other, to preserve the alterity of the Other, to *be* grateful, I must be ungrateful. Derrida explores a certain kind of "radical ingratitude" beyond all restitution. And this idea has a hermeneutical application. As the gift is preserved as gift only in a radical ingratitude, so the text is only preserved as text when one is in a certain way unfaithful to it. The text is not to be returned to its author.

As I have attempted to show, Derrida already in "Violence and Metaphysics" does not return Levinas's text to its author, but to another—namely, Heidegger. It is not a question of insisting upon Heidegger's influence on Levinas, which Levinas has never sought to deny. Derrida is concerned both with the extraordinary violence that Levinas seems to do to Heidegger's texts in order to arrive at his interpretations and with the tone of his remarks about Heidegger (*ED* 131/88). One is even tempted to speak here of an attempt at *parricide,* just as Derrida refers to parricide when recalling Levinas's attempt to break with Parmenides (*ED* 132–33/89). Derrida's references to the

"Letter on Humanism" show how little Levinas succeeds in distancing himself from Heidegger. How could Levinas attack Heidegger for having subordinated ethics to ontology when Heidegger goes to such pains to displace that question? Indeed Derrida's question of parricide could be juxtaposed with Levinas's own discussion of the impossibility of murder. Levinas interprets the command "Thou shalt not commit murder" not as a law to obey or disobey, but as the essence of the ethical relation, a necessity which we cannot evade. At one point in *Existence and Existents* Levinas refers us to Macbeth's inability to rid himself of Banquo (*EE* 101/62). On Derrida's reading, Levinas cannot rid himself of Heidegger's ghost. And so Derrida finds himself in a position to situate Levinas and the ethics he proposes with reference to the thought of Being: "Not only is the thought of Being not ethical violence, but it seems that no ethics—in Levinas's sense—can be opened without it" (*ED* 202/137). And again, "Levinas must ceaselessly suppose and practice the thought or precomprehension of Being in his discourse, even when he directs it against 'ontology.' . . . Ethico-metaphysical transcendence therefore presupposes ontological transcendence" (*ED* 208/141). So, according to Derrida, who sees at work here an instructive necessity, Levinas's metaphysics presupposes what it seeks to put in question in such a way that it remains haunted by it (see *ED* 195/133). And parricide proves just as difficult in the case of Parmenides. Derrida again and again draws attention to "some indestructible and unforeseeable resource of the Greek logos . . . by which he who attempts to repel it would always already be *overtaken*" (*ED* 165/111–12).

Nevertheless we would fail completely to recognize how far this early reading of Levinas accomplished the double movement of a deconstruction, if we saw in "Violence and Metaphysics" only an attempt to reassimilate Levinas to the tradition. The necessity which imposes itself on Levinas is that of "lodging oneself within traditional conceptuality in order to destroy it" (*ED* 165/111).[9] That is to say, if Levinas at times succumbs to philosophical discourse, this is not a failing but, according to Derrida, the only way he can renounce it. The question which Derrida does not clearly pose, but which his essay seems to provoke, is whether Levinas knew that that was what he was doing. And because Derrida seems sometimes to indicate that he did not, the reader of Levinas who disagrees is likely to ask whether Derrida's reading of Levinas must not be corrected, just as Derrida himself corrected Levinas's reading of Heidegger.

So, for example, Derrida seems to have thought that Levinas opposed infinity to totality and ethical metaphysics to the Western philosophical tradition of ontology. If this were the case, it could be shown, by what Derrida elsewhere calls "a Hegelian law," to be self-defeating: "the revolution against reason can be made only within it" (*ED* 59/36). The attempt to overcome philosophy by situating oneself outside it remains within the order of the same. This is what underlies Derrida's attempt to show how the negative prefix of the very word *infinity* renders "unthinkable, impossible, unutterable" Levinas's attempt to construe a positive infinity (*ED* 168/114). But then the question arises as to whether certain remarks that Derrida makes later in the essay are to be understood as developments of this objection or as a renewed exposition of Levinas. For example, when Derrida writes: "How could there be a 'play of the Same' if alterity itself was not already *in* the Same, with a meaning of inclusion doubtless betrayed by the word *in*? Without alterity *in* the same, how could the 'play of the Same' occur, in the sense of playful activity, or of dislocation, in a machine or organic totality which *plays* or *works?*" (*ED* 186/126–27). Is Derrida here explicating Levinas or correcting him? The "in" of *in*finity can be understood not simply negatively, but also as conveying the sense of "inclusion" that Derrida seems to think that he is bringing to Levinas. Levinas not only explicitly evokes this sense of inclusion in the 1975 essay "God and Philosophy"; the sense in which infinity is already *in* the finite provides *Totality and Infinity* with its structure, guiding the descriptions of, for example, both desire and labor.[10] Similarly, because of his charge of ahistoricism against Levinas, Derrida might be thought not to have recognized the extent to which another conception of history—other than Hegel's totalizing history—already pervaded *Totality and Infinity,* not least in the use made there of Plato and Descartes to say the beyond Being from within Western ontology. In *Otherwise Than Being or Beyond Essence* Levinas refers explicitly to this other history of the West, which announces the beyond of Being within Western ontology.[11] But as Levinas's *explicit* recognition of this "history of the departures from totality" (*ED* 173/117) comes only after Derrida misses it, it could be suggested that Derrida has again anticipated Levinas as much as he has overlooked what was always to be found there. It would be curious indeed simply to dismiss these moments in Derrida's essay as instances of criticism which failed, when their failure is only that they fail as criticisms, that is, fail to redirect Levinas's thinking elsewhere. It is not only in his discussion of history that Derrida seems to confirm what—at least retrospectively—appears to have been always at the core of Levinas's thinking. There is no need to insist that Levinas's subsequent development shows the marks of his having read carefully and learned from Derrida's "Violence and Metaphysics"—although there is evidence for such an assertion. A seemingly grand claim like that in fact reduces the question to one of influence, a notion whose philosophical value is questionable, as Derrida himself observes (*ED* 164/110). The affinity between the course Levinas actually follows and that which Derrida lays out for him raises the question of the character of the dialogue between thinkers after Heidegger. And incidentally it also serves both to establish the rigor of Derrida's reading and to contradict the accusation of arbitrariness which is commonly brought against him.

That said, it does seem that Derrida's gesture of distinguishing Levinas's intentions from his text, the classic early deconstructive mechanism for the production of a doubled text, seems somewhat forced in this case: "Levinas is resigned to betraying his own intentions in his philosophical discourse" (*ED* 224/151). Certainly Derrida could not have replaced this distinction with the distinction between a text and its standard interpretation, which is the means Derrida tends to use in order to "double" Heidegger without having to make recourse to indiscreet conjectures about intentions. It was Derrida who in some ways set the standard reading of Levinas by offering the first extended reading of him; and no doubt against Derrida's intentions what was adopted from "Violence and Metaphysics" was the idea that certain of Levinas's central terms were incoherent. For this understanding of Derrida's essay disregards the strategy guiding it, as I have tried to show elsewhere.[12] Yet even though Levinas's announcement in *Time and the Other* that he intended to break with the tradition of Parmenides was not without a certain naive innocence—as indeed he showed an extraordinary presumption fourteen years later when he claimed to have successfully made the break (*TI* 247/269)—on what basis could Derrida insist that Levinas was naive in his use of philosophical language? No doubt Derrida maintains that there is a certain necessity whereby Levinas could not avoid the use of such language. But when Derrida writes that "Levinas is resigned to betraying his own intentions in his philosophical discourse," he seems to have had no warrant for attributing to Levinas the naive idea that one can break with a discourse simply by an edict, an edict which he is supposed to have betrayed. Already in *Totality and Infinity* Levinas shows himself to be fully aware of the difficulty of rupturing a tradition.

And yet to throw doubt on Derrida's use of the distinction between text and intention is not to correct Derrida. Derrida had already acknowledged that in Levinas's writing more than anywhere the distinction between intentions and stylistic gestures is a "violence of commentary" (*ED* 124 n./312 n. 7). The whole question of intention, of

how much Levinas or Derrida knew what they were doing, is not only
unimportant and often unanswerable; the interest in posing it arises
from the false assumption that the relation between Levinas and Derrida is to be viewed as if they were taking part in some sort of competition. When Levinas introduced the *trace* as "the presence of whoever,
strictly speaking, has never been there, of someone who is always past"
(*DEHH* 201/45) it was already with reference to the "unthinkable"
(*DEHH* 190/37). So when Derrida called the trace "impossible-
unthinkable-unstatable" he was not correcting Levinas, but instructing
us on how to maintain or preserve it in its denial of the (onto)logical
tradition on which it depends. Those commentators who have been
puzzled by the thought that Derrida could whole-heartedly reject
Levinas's concept of the trace one day and embrace it with equal enthusiasm the next read "Violence and Metaphysics" as a *critique*. Rather it
is by saying the unsayable, in resigning himself to "incoherent incoherence" (*ED* 224/151), that Levinas satisfies his "intentions." That
is the only way that, in Derrida's phrase, "the question of the relations
between belonging and the opening, the question of closure" can be
posed within language (*ED* 163/110). But it is important to recognize
that at the very beginning of the essay Derrida resigns himself to this
same "incoherent incoherence": "Therefore we will be incoherent, but
without systematically resigning ourselves to incoherence" (*ED*
125/84). A *systematic* incoherence is not a systematic *incoherence,* because it would in the end amount to a *coherent* incoherence.[13] And
Derrida warns against such a coherent incoherence whenever it threatens to deprive Levinas of absolute incoherent incoherency. That is what
Derrida means when at one point in "Violence and Metaphysics" he
refers to "a demonstration which contradicts what is demonstrated by
the very rigor and truth of its development" (*ED* 224/151). And it
explains the passage quoted earlier where Derrida describes the "Law of
laws" as a "coherence which breaks down the coherence of the discourse against coherence"; this is not a refutation of Levinas, but an
illustration of the only way his text can work. Only thereby can the
infinite concept be "hidden within the protest against the concept" (*ED*
164/111).

So Derrida by no means simply returns Levinas to Heidegger.
He shows how Levinas maintains the impossible discourse of the ethical and infinite relation to the Other. Over and beyond that, Derrida
"returns" Heidegger to Levinas. That is to say, he allows a Levinasian
interpretation of Heidegger. It is not the one which bears Levinas's
own name. Derrida neither confirms nor denies Levinas's central charge
against Heidegger that he shares the tradition's refusal of transcen-

dence. It is at all events a charge which can be brought against Derrida at least as readily as against Heidegger. But the remarkable pages at the end of "Violence and Metaphysics" which attempt to establish a proximity between Levinas and Heidegger have not, so far as I am aware, been taken up by any commentator. Derrida there writes of "the proximity of two 'eschatologies' which by opposed routes repeat and put into question the entire 'philosophical' adventure issued from Platonism" (*ED* 221/149). He suggests that God as positive infinity might be "the other name of Being." Not one word of Being among others (which Heidegger might accept, according to my interpretation of him), nor one eventual determination of the simplicity of Being (which is what Derrida imagines Heidegger might have accepted—*ED* 222/150). But Being and God, twin non-concepts, proving to be the same name! And as if this were not remarkable enough, Derrida adds that "the question about the Being of the existent would not only introduce—among others—the question about the existent-God; it already *would suppose* God as the very possibility of its question" (*ED* 223/150). No wonder there has been a conspiracy of silence! Derrida is here not simply gathering Levinas and Heidegger together. He is suggesting that the thought of infinity opens the question of the ontico-ontological difference, thereby raising the issue of the relative priority of Being and God, and thus in a certain sense the relative priority of Heidegger's thinking as compared with that of Levinas. In the light of Heidegger's discussion of the onto-theo-logical constitution of metaphysics Derrida's claim is extraordinary and all the more so for appearing in the context of an essay in which he has been severe with Levinas for failing to attend sufficiently closely to the letter of the "Letter on Humanism." But just as Derrida returns Levinas to Heidegger by showing that ethico-metaphysical transcendence presupposes ontological transcendence, so Heidegger is "returned" to Levinas, by the suggestion that the question of Being presupposes God. I am not commenting here on Derrida's reading of Heidegger, but, as Derrida himself might say, on the *necessity* which forbids Derrida from according to the subject-matter of either thinker an absolute priority over that of the other.

The response of deconstruction to the demand for an ethics was not, need not, and indeed should not be the one I suggested earlier. Ethics is not simply to be put in its place—even if that place is the exalted one of an "original ethics" which already contests the name and place traditionally given to ethics. Heidegger's original ethics can in no way be equated with Levinasian ethics. Indeed, more telling than the very little that Heidegger has to say about original ethics is the fact that

Heidegger constantly writes of the destiny of Being in ethical terms. For example, the very word *Schicklichkeit,* which in Heidegger's text evokes the destiny or sending of Being, also marks the fittingness of Being to which we should submit ourselves: "Rigor in meditation, carefulness in saying, frugality in words" (*W* 194/241). Have we not seen how Heidegger constantly enjoins us to come to abide in the truth of Being (*W* 191/239)? It is a tone which Derrida himself adopts at the beginning of "Violence and Metaphysics": "The injunction must be maintained." Perhaps on the basis of this ethical language one might attempt to reread Heidegger's answer to Beaufret as saying that ethics does indeed supplement ontology, not as a mere addition, but *in accordance with the logic of the supplement* and that this is the meaning of original ethics. Perhaps one could rejoin such an effort to that by which Derrida showed that the question of Being presupposes God. Or one could even apply Derrida's own caricature of the deconstructive strategy whereby overturning the hierarchy precedes its neutralization and could thereby come to suggest that Levinas's attempts to subordinate ontology to ethics serve only as the reversal of the traditional privilege accorded to ontology, whereas it is Heidegger with his notion of "original ethics" who attains to the second stage and renders the conceptual pair "undecidable."

But suppose one grants that it is in some sense an *ethical* demand that imposes itself on the thinker, a demand which says that he or she should abide in the truth of Being, "maintain the injunction," rather than, for example, write an ethics. How would this stand as a reply to the demand for an ethics? However rigorous, careful, and frugal that thinking might be, would we not also have to call it patronizing for addressing the demand for an ethics in this way? Do we not need to attend more humbly to the demand for an ethics?

What is the relation to thinking to the demands made on it from "elsewhere"? In the context of this question another meaning can be given to Aristotle's story of Heraclitus found at his stove by strangers come to visit him.[14] I have always felt uneasy about Heidegger's retelling of the story, not least because I cannot help wondering whether Heidegger could read the story without thinking of the numerous sightseers who came to catch a glimpse of him. Heidegger introduces the story about Heraclitus into the "Letter on Humanism" in order to deepen our appreciation of the Greek understanding of *ethos* as abode or dwelling place, even though the word appears nowhere in Aristotle's discussion of it. Fragment 119, ἦθος ἀνθρώπῳ δαίμων, is not to be read as "a man's character is his daimon," but as follows: "the abode is for man the open region for the presencing of god." The "here" of Heraclitus's invitation to the strangers—"even here the gods are present"—is read by Heidegger as a reference to the stove, "the ordinary place where every thing and every condition, every deed and thought is intimate and commonplace" (*W* 186–87/234). Both sayings of Heraclitus are thus to be understood as referring the familiar to the unfamiliar, the abode to the gods.

Heidegger refuses to speculate on whether or not these strangers might have understood Heraclitus's phrase. Having heard it, did they or did they not come to see everything otherwise? Certainly Heidegger seems to have a low opinion of them. Aristotle tells us nothing about their motives for wanting to visit Heraclitus; but Heidegger assumes that they merely want to be provided with "the material for entertaining conversation." They are described by Heidegger three times as "curious," and curiosity has in *Being and Time* the "everyday" characteristic of lacking an abode. It is because Heraclitus is, from the look of it, engaged in the everyday, like themselves, that they turn away disappointed. Furthermore, Heidegger's translation of Aristotle's story is already an expansion of it. It is Heidegger who provides the detail that the consternation of the strangers grew all the greater when Heraclitus issued his saying. And one effect of this addition is to complete the reader's perplexity as to both whether the statement was eventually understood by the strangers and how it came to be handed down, assuming for the sake of argument that the story is genuine. Who retold the story generation after generation? Did these curious strangers tell it as an amusing anecdote, not knowing what philosophers might subsequently make of it? Or did it at once enter into the philosophical repertoire, enthusiastically recalled because of the rigor, carefulness, and frugality of the response and the way it put the common people to shame? Or were there philosophers who were haunted by the fact that before the face of the stranger the thinker had so little to offer? Heidegger imagines "the frustrated curiosity of these faces" (*W* 186/234). Could philosophers be haunted by the memory of these disappointed faces as Macbeth was haunted by Banquo?

What could Heraclitus have offered to the strangers? Bread and wine after their journey? This would have been all the more disappointing, at least as Heidegger presents the story. The strangers came to see a thinker at work. They saw him in the mode of everyday existence and they turned away disappointed. But Heraclitus uttered a word which perhaps might have enabled him to see what they would already have seen, had they eyes to see at all. He gave them what they wanted, but

perhaps they never penetrated beyond the surface, which was all that
concerned them. What more could Heraclitus have said and done for
the strangers?

Heraclitus's saying went unrecognized, which is to say that it
went unreturned. Perhaps Heraclitus learned in the process that the
crucial question is not what one must do to fulfill one's obligations.
Perhaps he learned more from the encounter than they appear to have
done. Perhaps their response taught him that whatever we say as teachers or authors, it is never enough.[15] We always approach the Other
with empty hands. And yet would not this make Heraclitus all the more
correct when he said "Even here there are gods present"? Even here:
καὶ ἐνταῦθα: even now: at this very moment: *en ce moment même*. Not
in the sense Heidegger gives it: in every thing, condition, deed, and
thought. Not there only. But because the gods are present, the infinite
in the finite, in the encounter itself between thinker and strangers.[16]

And is it not in some sense the same story when the young friend
comes to Heidegger and asks about ethics? Heidegger does not record
exactly what he said on that occasion. Recalling the event in the "Letter
on Humanism," he says of *Being and Time* that "Where the essence of
man is thought so essentially, i.e., solely from the question concerning
the truth of Being, but still without elevating man to the center of
beings, a longing necessarily [*muss*] awakens for a peremptory directive
and for rules that say how man, experienced from eksistence towards
Being, ought to live in a fitting [*geschicklich*] manner" (*W* 183/231). A
hasty reading might suppose that Heidegger is doing no more in this
sentence than insisting—in his own inimitable language—on the impact made by his first great work: what can you expect after a book like
Being and Time than that young people, strangers even, would want to
live according to it? But it invites another reading. To demand an ethics
which will provide rules and directives no doubt misunderstands what
it means to live in a fitting manner, that is to say, according to the
destiny (*Geschick*) of Being. But that the demand is made in such a way,
that it arises out of a necessity—a necessity in the destiny of Being—
shows that the person who makes it abides in the destiny of Being and
responds to it in his or her own way. Heidegger in this passage effectively refers the demand for ethics to the truth of Being which conditions or dispatches ethics. And that means that the *demand* for ethics
itself arises from "original ethics." It is by refusing the demand for *an*
ethics that Heidegger ensures that he does not deny the person who
demanded it. To follow rules is to uproot oneself from dwelling. To
provide ethical directives is to condemn to the everyday the person who
adopts them.

Just as Heidegger sees the demand for an ethics as a destiny of Being, so for Levinas the demand would already be a manifestation of "the ethical relation." As Derrida himself presents Levinas: "Not a theoretical interrogation, however, but a total question, a distress and denuding, a supplication, a demanding prayer addressed to a freedom, that is to a commandment; [this is] the only possible ethical imperative, the only incarnated violence in that it is respect for the other" (*ED* 142/196). The demand for an ethics already enacts the ethical relation, is already "original ethics" as Levinas understands it, ethics in its primacy. But it seems that the demand for *an* ethics can only be satisfied by denying the ethical relation. It is as though the thinker were to respond by offering tablets of stone. It is, of course, no better a response to issue the instruction which refers ethics to the truth of Being. And yet it is at least the case that to refuse the demand is not necessarily to deny the relation.

The demand that deconstruction provide *an* ethics betrays not only traditional presuppositions about the possibility of generating ethical systems, but also a miscomprehension about the nature of deconstruction, confusing it for one philosophy among others. Hence in the face of the demand for an ethics, deconstruction can reply, in the course of its reading of Levinas that *the ethical relation is impossible and "the impossible has already occurred"* at this very moment. In other words, the ethical relation occurs in the face-to-face relation, as witnessed in the demand for an ethics itself, a demand which it is as impossible to satisfy as it is to refuse. To acknowledge this is to submit the demand for an ethics, not to instruction, but to deconstruction. And the *possibility* of ethics is referred, not to its actuality, but to its *impossibility*. This does not mean that writing ethical systems is impossible. Only that the attempt to do so is a denial of the ethical relation, though one which (fortunately) can never be complete; ontology denies the ethical relation when it presents its ethical system, but at the same time gives birth to it afresh in the saying of its said. The impossibility of murder.

Though the ethical relation as described by Levinas is thought both by logic and by deconstruction to be impossible, logic dismisses this "original ethics," while deconstruction maintains it by insisting on its impossibility. Deconstruction can—and to a certain extent does in "Violence and Metaphysics"—give a rigorous reading of Levinas which preserves the ethical relation without reducing it to the order of ontology. But the insistence that a λóγος of the ethical relation is impossible-unthinkable-unsayable might be said to preserve the *thought* of the ethical relation (a thought which is not yet also practice) rather than the ethical relation itself. The issue then is whether deconstruction enacts the ethical relation, as I have attempted to show Heidegger in the "Letter on Humanism" enacting it in his response to the young friend, or as Heraclitus perhaps enacted it in his dealings with the strangers, at least on a certain reading of Aristotle's story as retold by Heidegger. We might look at the way deconstruction seems rigorously to hold to the limits of thinking, not without a certain resignation, or at the way it responds with matchless energy to the apparently limitless appetite for more of its efforts. Of course, the *saying* of the said, its writerly saying, is also to be found in deconstruction—whenever it finds a "voice" of its own. But we find the ethical enactment above all in the way deconstruction ultimately refuses to adopt the standpoint of critique, renouncing the passing of judgments on its own behalf in its own voice.[17]

Notes

The following abbreviations are used in references in the text and in the notes:

AQ   Emmanuel Levinas, *Autrement qu'être ou au-delà de l'essence*; see note 9.

DEHH   Emmanuel Levinas, "La trace de l'autre," *En découvrant l'existence avec Husserl et Heidegger*; see note 8.

ED   Jacques Derrida, "Violence et metaphysique," *L'écriture et la différence*; see note 3.

EE   Emmanuel Levinas, *De l'existence à l'existant*; see note 6.

TEL   Jacques Derrida, "En ce moment même dans cet ouvrage me voici," *Textes pour Emmanuel Lévinas*; see note 7.

TI   Emmanuel Levinas, *Totalité et Infini*; see note 4.

W   Martin Heidegger, "Brief über den 'Humanismus,'" *Wegmarken*; see note 1.

1. Martin Heidegger, "Brief über den 'Humanismus,'" *Wegmarken* (Frankfurt am Main: Klostermann, 1967), p. 183; trans. F. A. Capuzzi and J. Glenn Gray, *Basic Writings*, ed. D. F. Krell (New York: Harper & Row, 1977), p. 231. Henceforth *W*.

2. On the issue of ethics as a supplement compare already Heidegger, *Sein und Zeit* (Tübingen: Niemeyer, 1967), p. 316; trans. John Macquarrie and Edward Robinson, *Being and Time* (Oxford: Blackwell, 1967), p. 364. On fundamental ontology see Heidegger, *Gesamtausgabe*, vol. 26, *Metaphysische Anfangsgründe der Logik* (Frankfurt am Main: Klostermann, 1978), pp. 196–202; trans. Michael Heim, *The Metaphysical Foundations of Logic* (Bloomington: Indiana University Press, 1984), pp. 154–59.

3. "First, let it be said, for our own reassurance: the route followed by Levinas's thought is such that all our questions already belong to his own interior dialogue, are displaced into his discourse and only listen to it, from many vantage points and in many ways." Jacques Derrida, "Violence et métaphysique," *L'écriture et la différence* (Paris: Seuil, 1967), p. 161; trans. Alan Bass, *Writing and Difference* (Chicago: University of Chicago Press, 1978), p. 109. Henceforth *ED*. The essay was first published in two parts in the *Revue de métaphysique et de morale* in 1964. A number of changes were made to the essay for its republication in 1967; most of them were minor, but a few of them

show Derrida engaged in the process of "Derridianising" his own text. I shall usually quote the second version, noting the changes where appropriate.

4. "My task does not consist in constructing ethics; I only try to find its meaning. . . . One can without doubt construct an ethics in function of what I have just said, but this is not my own theme." Emmanuel Levinas, *Éthique et infini* (Paris: Fayard, 1982), pp. 95–96; trans. Richard Cohen, *Ethics and Infinity* (Pittsburgh: Duquesne University Press, 1985), p. 90. But to agree that Levinas does not provide *an* ethics is not a straightforward issue. I shall make the point later in the essay that to write an ethics in the sense of a set of directives (and incidentally Aristotle's *Ethics* need not be read as being of that kind) is only possible while denying the ethical relation. The question then is whether maintenance of the ethical relation is not thereby accorded the status of a directive or a rule. My answer would be that Levinas understands it to be not so much an obligation which we must choose to follow, as an irremissible necessity. The sense in which this necessity cannot be evaded is precisely the same as that by which it is impossible to commit murder. Indeed "Thou shalt not commit murder" would mean to Levinas "it is impossible to annihilate the Other." Levinas refers to this as a "moral impossibility" and distinguishes it from "pure and simple impossibility." The interdiction dwells in this possibility "which precisely it forbids." *Totalité et Infini* (The Hague: Nijhoff, 1961), p. 209; trans. Alphonso Lingis, *Totality and Infinity* (Pittsburgh: Duquesne University Press, 1969), pp. 232–33. Henceforth *TI*. I would want to claim that Levinas's "moral impossibility" comes much closer to the sense of necessity governing Heidegger's history of Being than it does to logical impossibility. We can see yet again how Levinas's ethics of ethics is brought close to fundamental ontology, understood as a coming to abide in the sending of Being.

5. A further example of the convergence of Heidegger's "Letter on Humanism" and Derrida's "Violence and Metaphysics" occurs when Derrida says of Levinas that he has to "define metaphysical transcendence . . . as a not (yet) practical ethics" (*ED* 199/135). Derrida quotes the passage where Heidegger announces a thinking which is "neither theoretical nor practical" (*W* 192/240) and juxtaposes it to the remark in the preface to *Totality and Infinity* where Levinas says that he will refer both theory and practice to metaphysical transcendence (*TI* xvii/29).

6. Emmanuel Levinas, *De l'existence à l'existant* (Paris: Fontaine, 1947), p. 19; trans. Alphonso Lingis, *Existence and Existents* (The Hague: Nijhoff, 1978), p. 19. Henceforth *EE*.

7. Jacques Derrida, "En ce moment même dans cet ouvrage me voici," *Textes pour Emmanuel Lévinas,* ed. F. Laruelle (Paris: Jean-Michel Place, 1980), p. 24. Henceforth *TEL*.

8. Emmanuel Levinas, "La signification et le sens," *Humanisme de l'autre homme* (Montpellier: Fata Morgana, 1972), pp. 41–42. Also "La trace de l'autre," *En découvrant l'existence avec Husserl et Heidegger* (Paris: Vrin, 1974), p. 191; trans. Daniel Hoy, "On the Trail of the Other," *Philosophy Today,* vol. 10, no. 1 (Spring 1966), p. 37. Henceforth *DEHH*.

9. In "Tout Autrement," an essay written for an edition of *L'Arc* devoted to Derrida (no. 54, 1973, p. 35), Levinas is tempted by the thought of applying against Derrida the argument which Derrida had used against him in "Violence and Metaphysics"—specifically the argument which challenges the recourse to logocentric language in the fight against logocentric language. But Levinas turns his back on this argument on the grounds that it would bypass the "non-simultaneity" between *le dire* and *le dit,* the saying and the said. This shows very clearly the extent to which Levinas

believes that that distinction addresses Derrida. See, further, Levinas's *Autrement qu'être ou au-delà de l'essence* (The Hague: Nijhoff, 1974), pp. 56–61; trans Alphonso Lingis, *Otherwise Than Being or Beyond Essence* (The Hague: Nijhoff, 1981), pp. 43–48. Henceforth *AQ*. Derrida addresses this distinction himself in "En ce moment même dans cet ouvrage me voici" where he addresses it as the writing of the said and the saying of the written (*TEL* 27).

10. "Dieu et la philosophie," *De Dieu qui vient à l'idée* (Paris: Vrin, 1980), pp. 105–6; trans. Richard Cohen, *Philosophy Today*, 22, no. 2 (Summer 1978), p. 133. On the infinite in the finite see, for example, *TI* xi/23.

11. *AQ* 224–25/178. See further my essay "Levinas and Derrida: The Question of the Closure of Metaphysics," in Richard Cohen, ed., *Face to Face with Levinas* (Albany: SUNY, forthcoming 1986). Among the changes introduced in 1967 by Derrida to the 1964 version of "Violence and Metaphysics" a number are concerned with the concept of history. See for example *ED* 220/148 and 222/149.

12. See my essay "The Trace of Levinas in Derrida," in D. Wood and R. Bernasconi, eds., *Derrida and Différance,* (Coventry: Parousia Press, University of Warwick, 1985), pp. 17–44. To insist on the proximity of Derrida and Levinas is not to deny numerous differences between them, many of which are, of course, set out in "Violence and Metaphysics." The point is to develop an appreciation of Derrida's *strategy.* Compare, for example, Joseph Libertson, *Proximity, Levinas, Blanchot, Bataille and Communication,* Phaenomenologica 87 (The Hague: Martinus Nijhoff, 1982), p. 286 n.: "Derrida's essay . . . is a virulent attempt to reduce the pertinence and originality of all the Levinasian concepts, from a philosophical perspective which is surprisingly traditional. . . . Derrida's astonishing incomprehension of Levinas is noteworthy less for the ambiguity of its intention, which is a virtual constant in his theoretical practice, than for the extreme intimacy of the Levinasian text to those concepts (trace, *espacement,* supplementarity, temporal alteration in *différance,* etc.) which were to structure Derrida's own text."

13. By echoing the penultimate paragraph of Leszek Kolakowski's essay "In Praise of Inconsistency" in *Marxism and Beyond* (London: Pall Mall, 1969), p. 240. I do not mean to imply that the logic of inconsistency is "identical" with that of incoherency.

14. The source of the story is Aristotle's *De partibus animalium* 645a, 15–23. It is not usually included in collections of Heraclitus's sayings. Heidegger's retelling of the story can now be seen to have been extracted from his lecture course on Heraclitus held in the summer semester of 1943, so making all the more pressing the question of its place in the "Letter on Humanism." See *Gesamtausgabe,* vol. 55, *Heraklit* (Frankfurt am Main: Klostermann, 1979) pp. 6–10 and 22–23.

15. This is true even if the "more" that is required of us as teachers is that of holding back and refusing the demands of our students for more. Heidegger's discussion of the teacher-student relation recognizes this very clearly and can serve as another example in his work of the ethical relation. *Was heisst Denken?* (Tübingen, Niemeyer, 1954), p. 50; trans. F. D. Wieck and J. Glenn Gray, *What Is Called thinking?* (New York: Harper & Row, 1968), p. 15.

16. The attempt to refer Heidegger's discussion of the familiar and the unfamiliar (the gods) to Levinas's discussion of the finite and the infinite is not supposed to indicate that these two conceptual pairs are equivalent across the two thinkers. There is a pressing need for a discussion of Heidegger's notion of finitude (and also of the notion of infinity that he adopts from Hölderlin in later essays) in relation both to Levinas's and Derrida's discussion of these terms. I have not undertaken that task here; it cannot effectively be done without consideration of Hegel, particularly his *Glauben*

und Wissen. I offered a preliminary attempt to read Hegel's essay with a view to this issue in my lecture to the Hegel Society of Great Britain in September 1984.

17. As I have already mentioned, Derrida has explored the "traps" which attend gratitude on Levinas's discussion of it—"traps" which are not traps because, as Derrida points out, they are anterior to logic (*TEL* 25). It might therefore seem foolish—or even wrong of me—to express my thanks to Tina Chanter, Parvis Emad, David Krell, Kenneth Maly, John Sallis, and Charles Scott, all of whom have in various ways assisted me in the writing of this essay. So be it. There also has to be a place for the naming of friends.

Deconstruction— in Withdrawal?

4

Following Derrida

11

David Wood

Today, as you will soon gather, communication of information will always already have been exceeded. I am offering you something, I am opening myself up, I am risking myself, I am inviting you to follow me. I make no particular promises—to please, inform, stimulate, amuse— though there is always some hope of this. And I do not promise not to lead you astray, not to make feints. But I do not want you to have to listen out of courtesy. I would like to engage you, to have already engaged you.

But perhaps I have already let you anticipate too much. For now you will have already concluded that I am discussing the "ethics of communication." And my sensitivity to my position as speaker will mark me out as one who still harbors illusions of presence, of self-presence, of the presence of the writer to the reader, etc. Have I not learned the fundamental impersonality of speaking, of writing, of the production of signs? Are these very words not just another twitch, a final writhing in the last moments of the dying author?

Consider, I see myself writing, the multiplicity of contexts in which these words are being produced. Allow me this already oversimple schematization: (1) I am, "here and now," my ginger cat purring at my feet, in England, writing these words, reading them as I write them, monitoring them, thinking they *might* receive the right uptake. (2) I am, "here and now" (still in England), imagining an audience listening to my uttering these words at a later date, indeed an audience whose composition, in all sincerity, I could improve on only by acquiring the power of resurrection. (I would begin with philosophers whose names began with H.) (3) I anticipate that these words may be printed, published, distributed, and read, perhaps by people as yet unborn, and after my own death. Indeed it may be that between the (English) now of writing, and the (American) now of reading/speaking to you I will have passed away. It may be that one of my friends, or perhaps a stranger will be reading out these words. And then you will be thinking: how uncanny that he should have anticipated his own death! And how much pathos there is in these last words. And how disconcerting that we cannot reply to them, or ask for more, for elucidations. (4) And now that I am actually here, again, in Chicago, I can add a fourth: I am, here and now, reading this paper to you, speaking to you, in Chicago.

But it may be that you are not listening to me in Chicago, but reading me in Tokyo, perhaps even in "translation." This page (or that page) may have fallen from the wrapping round a fragile porcelain figure that has just arrived in the post. Do you not marvel at my prescience dear reader? And you, my living audience, supposing I have made it to Chicago, do you feel neglected when I address the reader? Or do you believe that subtly I am actually addressing *you,* that I am reminding *you* of these possibilities?

Can you be so sure? I have said that at one level, I am writing for an imagined (anticipated) audience, one that is (or would be) historically momentous. But the last time I spoke in America at a conference like this, Eugenio Donato was listening. Indeed I spoke about him, to him. And the time before that, Paul de Man was flourishing. Two great lights have since gone out, and each man's death diminishes me. People I imagine being here may no longer be anywhere. I can only guess the names of the ears my noise will be trickling into.

Clearly, too, whomever this is being written *for,* and even read or spoken to, it may yet be *addressed* to a quite different ear. To history? To postmodernity? To Rosemary? To the Other? Perhaps to Derrida "himself."

Suppose then, after all this, that the charges are dropped and I am no longer viewed as a naive reinscriber of the metaphysical value of "presence"? How then does the fragility of my beginning even begin to make sense? How can I be *offering* you something, *risking* myself, *opening* out, *inviting* you to follow me, when "you" are so radically put in question? But the issue is far more serious even than this. Surely I have begun with what is essentially a kind of plagiarism, a purloined strategy. And whether I admitted this, or invoked in my defense the metaphysical status of the idea of intellectual property that it involved, the consequence would be the same—that the "I" who could *offer, invite, open* out, *risk* . . . itself becomes a fiction. Sartre, *a propos* of *Being and Nothingness* once wrote that "Angst" was not something he had ever felt, but that it was a fashionable topic of conversation in Paris in the early 40s. Perhaps "risk" and "danger" are similarly just rhetorically intensifying. *Who* is at risk? And what danger can there be in these mere echoes of others' intrepid steps?

Let us say this—what is at stake, perhaps in all words addressed to a living audience—is what I shall call the *residual* question of the presence of the speaker, and of the act of speaking. Words are addressed, a paper is delivered, and everywhere we hear the workings of desire. These words are an invitation to an impossible event.

How friendly, you may say. The ball is in your court. You can say yes, no, maybe . . . Of course, it is not that simple. I have not explained what the impossible event is. You do not know what you are being invited to. How can you say yes or no? Etymology confirms these suspicions: invite → invito (from the Sanskrit *vak*—speak; *vak'as*—word; compare *vox* . . .). And the Oxford English Dictionary offers us many senses. To treat, feast, entertain. But also to summon, to challenge. And even to incite, attract, allure to transgression.

In issuing such a problematic invitation, I am, as I see it, following Derrida. I will pursue such a suggestion by explaining one or two ways in which invitation moves from openness to seduction and to a crisis of reading.

Let me take first a simple example, drawn from "Le retrait de la métaphore."[1] This essay begins with a discussion of metaphor that, let us say, becomes aware that it itself takes place *in* metaphor. The author comes to the conclusion that he cannot talk *about* metaphor without, as he puts it, "negotiating with it the loan I take from it in order to speak of it." On at least three occasions Derrida asks himself, or tells himself, or talks to the reader, about the necessary drifting or skidding of his writing about metaphor. Trying to prevent metaphor from creeping into his discussion of metaphor (which plays with transportation, vehicles, pilots in ships, etc.) is futile. Skidding, sliding, drifting are unavoidable.

The problem I want to pose is how should the critical reader respond to this? The reason *I* take it to be a problem is that Derrida is not just indulging himself but inciting himself to pursue every piece of slippage he comes across. What is meant to be a feature of language in general actually appears here only as a very willful, deliberate act of writing. Derrida doesn't begin to try to control metaphor. He claims he cannot control language, but in fact he is all the time in control—writing *about* metaphor precisely as he does, writing *about* slippage, and so forth. What is the reader to do? Are we to pretend that Derrida is just unable to control himself? Or what? The beginning, in other words, is a charade, a play. It is one that seeks our generous assent. The reader must accept that the horse *necessarily* runs away with the charioteer.

There are two points I am not disputing: (1) that discussions of metaphor are, indeed, often remarkably unaware of their own metaphors (Searle's paper on metaphor is a case in point),[2] (2) that the distinction between the literal and the metaphorical may indeed be systematically elusive. My point is that for the reader to follow, that is to accept, "go along with," these moves, he or she has to accept the pretence, the gambit, that Derrida's horse, and our horse, has always already bolted. This requires an elision of what is true of language itself and the special characteristics of a particular, highly calculating use of language. Derrida is just *playing victim,* like those bandits who pretend to be involved in a road accident and whose lifeless bodies spring up when the honest citizen stops.

My second case is in its implications far more important. It concerns the broader question of strategy and seduction.[3] We could put it like this: what is involved in acquiescing, going along with Derrida's deconstructive manoeuvres? I want to argue that the critical reader reaches a point of crisis in reading Derrida at which a decision both has to be and cannot be made. If for some, the question of *choice* does not arise, for the critical reader, it must. My question will be—what is it for the critical reader to *follow* Derrida?

Without wishing to privilege this early but seminal paper too much, consider some of the claims made for differance in the paper of that name. Using the language of transcendental causation (but persistently refusing its metaphysical implications), Derrida substitutes differance in place of any presence or origin of meaning. Differance, in which is condensed both deferment and differentiation, is what "produces" the mundane differences we encounter everyday. This term can be said to draw together the various powerful senses of difference generated by a whole range of thinkers—Saussure, Freud, Nietzsche, Heidegger, Levinas . . . Derrida writes ". . . one comes to posit presence . . . no longer as the absolutely central form of Being but as a 'determination' and as an 'effect' within a system which is no longer that of presence but of 'difference,' a system that no longer tolerates the opposition between activity and passivity, nor that of cause and effect, or of indetermination and determination, etc., such that in designating consciousness as an effect or a determination, one continues for strategic reasons that can be more or less lucidly deliberated, and systematically calculated—to operate according to the lexicon of that which one is de-limiting."[4]

The fundamental reason for this is that metaphysical thinking and ordinary language are inseparable, and that it is just not possible to operate on philosophy "from the outside"; there is no such "outside."

When Derrida introduces the term differance and begins to give it work to do (it "constitutes" or "produces" any code as a system of differences) he is very careful to repeatedly remind us that transcendental language is just provisional and inadequate. Its employment is merely strategic. Differance cannot be thought on the basis of old metaphysical oppositions, "which," he writes, "makes the thinking of it uneasy and uncomfortable."

With these words, Derrida simultaneously acknowledges our difficulty and disarms it of any critical force. Let us try to reopen the place of difficulty. First we notice Derrida's deferment to Saussure, to whom so much modern thought is indebted. There is no attempt to evaluate this model of language. Instead he offers us a kind of deepening of the principle of difference on which it rests. As an antidote to a phenomenological account of language, the force of this is clear. But to those of us who had also struggled with another tradition—with analytical philosophy, with ordinary language philosophy, who had followed Wittgenstein and Austin, this way of setting out seemed (and still seems) in need of justification. Let us put this to one side, however, for the central difficulty lies elsewhere.

I think we are offered two options: (*a*) We are asked to understand, or at least to acquiesce in sentences involving, the words "produce," "constitute," "possibility," "effect," without our being allowed to attribute to any of these terms either ordinary or philosophical significance. But if we had this ability to bracket out metaphysical implications, Derrida's position would be both far easier and far more difficult. It would be easier in that he could then exploit this ability of ours without question; it would be more difficult in that it would suggest that his whole programme of reading/writing rested on certain powers of abstinence that look remarkably like a transcription of Husserl's epoche. (*b*) We can understand these words in the old metaphysical way, but only for the time being. We are given warning that this grasp will soon be taken away from us. How we follow these instructions is surely doubly problematic. It is bad enough being asked to walk out on a branch that one knows is about to break. But the whole strategy rests on our actually crediting such terms as differance with a power to displace the foundational language of metaphysics, a power that they plainly do not have unless such terms as produce, constitute, etc., are understood out of erasure.

The key word in the early pages of the "Differance" essay is "*repartons*" ("Let us go on"). Is this an exhortation? A command? A request? An invitation? Who are *we*? Is Derrida addressing all his readers or only those who are still with him?

There are undoubtedly many responses to this. Let me suggest three. (1) It might be said that there is nothing special about this situation. Reading is always, or should always be an active, participatory affair. It is never possible to eliminate the reader's role. The occasions on which it seems to have happened are simply those in which the moves required conform to the reader's pre-existing prejudices. (2) There is a certain special insight and adventurousness required of the reader. The sedentary thinker will indeed be left behind. We have here a *selective* strategy, a book for the few, an esoteric text. If you bet nothing you win nothing. He who dares wins. (3) Finally, it could be said that our worries would disappear if a certain consequentialism were allowed to displace our foundational prejudices. We have nothing to lose by seeing where it all leads; we can judge the path later.

I will not attempt to judge this matter now. What I will say, briefly, is that not for the first time (for one can make the same remarks about Hegel, about Nietzsche, about Husserl, about Levinas, about Heidegger . . . and it is important that one can) Derrida opens up, within the framework of reading, albeit without thematizing it just here, the whole space of the relation to the Other, of the writer to the reader. And this relation is posed as one of necessary risk.

The status Derrida attributes to the Other seems to us fundamentally problematic. In his essay "Signature Evenement Context"[5] it is the absence of the Other, perhaps even the Other's absolute absence, that is the necessary condition for the legibility of writing. What he does not mention here (we would perhaps be repaid by a closer look at his readings of Levinas and Blanchot[6]) is the role the Other might play in the pathos of writing. In this respect, the writing we call philosophical, metaphysical, and even postmetaphysical or deconstructive may have every thing to do with the Other.

To help us pursue this possibility, I would first like to draw into our text a poem which, somewhat tentatively, I shall employ as a kind of grid.[7]

Voyage West

There was a time for discoveries—
For the headlands looming above in the
First light and the surf and the
Crying of gulls: for the curve of the
Coast north into secrecy.

That time is past.
The last lands have been peopled.
The oceans are known now.

Senora: once the maps have all been made
A man were better dead than find new continents.

A man would better never have been born
Than find upon the open ocean flowers
Drifted from islands where there are no islands,

Or midnight, out of sight of any land,
Smell on the altering air the odor of rosemary.

No fortune passes that misfortune—

To lift along the evening of the sky,
Certain as sun and sea, a new-found land

Steep from an ocean where no landfall can be.

Would it be wholly anachronistic to read in these lines an anticipatory commentary on the promise of deconstruction? Deconstruction
has presented itself as the only solution to a historically determined
situation which can briefly be termed the closure of philosophy. It has
heralded the possibility of a new kind of writing, one that neither makes
a radical break nor merely works from the inside, but one that weaves
together both strategies. And, what is crucial, refuses to understand
itself as relating to philosophy as a "negation" in a way that would
allow it to be merely absorbed in a dialectic of history. Deconstruction
claims in this sense to mark an absolute difference, not to be recupera-
ble! But suppose this were merely the dream of a new dawn, of a new
beginning.

In this poem, Archibald Macleish is warning against the tragedy
of false hope. Is deconstruction perhaps just a "smell on the altering
air," "flowers drifting from islands where there are no islands"? Or is it
not precisely an affirmation of ocean without nostalgia for new islands?
Does deconstruction offer a way for philosophy to carry on, to sur-vive,
or does it simply strew flowers on philosophy's watery grave?

The reading underlying such exorbitant questions is not without
its difficulties. I merely note that the reader sensitive to deconstructive
manoeuvres could easily refocus the question away from the smell (the

odor of rosemary) and onto the "altering air," away from the flowers to their drifting. And the question about whether deconstruction offers a way for philosophy to carry on leaves open the issue of whether one actually accepts its diagnosis of philosophy.

Unless we read this whole poem ironically (and I shall leave this problem unexplored), Macleish is operating with a fairly clear distinction between truth and illusion, innocent adventure and tragic mirage. We are warned against the flowers that drift from "islands where there are no islands." This formulation is not the affirmation of a paradoxical supplementation of origin (as in "trace which is not a trace of anything" [Derrida]). The "islands where there are no islands" are illusions we should steer clear of.

When Heidegger reads poetry he often picks out those poems and poets for which what is in question is *language,* its limits and productive possibilities, poems which are reflexive, and, perhaps, performative. One thinks of his account (in "The Nature of Language") of Stephan Georg's "The Word" ("Das Wort") (1919). Macleish not only does not do this here, he seems even to ignore language's own possibilities. For one way in which the distinction between truth and illusion, between real and apparent islands can surely be made problematic, is through language. The term fiction is perhaps a perfect condensation of such ambivalence. Fiction is both negative, error, false, and also productive, creative, even suggesting a certain coherence. What Macleish does not ask himself is whether language itself can supply new horizons, new islands. We have, as it happens, already anticipated a negative answer to this. The account Nietzsche gives of the closure of metaphysics (*Beyond Good and Evil,* section 20) is cast precisely in terms of a "prison-house of language" thesis. Nonetheless, it has been the belief of a whole string of philosophers (Nietzsche, Heidegger, Levinas, Bataille . . .)—who have even risked their labels in pursuing it—that by a change of style, by a changed relation to language, or some such move, something new can be allowed to happen.

Allow me, for a few minutes, a diversion. In the early days of April, in about 1977 or 1978, I learned at the ordinary empirical level a truth to which Derrida's meditations on the uncertainties of the postal services (on the possibility of messages not getting through, letters not being delivered, communicative intentions not being realised), only later gave theoretical significance.

I tore out of my daily newspaper a three- or four-page Supplement, carefully folded it up, slid it into a brown envelope, addressed it to Jacques Derrida at the École Normale, and popped it into the letter box. Thinking he might be in America, I added *Please Forward* on the outside, even adding a French translation. Well, it never arrived. I conjectured that it had indeed been forwarded to other continents, and then sent on again, following Derrida around the globe, until it attained sufficient momentum to be able to circulate freely within the international postal system long after its address had been effaced by the wear and tear of its travels. There, perhaps, it continues to this day, without origin or τέλος, a graphic illustration of the errance of writing. But the answer to its non-arrival may be found in its content. You must all have seen prominently displayed at least in most American airports a large sign proclaiming that "Security is no joking matter." It cautions against answering the questions of security staff in anything other than a totally serious manner. (If asked whether you have a weapon, and you reply that you have a fully armed Sherman tank in your bag, they will search to find it.) This is not the place, perhaps, to amplify on the theoretical connections between the general concept of security and that of seriousness. I merely offer you this sign in a light-hearted way to suggest an explanation for the non-arrival of my little folded bundle. It was intercepted by the seriousness police.

Suppose it had been received, carefully slit open, and unfolded, what would the addressee have discovered? What was this Supplement to a newspaper called *The Guardian*? It had caused a considerable stir in England. Many people had written in requesting travel brochures, people who thought they had found a new place to go on holiday. In fact, as they discovered, it was language that had gone on holiday. The Supplement was devoted to a political/cultural/economic/geographical profile of the islands of San Seriffe, with its golden sands, happy fun-loving people, and benign military dictatorship. A great deal could be said about San Seriffe. Indeed one could say almost anything about it. To forestall those readers who would seek it out on their maps, it was explained that the island, formed out of light volcanic rock, somewhat unusually had cracked free from the sea-bed, and now drifted over the oceans of the world, a floating paradise.

But let us stop this drifting and be serious for a minute. San Seriffe is a fiction, the veritable incarnation of the floating signifier. Its very name testifies to its status as a (typo-)graphical construction. San Seriffe is surely an "island where there are no islands," and I am certain that boats visiting its bustling harbor would often cleave waters strewn with flowers. Macleish, on our reading, was offering us a choice between the resignation of closure and false hopes. Does not the magical island of San Seriffe show that it is precisely through language or through some reformation or deformation of language that a third way might be charted? And is it not deconstruction's path to offer us a third way—neither more of the same, nor simple otherness, but some inter-weaving of the two?

We shall return to this poem, but first, another diversion. I would like to offer a brief note to a footnote to *La Carte postale.*[8] On August 22, 1979, Derrida, in the middle of typing a letter that had mentioned the names Freud and Heidegger (in that order) received a collect call from the United States. He writes: *"La téléphoniste américaine me demande si j'accepte un 'collect call' de la part de Martin (elle dit Martine ou martini) Heidegger."* Derrida refused the call, saying "It's a joke, I do not accept."

It so happens that open on my desk while I was reading this foot-note, was Derrida's *Marges,* containing a paper to which I have already referred—"Signature Événement Contexte," a paper which I had heard "live" some ten years earlier in Montreal. And as chance would have it again, the book was open at the page on which Derrida was diagnosing Austin's exclusion, at the beginning of *How to Do Things with Words,* of, "along with what he calls the sea-changes,[9] the 'non-serious,' the 'parasitic,' the 'etiolations.'" Derrida wonders whether the possibility of language falling into non-seriousness is the possibility of its failure, or an *essential* possibility. Might not this risk be its "internal and positive condition of possibility," he asks, "this outside its inside"? And so on.

When I read "It's a joke, I do not accept," my reaction was strange. The words immediately fragmented into a matrix, and re-formed themselves into different patterns: "It's no joke, I accept"; "It's no joke, I do not accept"; "It's a joke, I accept." The law that favoured "It's a joke, I do not accept" was the law of exclusion, of refusal. No expenditure without reserve here. In fact, Derrida even profits from it, in the shape of an interesting question. ("Who should pay, the caller or the called . . . a very difficult question") even as he pretends that the footnote itself is a note of thanks, a kind of payment. But let's be serious! Suppose that we respond to the call seriously, what then?

Derrida *refused* the call. We have to ask what was actually refused. Was it (1) the possibility that Heidegger might have made a radical break with the way of life of Black Forest peasants, abandoned the "provinces" for that radically deracinated and deracinating world we call America? (2) the possibility that Heidegger might have survived death, or Derrida's treatment of him? (3) the possibility that Heidegger was a woman? We take especial delight in the way in which Derrida openly suppresses this possibility (*"un 'collect call' de la part de Martin 'elle dit Martine ou martini' Heidegger"*).

And what, we might ask, was the nature of the call? We may think that because the call was refused we will never know. But we can ask whether this refusal did not involve a certain recognition. Consider, just for a moment, *what calls?* In connection with Heidegger we would re-call two possibilities: the call of Being and the call of conscience. Der-rida's refusal of either would be understandable. But let us not forget that the call was beyond the grave, for Heidegger had, by this time, passed on. His time had already come. Perhaps then, the call was the last call of all, the call of death?[10] Why, then, did Derrida refuse the call? At this point we might remind ourselves that it was a collect call. This makes the "es gibt Sein" reading rather less plausible, and strengthens the suggestion that it is death that speaks, that wants to collect its dues. Derrida refuses. This, you may say, is understandable. And yet does not Derrida, in his writing about Bataille, about Blanchot, about Shelley, not to mention Hegel, Husserl, and others, precisely negotiate for him-self and indeed for others the most intimate relation with death? Does not Derrida, in effect, and in his own way, affirm death? What charges would there be left for death to collect?

There is a final possibility—that we should not have asked *what* calls but *who*. There are many clues. The name given, like Heidegger's Dasein, is sexually indeterminate (Martin/Martine). It is the name of one whose voice has been extinguished by death, a radical absence. And it is mediated, absolutely, through an operator, who is both an indi-vidual (indeed a woman), and yet not an individual. We now know, surely, who it is that calls. It is the Other. And if Levinas is right about Heidegger, it would not be inappropriate for Heidegger to be the name used on the *Fern*sprecher, for the question of the Other is still critical for those who have divided up his philosophical legacy—not least for Derrida.

You see the outrageous privilege I allow myself—to give new life, new possibilities of death, to Derrida's lines—the absolute privilege of the reader. Let us suppose that our mineshafts have struck two rich veins—that of death and that of the Other. And that "Heidegger," at least for the moment, is a clue—that he might be the name of un-finished business, that his formulations might still give us more to think, that in some way, he lives on.

I will now confirm this by another strangly parallel example, from another entry (June 6, 1977) in *La Carte postale*.[11] Derrida had just given a seminar on "La differance," by then already ten years old, at Balliol College, Oxford. He was stretched out on the grass of the quad-rangle where the discussion following his paper was to take place. A very handsome student, and I quote here, "thought to provoke me, and, I think seduce me a little by asking me why I did not commit suicide. It was in his view the only way of following up ('faire suivre,' in Derrida's words) my 'theoretical discourse,' the only way of being consistent and bringing about an event."

Not surprisingly, Derrida gives no direct answer.

The question is not entirely perspicuous. Derrida tells us the question only in indirect speech. We do not hear the exact words. As I recall, it was actually posed at greater length than Derrida allows. I remember only trivia—the creeping shadows of the trees over the lawn, and the signature scored on the soles of Derrida's upturned shoes, that would leave its imprint on the soft verge of the lawn when he walked away. Perhaps Camus, for whom suicide is the only serious philosophical question, is being cited. Or perhaps something was being made of the role of "difference" in the Stoic discussion of death. The Stoic affirms that he is indifferent to death. He is asked why, then, he does not commit suicide, and answers "because it would make no difference."

Perhaps, finally, we might note Derrida's setting aside, at the end of "La differance," what he calls Heideggerian hope. The questioner would then be asking—what sort of future for philosophy is provided by laughter, dance, and ". . . an affirmation foreign to all dialectics"?

The phone-call from America was, we are told, "a joke." The question on the Balliol lawn was a "provocation, perhaps a seduction." A strange couple. And strange, too, if death should be their shared theme. Derrida refused the phone-call. What did he do to the question? "Instead of arguing . . . I responded with a pirouette, by returning his question to him . . . ." A strange parallel. The relation to the Other exhibits an extraordinary inversion, however. In each case, there is anonymity, although in different ways. Derrida never discovers the proper name of his transatlantic caller. He is offered a pseudonym, and that indeterminate—between sex (Martin/Martine) and between category of sign, that is, between proper name and brand name (Martin[e]/ Martini). Derrida calls him Martin in his footnote. The caller is a pseudonymous *absence,* moreover one mediated by an unnamed operator. On the Balliol lawn, the interlocutor is totally present, and yet unnamed. We do not know whether Derrida omits to mention his name, or simply does not know it. For the record I will tell you the name of this Adonis. It, too, was Martin.

So—a call, a question, some conceits. Sheer whimsy, perhaps, and flimsy at that. And yet so much has already come into play. Let us try to be somewhat more explicit in this last section about what the relationship between writing, death, and the Other might come to, aware as I was very much am, how much more needs to be said, how I should have systematized Derrida's treatment of Husserl, Freud,

Blanchot, Bataille, Shelley, Heidegger, etc. That I have not done so is a sign only of my own scholarly finitude, not of some lofty gesture. We are guided by the thought that the historical fate of Derrida's writing will, of course, depend on his readers, those who come after him.

We could conveniently begin with Derrida's early discussions of writing as a break with the metaphysics of presence and self-presence, especially phenomenological consciousness. Perhaps I could quote from "The End of the Book and the Beginning of Writing." "What writing itself, in its non-phonetic movement, betrays is life. It menaces at once the breath, the spirit, and history as the spirit's relationship with itself. It is their end, their finitude, their paralysis."[12]

Elsewhere he writes that "the metaphysics of the logos, of presence, and consciousness, must reflect upon writing as its death."[13] Writing is the death of presence in that it inscribes any meaning in a play or economy of signification, which essentially disperses any sense—immediate or mediated—of self-presence, of absolute interiority, or self-relatedness. Husserl's founding of meaning in his own "living presence," as Derrida has shown, perfectly exemplifies the threat writing poses to "life." We have two main responses to this.

(1) The words "life" and "death" are, in this very movement, transformed, and their opposition subverted. Dispersion, differance, mark the end of a certain illusion of life that we call self-presence. What this opens up is the possibility of a reinscription, a re-working, of these values within the general problematic of writing. If writing is a supplement to my living presence without which I would not be who I am (I am thinking of Rousseau[14]), is not writing essential to "life" in some sense freed from its traditional metaphysical signification? Is not Derrida, via writing, simply giving voice to a sense of "life" which even in its vulgar forms (as "struggle," as "disappointment," as "vale of tears," as "for the living," as "bed of nails" or as a "bed of roses") is postmetaphysical, shorn of any illusions of "presence"? In the old metaphysical sense, who, apart from Husserl, is still talking about living?

(2) We find in Derrida's formulation (which we could summarize as "writing is the death of presence") a definite weighting towards the self-dispersal of meaning. In his account of Husserl's inner speech which, it is worth recalling, Husserl set up to provide an ideal pure ground of meaning free from the dispersive dangers of *outer* communication, what Derrida focuses on is the way both the "imagination" and the temporal present have an essential relation to what is "other." But *we* can ask: what of the fate of public speech/writing? How do the concepts of life/death as they function here involve a relation to the Other?

I wanted to say, at this point, that this is an impossibly difficult question to discuss in such a short time, that I would need a book. Then, protected by its seriousness, its weightiness, its table of contents, its security apparatus, I might be able to offer myself up to you. But only a transcendental book could afford such protection, as everyone who has been reviewed knows well. I wanted to say that I would not attempt to tell the whole story of writing, death, and the Other, that I would be selective. And albeit in a performative way I have already let slip the focus I have in fact selected. I will call it the *vulnerability* of the writer. If we think of "writing" in its widest sense, this becomes the question of vulnerability "as such." I will try to broach this question economically and without fuss, fully aware that I am taking certain things for granted, and that I am not fully justifying this focus.

What is the *question* of vulnerability? I thought it was just one. In fact, it is several. Most obviously, what sense can be given to vulnerability after the death of the subject, the death of the author? Is there anything left to defend, to protect, to be threatened? Would not affirmation, dissemination, self-dispersal make the question of vulnerability into a relic of an outdated logocentrism, a fundamentally residual problem?

There is no doubt that the question of vulnerability can take a hysterical form. As proof, let me quote from an early draft of this paper.

"For the last decade and a half I have followed Derrida around this Western world . . . I speak today, however, not as a camp-follower, but as his Reader, one of the names of Fate, one of the dark birds circling on high. . . . I begin, then, with an act of displacement, of dramatization, in which I don a mask, the better to speak through. Let me call myself Death. Here, at this point, I feel a mild sense of comfort. I have found a way to begin. And yet there is also the greatest trembling and striving. He who plays with fire. . . . He who lives by the sword. . . . For I, too, am writing, and you will be the death of me, you who rake through the ashes of my words for the fragments that please you, you who disperse, distort, forget, ignore . . . even enjoy; are you not already preparing to kill? The writer, after all, lacks a face. . . ."

It went on like this. Perhaps you can see how I needed the safety of quotation marks before I could let it out. Here the reader, the Other, is the source of all misunderstanding, of all loss of meaning, and of pain. The question is—is this simply the price we have to pay for that *necessary* opening to the Other to which we give the name of writing, or are all such negative, protective responses simply, as we called them, residues of those illusions of ego that an affirmative dissemination might dispense with? (Do we learn anything from the keen control that

Derrida so clearly exercises over his writing and his "natural" concern that it not be misunderstood, that his strategies succeed?) The reader, quite as much as being a threat, it might be said, is the condition of my life, my living-on. And yet it is just as such that the reader poses his/her threat. For the reader has the power to appropriate my legacy, to turn it to his (or her) advantage. One thinks of Husserl's disappointment with Heidegger. One can only speculate about Derrida's attitude to Derrideans, those admiring offspring, those who already seek to divide the estate.

What is true of translation—that one lives on, survives, continues—at the very moment of one's betrayal is equally true of reading in general. (Better read than dead?) Interestingly, the reader, and even more a seated audience, is in the same position: open to pleasure, *jouissance,* ecstasy, but equally, lacking earlids, to boredom, frustration, insult, outrage, and so on. Perhaps to listen, to read, is equally to risk a little death. Perhaps, then, both reader and writer are engaged in a life-and-death struggle that never ends, and is never resolved.

It may be that the silent and hidden object of this discussion will one day turn out to be desire, and the economy of desire. Only then, perhaps, will we be able to make sense of such concepts as risk and danger, and only then will the undecidability of life/death and the whole question of vulnerability get articulated.

I would like now, before concluding, to offer some brief and tentative thoughts about the desire of deconstruction "itself"—tentative because what I shall say is opaque to me both in its force and its motivation.

Deconstruction is intimately concerned with power. The key to what Derrida called the general strategy of deconstruction[15] is the discovery of a conceptual opposition working within a text that structures that text by the systematic privilege given to one of the terms in the opposition. By inversion and displacement that power-play is exposed and, perhaps, unraveled. It must have been asked before, but does not the deployer of such strategies of reading actually acquire, for him/herself or for their own texts, enormous power? But of course, it may be said, and what is wrong with that? Power is the natural corollary of a productive, insightful reading. If the alternative is the "deaf passivity of commentary" who would want anything else? So when someone laments, as I heard recently, that he had been deconstructed, he is suffering from a misapprehension, his suffering *is* a misapprehension. But in what way? Should one affirm and encourage the deconstruction of one's own writing, perhaps even be honoured to be so chosen? Or should one simply enjoy the spectacle of something one never really owned (one's writing) being undone? Should one seek deconstruction, acquiesce in it, avoid it, or what? The case for saying that the cry "I have been deconstructed. Alas, I am undone!" is a naive one is surely that deconstruction is not destructive, not the same thing as criticism. Any philosophical text, and as such, can be deconstructed. (So, too, can any deconstructive text.) We should not worry. The reason the worry remains, of course, is that the successfully deconstructed text, at least in one respect or at one level, loses its power (which is why, for strategic reasons, Derrida has privileged Marx's writings). Surely we need to ask again: What about deconstruction? What of its desire?

A sceptical friend of mine put his difficulty this way: "everything I read of Derrida's has one consequence—the production of an invulnerable discourse—a kind of postmodern omnipotence. It is said that deconstruction is not a position. So it cannot be attacked! It is said that deconstruction 'is' not, at all, that it is not an 'is.' All the better, for that makes 'it' completely immune to criticism. Insofar as deconstruction is the absolute anticipation of philosophy[16] it is the renewal of the fundamental desire of Hegelian thought. And insofar as it is the interweaving of the only two possibilities of thinking beyond the closure of philosophy, it denies the possibility of any serious competition. Deconstruction has sacrificed the name of philosophy the better to realize its fundamental desire—total anticipation." If one were to pursue this sceptical line of thought, one would add that the admission that any deconstructive reading is, in principle, open to deconstruction is no limitation at all—it simply confirms the practice of deconstruction in its position of invulnerability.

Now, what is being said here is, of course, paradoxical. If deconstruction is immune to criticism, then these remarks must fail (as criticism). If they are a successful criticism, then they must be false, for deconstruction would then be open to criticism. The simplest way to round this would be to suggest that while it can always, in a certain way, handle straightforward philosophical objections, the question of its own power, vulnerability, desire, might prove to be its Achilles heel.

I am quite aware that an adequate discussion of these questions could only really follow a careful consideration of Derrida's texts. On other occasions I have done just that. For now, I shall simply accentuate the difficulty of judging deconstruction in this way by saying that the reason this question of desire, vulnerability, and so forth, is not posed more insistently rests on the continuing power of deconstruction to excite, to allure to transgression, to open up texts to previously unheard of readings, to raise questions where none had appeared before, and to preserve the space of questioning where others (such as Heidegger and Levinas) have opened it up.

We have repeatedly attempted to bring together the questions of writing, death, and the relation to the Other. Indeed we raised the whole question of deconstruction within the context of "vulnerability." Is it not curious that Derrida seems to suspend the question of the Other at one of the critical points in his writings at which these themes converge? Discussing Levinas, he talks of the questions surrounding the death of philosophy as "the only questions today capable of founding the community, within the world, of those who are still called philosophers . . . a community of the question about the possibility of the question."[17] This is in many ways a satisfying formulation, which describes the horizon of such "events" as this paper, but does it not rest on an unproblematized notion of "community"?

It will not completely resolve the question of the relative claim of the primary of the desire for the Other or the desire for "presence" (which is one way of formulating our central question) but I would like to end by returning to Macleish, and to the poem we discussed earlier. For our reading was, of course, a subterfuge, a deferral, a holding-back. Is the poem really about the illusory dreams of a new kind of writing or thinking that would not be reappropriated by history? "There was a time for discoveries . . ."—is that about the closure of metaphysics? Is the "first light" a version of "*lichtung*"? Is "the crying of gulls" the anonymous call of Being? Perhaps not.

The surf of any such reading breaks on the words that follow— "for the curve north into secrecy." And if that is not clue enough, the secret is soon upon us, unveiled:

> *Senora:* once the maps have all been made
> A man were better dead than find new continents
>
> A man would better never have been born
> Than find upon the open ocean flowers
> Drifted from islands where there are no islands,
>
> Or midnight, out of sight of any land,
> Smell on the altering air the odor of rosemary.
>
>   Rosemary?

Suppose truth were a woman, what then?

Notes

1. "Le retrait de la métaphore," in *Poésie* (Fall 1978); "The *Retrait* of Metaphor, trans. F. Gasdner et al., *Enclitic* 2, no. 2 (Fall 1978): 5–33.

2. See his "Metaphor," in *Metaphor and Thought,* ed. A. Ortony (Cambridge: Cambridge University Press, 1979).

3. I have "dealt with" the question of strategy more fully in a number of other places. See, for instance, "Style and Strategy at the Limits of Philosophy: Heidegger and Derrida," *The Monist* 63, no. 4 (October 1980): 494–511, and "Difference and the Problem of Strategy," in *Derrida and Différance,* ed. D. C. Wood and R. Bernasconi (Warwick: Parousia Press, 1985), pp. 93–106.

4. Jacques Derrida, *Marges de la philosophie* (Paris: Minuit, 1972), pp. 17–18; *Margins of Philosophy,* trans. Alan Bass (Chicago: University of Chicago Press, 1982), pp. 16–17.

5. Jacques Derrida, "Signature Evénément Contexte," in *Marges* (see note 4), Fr. pp. 365–93; Eng. pp. 307–30.

6. See, for example, "Violence et métaphysique" in *L'écriture et la différence* (Paris: Seuil, 1967), pp. 117–228; *Writing and Difference,* trans. Alan Bass (Chicago: University of Chicago Press, 1978), pp. 79–195, on Levinas; "Living On / Border Lines," in *Deconstruction and Criticism* (New York: Seabury Press, 1979), "on" Blanchot (and others).

7. Archibald Macleish, "Voyage West," in his *Collected Poems* (Boston: Houghton Mifflin, 1962).

8. Jacques Derrida, *La Carte postale: De Socrate à Freud et au-delà* (Paris: Flammarion, 1980), p. 25.

9. I make no attempt to connect Austin's "sea-change" to either San Seriffe or to Macleish's "open ocean."

10. At the risk of seeming to celebrate the victory of metonymy over thought, I might add that the "Martini" possibility led me to thinking about Italian philosophers, and thence to Benedetto Croce's *What Is Living and What Is Dead in Hegel's Philosophy,* and to smile at the marvelous ease with which one might be able to draw that distinction in some less problematic space.

11. *La Carte postale,* p. 19.

12. See *De la grammatologie* (Paris: Minuit, 1967), p. 40; *Of Grammatology,* trans. Gayatri Ch. Spivak (Baltimore: Johns Hopkins University Press, 1976), p. 25.

13. "Linguistique et grammatologie" in *De la grammatologie,* Fr. p. 108; Eng. p. 73.

14. See Derrida's "ce dangereux supplément . . ." (on Rousseau) in *De la grammatologie.*

15. Jacques Derrida, *Positions* (Paris: Minuit, 1972); *Positions,* trans. Alan Bass (Chicago: University of Chicago Press, 1981).

16. The paper by Rodolphe Gasché, for all its many virtues, might seem to confirm such a judgment.

17. "Violence et métaphysique" (see note 6 above), Fr. p. 118; Eng. p. 80.

Geschlecht II: Heidegger's Hand

12

Jacques Derrida

Translated by John P. Leavey, Jr.

I must begin with some precautions. They all come down to asking your pardon and indulgence for what in particular touches on the form and the status of this "lecture," this reading, on all the presuppositions I ask you to take account of. In effect, I presuppose the reading of a brief and modest essay published under the title *"Geschlecht:* sexual difference, ontological difference." This essay, published and translated more than a year ago,[1] began some work I have taken up again only this year in the course of a seminar I am giving in Paris under the title "Philosophical Nationality and Nationalism." For lack of time I can reconstitute neither the introductory article entitled *"Geschlecht"* (it treats of the motif of sexual difference in a course almost contemporary with *Sein und Zeit*), nor all the developments that form, in my seminar on "Philosophical Nationality and Nationalism," the contextual landscape of the reflections I shall present to you today. Nevertheless I shall strive to make the presentation of these few reflections, still preliminary, as intelligible and independent of all these invisible contexts as possible. Another precaution, another call for your pardon and indulgence: for lack of time, I shall present only a part, or rather several fragments, at times a bit discontinuous, of the work I am following this year in the slow rhythm of a seminar engaged in a difficult reading, one that I would like to be as meticulous and careful as possible, of certain Heidegger texts, notably *Was heisst Denken?* and above all the lecture on Trakl in *Unterwegs zur Sprache.*

I want to thank John Leavey very warmly for the invaluable and decisive aid he gave me, once more, in the translation and the presentation of this unfinished work.

We are going to speak then of Heidegger.
We are also going to speak of monstrosity.

We are going to speak of the word "*Geschlecht*." I am not going to translate it for the moment. Doubtless I shall translate it at no moment. But you know that, according to the contexts that come to determine this word, it can be translated by sex, race, species, genus, gender, stock, family, generation or genealogy, community. In the seminar on "Philosophical Nationality and Nationalism," before studying certain texts of Marx, Quinet, Michelet, Toqueville, Wittgenstein, Adorno, Hannah Arendt, we had encountered the word *Geschlecht* in a very sketchy reading of Fichte: " . . . *was an Geistigkeit und Freiheit dieser Geistigkeit glaubt, und die ewige Fortbildung dieser Geistigkeit durch Freiheit will, das, wo es auch geboren sei und in welcher Sprache es rede,* ist unsers Geschlechts, *es gehört uns an und es wird sich zu uns tun*" (seventh of the *Discourses to the German Nation* [*Reden an die Deutsche Nation*]).[2] The French translation neglects to translate the word *Geschlecht,* no doubt because the translation was done during or just after the war, I think, by S. Jankelevitch, and under conditions that made the word "race" particularly dangerous and moreover not pertinent for translating Fichte. But what does Fichte mean when he develops in this way what he calls then his fundamental principle (*Grundsatz*), to wit, that of a circle (*Kreis*) or an alliance (*Bund*), of an engagement (we had spoken much of this engagement in the seminar's preceding sessions) that constitutes precisely belonging to "our *Geschlecht*"? All those who believe in spirituality and the freedom of that spirit, all those who want the eternal and progressive formation of this spirituality through freedom (*die ewige Fortbildung:* and if Fichte is "nationalistic," in a sense rather enigmatic so that we can speak of it here very quickly, he is so as a *progressive,* a republican, and a cosmopolitist; one of the themes of the seminar I am currently working on concerns just the paradoxical but regular association of nationalism with a cosmopolitanism and with a humanism), they all are part of our *Geschlecht,* they all belong to us and have to do business with us, wherever they are born or whatever tongue [*langue*] they speak. So this *Geschlecht* is not determined by birth, native soil, or race, has nothing to do with the natural or even the linguistic, at least in the usual sense of this term, for we were able to recognize in Fichte a kind of claim of the idiom, of the idiom of the German idiom. Certain citizens, German by birth, remain strangers to this idiom of the idiom; certain non-Germans can attain it since, engaging themselves in this circle or this alliance of spiritual freedom and its infinite progress, they would belong to "our *Geschlecht*." The sole analytic and unimpeachable determination of "*Geschlecht*" in this context is the "we," the belonging to the "we" who are speaking at this moment, at the moment when Fichte addresses himself to this supposed but still to be constituted community, a community that *stricto sensu* is neither political, nor racial, nor linguistic, but that can receive his allocution, his address, or his apostrophe (*Rede an* . . .), and can think with him, can say "we" in some language and from whatever birthplace. *Geschlecht* is an ensemble, a gathering together (one could say *Versammlung*), an organic community in a nonnatural but spiritual sense, that believes in the infinite progress of the spirit through freedom. So it is an infinite "we," a "we" that announces itself to itself from the infinity of a τέλος of freedom and spirituality, and that promises, engages, or allies itself according to the circle (*Kreis, Bund*) of this infinite will. How is "*Geschlecht*" to be translated under these conditions? Fichte uses a word that *already* has in his language a vast wealth of semantic determinations, and he speaks *German*. Despite what he says: anyone, in whatever language he or she speaks, "*ist unsers Geschlechts,*" he says this in German, and this *Geschlecht* is an essential *Deutschheit*. Even if the word "*Geschlecht*" has rigorous content only from out of the "we" instituted by that very address, it also includes connotations indispensable to the minimal intelligibility of discourse, and these connotations belong irreducibly to German, to a German more essential than all the phenomena of empiric Germanness, but to some German. All these connoted senses are copresent in the use of the word "*Geschlecht,*" they virtually appear in that use, but no sense is fully satisfying. How is one to translate? One can recoil before the risk and omit the word, as the French translator did. One can also judge the word so open and undetermined by the concept it designates, to wit, a "we" as spiritual freedom engaged toward the infinity of its progress, that the omission of this word does not lose much. The "we" finally comes down to the humanity of man, to the teleological essence of a humanity that is announced *par excellence* in *Deutschheit*. "*Menschengeschlecht*" is often said for "*genre humain,*" "humankind," "human species," "human race." In the Heidegger text we shall be concerned with in a few minutes, the French translators sometimes speak of *genre humain* for *Geschlecht* and sometimes very simply of species.

For here the question is nothing less, I venture to say, than the problem of man, of man's humanity, and of humanism. But situated where language no longer lets itself be effaced. Already for Fichte, it is not the same thing to say the "humanity" of man and *Menschlichkeit*. When he says "ist unsers Geschlechts," he is thinking of *Menschlichkeit* and not of *Humanität* of Latin ancestry. The fourth *Discourse* . . . is by far consonant with those Heidegger texts to come on Latinness. Fichte distinguishes the dead language "cut off from the living root"[3] and the living language animated by an inspiriting breath. When a language, from its first phonemes, arises from the common and uninterrupted life of a people whose intuitions that language continues to espouse, the invasion of a foreign people changes nothing; the intruders can rise only up to this primordial language, unless one day they can assimilate the intuitions of the *Stammvolk*, of the people-stock for whom these intuitions are inseparable from the language: ". . . und so bilden nicht sie die Sprache, sondern die Sprache bildet sie,"[4] they do not form the language, the language forms them. Conversely, when a people adopts another language [*langue*] developed in the designation of suprasensible things, without however totally handing itself over to the influence of this foreign language, the sensible language [*langage*] is not altered by this event. In all peoples, Fichte notes, children learn that part of the language turned toward sensible things as if the signs for those things were arbitrary (*willkürlich*). The children must reconstitute the past development of the national language. But in this sensible sphere (*in diesem sinnlichen Umkreise*), each sign (*Zeichen*) can become altogether clear thanks to vision or the immediate contact with the designated or signified thing (*Bezeichneten*). Here I stress the sign (*Zeichen*), for in a moment we shall come to the sign as monstrosity. In this passage Fichte uses the word *Geschlecht* in the narrow sense of generation: "At most, the result of this would be that the first generation (*das erste Geschlecht*) of a people which thus changed its language would be compelled when adults/men (*Männer*) to go back to the years of childhood."[5]

Here Fichte is bent on distinguishing *Humanität* and *Menschlichkeit*. For a German these words of Latin origin (*Humanität, Popularität, Liberalität*) resound as if they were void of sense, even if they appear sublime and make etymology something of interest [*rendent curieux d'étymologie*]. Besides, it's the same in the Latin or neo-Latin peoples who know nothing of the etymology and believe these words belong to their maternal tongue (*Muttersprache*). But say *Menschlichkeit* to a German, you would be understood without any other historical explanation (*ohne weitere historische Erklärung*). Besides, it is useless to state that a man is a man and to speak of the *Menschlichkeit* of a man about whom one knows very well that he is not an ape or a savage beast. A Roman would not have responded in that way, Fichte believes, because if, for the German, *Menschheit* or *Menschlichkeit* always remains a sensible concept (*ein sinnlicher Begriff*), for the Roman *humanitas* had become the symbol (*Sinnbilde*) of a suprasensible (*übersinnlichen*) idea. From their origins, the Germans, they too, have joined together concrete intuitions in an intellectual concept of humanity, always opposed to animality; and one would surely be wrong to see in the intuitive relation they preserve with *Menschheit* a sign of inferiority with respect to the Romans. Nevertheless, the artificial introduction of words of foreign origin, singularly Roman, into the German tongue risks debasing the moral level of their own way of thinking (*ihre sittliche Denkart . . . herunterstimmen*). But there is concerning language [*langage*], image, and symbol (*Sinnbild*) an "ineradicable nature" of the "national imagination (*Nationaleinbildungskraft*)."[6]

   This schematic recall seemed necessary to me for two reasons. On the one hand, in order to underline the difficulty of translating this sensible, critical, and sensitive [*névralgique*] word *Geschlecht;* on the other hand, in order to indicate its irreducible bond to the question of humanity versus animality, and of a humanity whose name, as the bond of the name to the "thing," if one can say that, remains as problematic as that of the language in which the name is written. What does one say when one says *Menschheit, Humanitas, Humanität, mankind,* etc., or when one says *Geschlecht* or *Menschengeschlecht?* Is one saying the same thing? I also recall in passing the criticism Marx addressed in *The German Ideology* to the socialist Grun whose nationalism appealed, according to Marx's ironic expression, to a "human nationality" better represented by the Germans (socialists) than by the other socialists (French, American, or Belgian).

   In the letter addressed in November 1945 to the Academic Rectorate of Albert-Ludwig University, Heidegger explains his own attitude during the Nazi period. He had thought, he said, that he would be able to distinguish between the national and nationalism, that is, between the national and a biologicist and racist ideology: "I thought that Hitler, after taking responsibility in 1933 for the whole people, would venture to extricate himself from the Party and its doctrine, and that the whole would meet on the terrain of a renovation and a gathering together with a view to a responsibility for the West. This conviction was an error that I recognized from the events of 30 June 1934. I, of course, had intervened in 1933 to say yes to the national and the social (and not to nationalism) and not to the intellectual and metaphysical grounds on which the biologism of the Party doctrine rested, because the social and the national, as I saw them, were not essentially tied to a biologicist and racist ideology."[7] The condemnation of biologism and racism, as of the whole ideological discourse of Rosenberg, inspires numerous Heidegger texts, whether it be the Discourse of the Rectorate or the courses on Hölderlin and Nietzsche, whether it be also the question of technology, always put in perspective against the utilization of knowledge for technical and utilitarian ends, against the Nazis' professionalization and their making university knowledge profitable. I shall not reopen today the dossier of Heidegger's "politics." I have done that in other seminars, and we have today a rather large number of texts available for deciphering the classic and henceforth a bit academic dimensions of this problem. But all that I shall now attempt will keep an indirect relation to another, perhaps less visible, dimension of the same drama. Today, I shall begin then by speaking of that monstrosity I announced a few moments ago. This will be another detour through the question of man (*Mensch* or *homo*) and of the "we" that gives its enigmatic content to a *Geschlecht*.

Why "monster"? Not in order to make the thing pathetic, nor because we are always near some monstrous *Unheimlichkeit* when we are prowling around the nationalist thing and the thing named *Geschlecht*. What is *un monstre*? You know the polysemic gamut of this word, the uses one can make of it, for example concerning norms and forms, species and genus/gender: thus concerning *Geschlecht*. I shall begin by privileging here another course [*direction*]. It goes in the direction, the *sens,* of a less known sense, since in French *la monstre* (a changing of gender, sex, or *Geschlecht*) has the poetico-musical sense of a diagram that *shows* [*montre*] in a piece of music the number of verses and the number of syllables assigned to the poet. *Monstrer* is *montrer* (to show or demonstrate), and *une monstre* is *une montre* (a watch). I am already settled in the untranslatable idiom of my language, for I certainly intend to speak to you about translation. *La monstre,* then, prescribes the divisions of a line of verse for a melody. *Le monstre* or *la monstre* is what shows in order to warn or put on guard. In the past *la montre,* in French, was written *la monstre.*

I chose this melo-poetic example because the monster I am going to speak to you about comes from a well-known poem of Hölderlin, "Mnemosyne," that Heidegger often contemplates, interrogates, and interprets. In the second of its three versions, the one that Heidegger cites in *Was heisst Denken?* one reads the famous stanza:

> Ein Zeichen sind wir, deutungslos,
> Schmerzlos sind wir, und haben fast
> Die Sprache in der Fremde verloren.[8]

Among the three French translations of this poem, there is the one by the translators of *Was heisst Denken?,* Aloys Becker and Gérard Granel. Translating Hölderlin in Heidegger, this translation uses the word *monstre* (for *Zeichen*), in a style that had first seemed to me a bit mannered and gallicizing, but which on reflection seemed to me in any case to give occasion for thought.

Nous sommes un monstre privé de sens
Nous sommes hors douleur
Et nous avons perdu
Presque la langue à l'étranger.⁹

We are a "monster" void of sense
We are outside sorrow
And have nearly lost
Our tongue in foreign lands.

Leaving aside the allusion to the tongue lost in foreign lands, which would lead me back too quickly to the seminar on nationality, I want to stress first the "we, 'monster.'" We are a monster, and singular, a sign that shows and warns, but all the more singular since, showing, signifying, designating, this sign is void of sense (*deutungslos*). It says itself void of sense, simply and doubly monster, this "we": we are sign— showing, informing, warning, pointing as sign toward, but in truth toward nothing, a sign out of the way [*à l'écart*], in a gapped relation to the sign [*en écart par rapport au signe*], display [*montre*] that deviates from the display or monstration, a monster that shows [*montre*] nothing. This gap of the sign to itself and to its so-called normal function, isn't it already a monstrosity of monstrasity [*monstrosité*], a monstrosity of monstration? And that is we, we inasmuch as we have nearly lost our tongue in foreign lands, perhaps in a translation. But this we, the monster, is it man?

The translation of *Zeichen* by *monstre* has a triple virtue. It recalls a motif at work ever since *Sein und Zeit*: the bond between *Zeichen* and *zeigen* or *Aufzeigung,* between the sign and monstration. Paragraph 17 (*Verweisung und Zeichen*) analyzed the *Zeigen eines Zeichens,* the showing of the sign, and lightly touches in passing the question of the fetish. In *Unterwegs zur Sprache, Zeichen* and *Zeigen* are linked with *Sagen,* more precisely with the High German idiom *Sagan:* "'*Sagan*' heisst: *zeigen, erscheinen-, sehen- und hören-lassen.*"¹⁰ Farther on: "To name the said (*die Sage*) we employ an old word, well warranted but no longer in use: *die Zeige (la monstre)*"¹¹ (word underlined by Heidegger who has moreover just cited Trakl, to whom we shall return in a few minutes). The second virtue of the French translation by "*monstre*" has value only in the Latin idiom, since the translation stresses this gap concerning the normality of the sign, of a sign that for once is not what it should be, shows or signifies nothing, shows the *pas de sens,* no-sense, and announces the loss of the tongue. The third virtue of this translation poses the question of man. I omit here a long development that seems necessary to me on what deeply binds a certain humanism, a certain nationalism, and a certain Europocentric universalism, and I hastily move toward the interpretation of "Mnemosyne" by Heidegger. The "we" of *"Ein Zeichen sind wir,"* is it indeed a "we men"? Numerous indications would give one the thought that the response of the poem remains rather ambiguous. If "we" were "we men," this humanity would be determined in a way justly rather monstrous, apart from the norm, and notably from the humanist norm. But Heidegger's interpretation that prepares and gives access to this Hölderlin citation says something about man, and then too about *Geschlecht,* about the *Geschlecht* and the word *"Geschlecht"* that still awaits us in the text on Trakl, in *Unterwegs zur Sprache.*

The hand will be the (monstrous) sign [*le monstre*], the proper of man as (monstrous) sign, in the sense of *Zeichen.* "The hand reaches and extends, receives and welcomes—and not just things: the hand extends itself, and receives its own welcome in the hand of the other. The hand keeps. The hand carries. The hand designs and signs, presumably because man is a (monstrous) sign (*Die Hand zeichnet, vermutlich weil der Mensch ein Zeichen ist*)."[12]

This seminar of 1951–52 is later than the "Letter on Humanism" that withdraws the question of being from the metaphysical or ontotheological horizon of classic humanism: *Dasein* is not the *homo* of this humanism. So we are not going to suspect Heidegger of simply falling back into that humanism there. On the other hand, the date and the thematic of this passage accord it to that thought of the gift, of giving, and of the *es gibt* that overflows without reversing the anterior formation of the question of the sense of Being.

(In order to situate more precisely what one could call here the thought of the hand, but just as well the hand of thought, of a thought of the human *Geschlecht,* of a thought claiming to be nonmetaphysical, let us remark that this develops itself in one moment of the seminar [Recapitulations and Transitions from the First to the Second Hour][13] that repeats the question of the teaching of thought, in particular in the university, as the place of sciences and technics. It is in this passage that I cut out, so to speak, the form and the passage of the hand: the hand of Heidegger. The issue of *L'Herne* in which I published "*Geschlecht* I" bore on its cover a photograph of Heidegger showing him, a studied and significant choice, holding his pen with both hands above a manuscript. Even if he never used it, Nietzsche was the first thinker of the West to have a typewriter, whose photograph we know. Heidegger himself could write only with the pen, with the hand of a craftsman and not a mechanic, as the text in which we are going to become interested prescribes. Since then I have studied all the published photographs of Heidegger, especially in an album bought at Freiburg when I had given a lecture there on Heidegger in 1979. The play and the theater of hands in that album would merit a whole seminar. If I did not forgo that, I would stress the deliberately craftsman-like staging of the hand play, of the monstration and demonstration that is exhibited there, whether it be a matter of the handling [*maintenance*] of the pen, of the maneuver of the cane that shows rather than supports, or of the water bucket near the fountain. The demonstration of hands is as gripping in the accompaniment of the discourse. On the cover of the catalog, the only thing that overflows the frame, that of the window but also of the photo, is Heidegger's hand.)

The hand is monstrasity [*monstrosité*], the proper of man as the being of monstration. This distinguishes him from every other *Geschlecht*, and above all from the ape.

The hand cannot be spoken about without speaking of technics.

Heidegger just recalled that the problem of university teaching resulted from the fact that the sciences belong to the essence of technics: not to technics, but to the essence of technics. Technics remains plunged in a fog for which no one is responsible, neither science, nor the scientists, nor man in general. Simply what gives rise the most to thinking (*das Bedenklichste*) is that *we* do not yet think. Who, we? All of us, Heidegger specifies, including him who speaks here and even him the very first (*der Sprecher mit einbegriffen, er sogar zuerst*). To be the first among those who do not yet think—is that to think more or less the "not yet" of what gives rise the most to thinking, to wit, that we do not yet think? The first, here, the one who speaks and shows himself in speaking thus, designating himself in the third person, *der Sprecher*, is he the first because he already thinks that we do not yet think and already says so? Or indeed is he the first not yet to think, then the last to think already that we do not yet think, which would not nonetheless prevent him from speaking in order to be the first to say this? I leave these questions that would merit long developments on the auto-situation of this speaking that claims to teach while speaking of teaching and claims to think what is learning and first of all learning to think. "That is why," Heidegger continues, "we are here attempting to learn thinking (*Darum versuchen wir hier, das Denken zu lernen*)."[14] But what is learning, in French *apprendre*? The response, untranslatable in its literalness, passes through a very subtle craft work, a work of the hand and of the pen among the words *entsprechen, Entsprechung, zusprechen, Zuspruch*. Let me, instead of translating, roughly summarize: to learn, *apprendre,* is to relate what we are doing to a correspondence (*Entsprechung*) in us with the essential (*wesenhaft*). To illustrate this accord with the essence, here is the traditional example of philosophical didactics, that of the joiner, of the apprentice joiner. Heidegger chooses the word *Schreiner* rather than *Tischler,* for he intends to speak of an apprentice joiner (*Schreinerlehrling*) who works on a cabinet (*Schrein*). Now he will say later that "Perhaps thinking, too, is just something like building a cabinet (*wie das Bauen an einem Schrein*)."[15] The apprentice cabinetmaker learns not only to use tools, not only to familiarize himself with the use, the utility, the toolness [*outilité*] of things for making. If he is a "true cabinetmaker (*ein echter Schreiner*)," he inclines [*se porte*] or relates himself to the different ways of the wood itself, accords himself with the forms that sleep in the wood as it enters man's dwelling (*in das Wohnen des Menschen*). The true joiner accords himself with the hidden plenitude of the wood's essence, and not with the tool and the use value. But with the hidden plenitude insofar as it enters the inhabited place (I stress here this value of *place* or *site* for reasons that will appear later), and inhabited by *man.* There is no craft, *métier,* of the joiner without this correspondence between the essence of the wood and the essence of man as the being who inhabits. In German *métier* is said *Handwerk,* work of the hand, handiwork, handling, if not maneuver. When the French must translate *Handwerk* by *métier,* perhaps that is legitimate and cannot be avoided, but it is a bad maneuver, a poor craft of translation, because in it the hand is lost. And reintroduced in that translation is what Heidegger wants to avoid, the service rendered, utility, the office, the *ministerium,* from which, I believe, the word *métier* comes. *Handwerk,* the noble *métier,* is a manual *métier* that is not ordered, like any other profession, to public use or interest or in pursuit of profit. This noble *métier,* as *Handwerk,* will also be that of the thinker or the teacher who teaches thinking (the teacher is not necessarily the professor of philosophy). Without this accord with the essence of the wood, itself accorded to man's dwelling, the activity would be empty. It would remain just activity (*Beschäftigung*) oriented by trade (*Geschäft*), commerce, and the taste for profit. Implicit, the hierarchizing and the evaluation are no less clear: on the one hand, but also above, towards the best, handiwork (*Handwerk*) guided by the essence of the human dwelling, by the wood of the hut [*la hûte*] rather than by the metal or glass of the cities; on the other hand, but also below, the activity that cuts the hand off from the essential, useful activity, utilitarianism guided by capital. To be sure, as Heidegger recognizes, the inauthentic can always contaminate the authentic, the authentic cabinetmaker can become a furniture dealer for "large stores" (supermarkets), the artisan of the dwelling or habitat can become the international corporation named, I think, "Habitat." The hand is in danger. Always: "All hand-iwork (*Handwerk*), all human dealings (*Handeln*) are constantly in that danger. The writing of poetry (*Das Dichten*) is no more exempt from it than is thinking (*das Denken*)."[16] The analogy is double: between *Di-chten* and *Denken* on the one hand, but also, on the other, between the two, poetry and thought, and the authentic handiwork (*Handwerk*). To think is a handiwork, says Heidegger explicitly. He says it without any dodge and without even that "perhaps (*vielleicht*)" that had moderated the analogy of thought with the manufacture of the cabinet that is "per-haps" like thought. Here, without analogy and without "perhaps," Heidegger declares: "At any rate, it [thinking, *das Denken*] is a hand-work (*Es ist jedenfalls ein Hand-Werk*, a word of the hand, in two words)."[17]

This does not mean that one is thinking *with* one's hands, as is said in English and French that one speaks *with* one's hands when one's discourse is accompanied with voluble gestures, or that one thinks *with* one's feet, *avec ses pieds*, when one is, as French has it, *bête comme ses pieds*, too stupid for words. What does Heidegger mean then, and why does he choose here the hand, whereas elsewhere he more readily ac-cords thought to light or to *Lichtung*, one would say to the eye, or else to hearing and the voice?

Three remarks to prepare a response here.

(1) I have chosen this text in order to introduce a reading of *Geschlecht*. In this text Heidegger in effect binds thinking, and not only philosophy, to a thought or to a situation of the body (*Leib*), the body of man and of human being (*Menschheit*). That will permit us to glimpse a dimension of *Geschlecht* as sex or sexual difference apropos what is said or not said [*tu*] about the hand. Thinking is not cerebral or disincarnate; the relation to the essence of being is a certain *manner* of *Dasein* as *Leib*. (I take the liberty to refer to what I said on this subject in the first article on *Geschlecht*.)

(2) Heidegger privileges the hand when, speaking of the relations between thought and the craft of teaching, he distinguishes between the current profession (an activity, *Beschäftigung*, oriented by useful service [*service utile*] and the pursuit of profit, *Geschäft*), and on the other hand, the authentic *Hand-Werk*. Now to define the *Hand-Werk*, which is not a profession, one must think *Werk*, work, but also *Hand* and *Handeln* that cannot be translated by "dealings" or "*agir*." The hand must be thought. But the hand cannot be thought as a thing, a being, even less an object. The hand thinks before being thought; it is thought, a thought, thinking [*la pensée*].

(3) My third remark will be more narrowly tied to a classic treatment of Heidegger's "politics" in the national-socialist context. In all his self-justifications after the war, Heidegger presents his discourse on the essence of technics as a protest, an act of *resistance* barely disguised *against:* (*a*) the professionalization of university studies to which the Nazis and their official ideologues have surrendered themselves. Heidegger recalls this concerning his *Rectorate Discourse* that in effect is raised against the professionalization that is also a technologization of studies. (*b*) the submission of the national-socialist philosophy to the dominion and imperatives of technical productivity. The meditation on the authentic *Hand-Werk* also has the sense of an artisanalist protest against the hand's effacement or debasement in the industrial automation of modern mechanization. This strategy has, one suspects, equivocal effects: it opens up to an archaistic reaction toward the rustic artisan class and denounces business or capital, notions whose associations then are well known. In addition, with the division of labor, what is called "intellectual work" is what implicitly finds itself thus discredited.

Having said this, I want to underscore again the idiomaticity in what Heidegger says to us about the hand: *"Mit der Hand hat es eine eigene Bewandtnis."*[18] With the hand one is dealing with a thing entirely particular, one's own, proper, singular. *Une chose à part* (a thing apart), as the French translation says while running the risk of letting one think of a separate thing, of a separate substance, as Descartes said of the hand that it was a part of the body, to be sure, but was endowed with such independence that it could also be considered as a complete substance apart and almost separable. Heidegger does not say in this sense that the hand is a thing apart. In that the hand has any proper or particular of its own (*eigene*), it is not a part of the organic body, as the common representation (*gewöhnliche Vorstellung*) claims and against which Heidegger invites us to think.

The hand's being (*das Wesen der Hand*) does not let itself be determined as a bodily organ of gripping (*als ein leibliches Greiforgan*). It is not an organic part of the body intended [*destinée*] for grasping, taking hold [*prendre*], indeed for scratching, let us add even for catching on [*prendre*], comprehending, conceiving, if one passes from *Greif* to *begreifen* and to *Begriff*. Heidegger could not not let the thing say itself, and one can follow here, I have tried to do it elsewhere, the whole problematic of the philosophical "metaphor," in particular in Hegel, who presents the *Begriff* as the intellectual or intelligible structure "relieving" (*aufhebend*) the sensible act of grasping, *begreifen*, of comprehending by taking hold of, by laying one's hands on, mastering and manipulating. If there is a thought of the hand or a hand of thought, as Heidegger gives us to think, it is not of the order of conceptual grasping. Rather this thought of the hand belongs to the essence of the *gift*, of a giving that would give, if this is possible, without taking hold of anything. If the hand is also, no one can deny this, an organ for gripping (*Greiforgan*), that is not its essence, is not the hand's essence in the human being. This critique of organicism and biologism also has the political destination I spoke of a moment ago. But does that suffice to justify this critique?

Here in effect occurs a sentence that at bottom seems to me Heidegger's most significant, symptomatic, and seriously dogmatic. Dogmatic also means metaphysical, coming under one of those "common representations" that risk compromising the whole force and necessity of the discourse right here. This sentence in sum comes down to distinguishing the human *Geschlecht*, our *Geschlecht*, and the animal *Geschlecht*, called "animal." I think, and I have often thought I must underscore this, that the manner, lateral or central, in which a thinker or scientist spoke of the said "animalness" constituted a decisive symptom concerning the essential axiomatic of the given discourse. No more than anybody else, classic or modern, does Heidegger seem to me here to escape this rule when he writes: "Apes, *for example* [my emphasis, J.D.], have organs that can grasp, but they have no hand (*Greiforgane besitzt z. B. der Affe, aber er hat keine Hand*)."[19]

Dogmatic in its form, this traditional statement presupposes an empiric or positive knowledge whose titles, proofs, and signs are never shown [*montrés*]. Like most of those who, as philosophers or persons of good sense, speak of animality, Heidegger takes no account of a certain "zoological knowledge" that accumulates, is differentiated, and becomes more refined concerning what is brought together under this so general and confused word animality. He does not criticize it and does not even examine the sorts of presuppositions, metaphysical or otherwise, it can harbor. This nonknowing raised to a tranquil knowing, then exhibited as essential proposition about the essence of an ape's prehensile organs, an ape that would have no hand, this is not only, in its form, a kind of empirico-dogmatic ἅπαξ λεγόμενον misled or misleading in the middle of a discourse keeping itself to the height of the most demanding thought, beyond philosophy and science. In its very content, this proposition marks the text's essential scene, marks it with a humanism that wanted certainly to be nonmetaphysical—Heidegger underscores this in the following paragraph—but with a humanism that, between a human *Geschlecht* one wants to withdraw from the biologistic determination (for the reasons I just stated) and an animality one encloses in its organico-

biologic programs, inscribes not *some* differences but an absolute oppositional limit. Elsewhere I have tried to show that, as every opposition
does, this absolute oppositional limit effaces the differences and leads
back, following the most resistant metaphysico-dialectic tradition, to the
homogeneous. What Heidegger says of the ape without hand—and
then, as we are going to see, without thinking, language, gift—is not
only dogmatic in its form because Heidegger knows nothing about this
and wants to know nothing, has no doubt studied neither the zoologists
(even were it to criticize them)[20] nor the apes in the Black Forest. It is
serious because what he says traces a system of limits within which
everything he says of man's hand takes on sense and value. Since such a
delimitation is problematic, the name of man, his *Geschlecht,* becomes
problematic itself. For it names what has the hand, and so thinking,
speech or language, and openness to the gift.

Man's hand then will be a thing apart not as separable organ but
because it is different, dissimilar (*verschieden*) from all prehensile organs
(paws, claws, talons); man's hand is far from these in an infinite way
(*unendlich*) through the abyss of its being (*durch einen Abgrund des
Wesens*). This abyss is speech and thought. "Only a being who can speak,
that is, think, can have the hand and can be handy (*in der Handhabung*) in
achieving works of handicraft (*Nur ein Wesen, das spricht, d. h. denkt,
kann die Hand haben und in der Handhabung Werke der Hand voll-
bringen*)." Man's hand is thought ever since thought, but thought is
thought ever since speaking or language. That is the order Heidegger
opposes to metaphysics: "Only when man speaks, does he think—not
the other way around, as metaphysics still believes (*Doch nur insofern der
Mensch spricht, denkt er; nicht umgekehrt, wie die Metaphysik es noch
meint*)."[21]

The essential moment of this meditation opens onto what I shall
call the hand's double *vocation.* I use the word vocation to recall that, in
its destination (*Bestimmung*), the hand holds on to speaking. This vocation is double, but gathered together or crossed in the same hand: to
show [*montrer*] or point out (*zeigen, Zeichen*) and to give or give itself, in
a word the *monstrasity* [monstrosité] *of the gift or of what gives itself.*

> But the work of the hand (*das Werk der Hand*) is richer than we commonly
> imagine [*meinen:* we believe, have the opinion]. The hand does not only
> grasp and catch (*greift und fängt nicht nur*), or push and pull. The hand
> reaches and extends, receives and welcomes [*reicht und empfängt:* the
> German consonances must be heard: *greift, fängt/reicht, empfängt*]—and
> not just things: the hand extends itself, and receives its own welcome in the
> hand of the other. The hand holds (*hält*). The hand carries (*trägt*).[22]

This passage from the transitive gift, if such can be said, to the gift of what gives *itself,* which gives itself as being-able-to-give, which gives the gift, this passage from the hand that gives something to the hand that gives *itself* is evidently decisive. We find again a passage of the same type or the same structure in the following sentence: not only does man's hand point out and show, but man is himself a sign, a monstrous sign [*un monstre*], what begins the citation and the interpretation of "Mnemosyne," on the following page.

> The hand designs and signs (*zeichnet*), presumably because man is a (monstrous) sign (*ein Zeichen ist*). Two hands fold into one [*falten sich:* also, join together], a gesture meant to carry man into the great simplicity [*Einfalt;* I am not sure of comprehending this sentence that plays on *sich falten* and *Einfalt;* whether it be a matter of prayer or of more common gestures, what matters above all is that the hands can touch each other as such, in auto-affection, even at the touch of the other's hand in the gift of the hand; this implies that the hands can also *show themselves*]. The hand is all this, and this is the true hand work (*das eigentliche Hand-Werk*). Everything is rooted here that is commonly known as handicraft (*Handwerk*), and commonly we go no further. But the hand's gestures [*Gebärden:* a word worked over very much by Heidegger in other texts too] run everywhere through language [or through the tongue], in their most perfect purity precisely when man speaks by being silent. And only when man speaks, does he think—not the other way around, as metaphysics still believes. Every motion of the hand in every one of its works carries itself (*sich trägt*) through the element of thinking, every bearing of the hand bears itself (*gebärdet sich*) in that element. All the work of the hand is rooted in thinking. Therefore, thinking (*das Denken*) itself is man's simplest, and for that reason hardest, *Hand-Werk,* if it would be properly accomplished (*eigens*).[23]

The nerve of the argument seems to me reducible to the assured opposition of *giving* and *taking:* man's hand *gives and gives itself, gives* and *is given,* like thought or like what gives itself to be thought and what we do not yet think, whereas the organ of the ape or of man as a simple animal, indeed as an *animal rationale,* can only *take hold of, grasp, lay hands on the thing.* The organ can *only* take hold of and manipulate the thing insofar as, in any case, it does not have to deal with the thing *as such,* does not let the thing be what it is in its essence. The organ has no access to the essence of the being [*étant*] *as such (see Gesamtausgabe* 29/30, p. 290). For lack of time I must refer to a seminar already of long standing in which we had been able to problematize this opposition between giving and taking, or two ways of *taking*, human and animal; only the human would be granted the possibility of giving. Nothing is less assured than the distinction between *giving* and *taking*, at once in the Indo-European languages we speak (here I am referring to a famous text of Benveniste, "Gift and Exchange in the Indo-European Vocabulary," in *Problems in General Linguistics*, trans. M. E. Meek [Coral Gables: Univ. of Miami Press, 1971]) and in the experience of an economy—symbolic or imaginary, conscious or unconscious, all these values remaining precisely to be reelaborated from the precariousness of that opposition of the gift and of the grip, of the gift that presents and the gift that grips or holds or takes back, of the gift that does good and of the gift that does bad, of the present [*cadeau*] and of the poison (*gift/Gift* or φάρμακον, etc.).

For lack of time I shall not analyze any more the immense role the hand or the word *Hand* more or less directly plays in the whole Heideggerian conceptuality since *Sein und Zeit*, notably in the determination of presence according to the mode of *Vorhandenheit* or *Zuhandenheit*. The first is translated more or less well in French by "*étant subsistant*" and better in English by "presence-at-hand"; the second by "*être disponible*," as "being available" like a tool or implement, and better, since the English can keep the hand, by "ready-to-hand," "readiness-to-hand." *Dasein* is neither *vorhanden* nor *zuhanden*. Its mode of presence is otherwise, but it must indeed have the hand in order to relate itself to the other modes of presence.

The question posed by *Sein und Zeit* (§ 15) gathers together the greatest force of its economy in the German idiom and in that idiom in the Heideggerian idiom: is or is not *Vorhandenheit* founded (*fundiert*) on *Zuhandenheit*? Literally: what is the relation to the hand that founds the other in the relation of *Dasein* to the Being of beings that it is not (*Vorhandensein* and *Zuhandensein*)? What hand founds the other? The hand that is related to the thing as maneuverable tool or the hand as relation to the thing as subsisting and independent object? Here I cannot reconstitute either the stake of this question decisive for the whole strategy of *Sein und Zeit*, or Heidegger's original course for deconstructing the classical order of foundation (the end of § 15). But as this whole passage is also an analysis of *Handeln*, of the action or the practice as a gesture of the hand in its relation to sight, and thus a placement in a new perspective of what is called the πρᾶξις/θεωρία opposition, let us recall that for Heidegger "'practical' behavior" is not "'atheoretical.'"[24] And I am only going to cite some lines in order to draw out two guiding threads:

The Greeks had an appropriate term for "Things": πράγματα—that is to say, that which one has to do with (*zu tun*) in one's concernful dealings (*im besorgenden Umgang*) (πρᾶξις). But ontologically, the specifically "pragmatic" character of the πράγματα is just what the Greeks left in obscurity (*im Dunkeln*) [in sum the Greeks were beginning to leave *Zuhandenheit* of the tool in obscurity to the benefit of *Vorhandenheit* of the subsisting object: one could say that they were inaugurating the whole classical ontology while leaving a hand in the dark, while leaving a hand to bring umbrage to the other, while substituting, in a violent hierarchizing, one hand experience for another]; they thought of these "proximally" as "mere Things (*blosse Dinge*)." We call those entities which we encounter in concern (*im Besorgen*) "*equipment (Zeug)*." In our dealings [in common life, *im Ungang*, in daily and social surroundings] we come across equipment for writing, sewing, working, transportation, measurement [I cite a very inadequate translation for *Schreibzeug, Nähzeug, Werk-, Fahr-, Messzeug*]. The kind of Being which equipment (*Zeug*) possesses must be exhibited. The clue for doing this lies in our first defining [*Umgrenzung:* delimiting] what makes an item of equipment—namely, its equipmentality (*Zeughaftigkeit*).[25]

This mode of being will be precisely *Zuhandenheit* (*readiness-to-hand*). And Heidegger begins, in order to speak about it in the following paragraph, by taking up the examples that he has in a way near at hand: the writing desk (*Schreibzeug*), pen (*Feder*), ink (*Tinte*), paper (*Papier*), what is happily called *le sous-main* in French, the blotting pad (*Unterlage*), the table, lamp, furniture, and, his eyes looking up a bit above his hands writing, the windows, doors, the room.

Here now are the two threads I would like to draw, by hand, from this text, in order to make them guiding threads, clues, or in order to sew and write also a bit in my manner.

(1) The first concerns πρᾶξις and πράγματα. I had already written all this when John Sallis, whom I want to thank for this, drew my attention to a much later passage of Heidegger. It punctuates in a gripping way this long maneuver that makes of the *path of thinking* and of the question of the sense of Being a long and continuous meditation *of/on* the hand. Heidegger always says of thought that it is a path, on the way (*Unterwegs*); but on the way, on the march, the thinker is unceasingly occupied with a thought of the hand. Long after *Sein und Zeit,* which does not speak *thematically* of the hand while analyzing *Vorhanden-* and *Zuhandenheit,* but ten years before *Was heisst Denken?* which thematizes these, there is that seminar on Parmenides that, in 1942–43, takes up

again the meditation on πρᾶγμα and πρᾶξις. Although the German word *Handlung* is not the literal translation of πρᾶγμα, it just touches, if one comprehends well, it meets "the primordially essential being of πρᾶγμα (*das ursprünglich wesentliche Wesen von* πρᾶγμα)," since these πράγματα present themselves, as "*Vorhandenen*" and "*Zuhandenen,*" in the domain of the hand (*im Bereich der "Hand*").[26] All the motifs of *Was heisst Denken?* are already in place. Only the being that, like man, "has" speech (*Wort*, μῦθος, λόγος) can and must have the hand thanks to which prayer can occur, but also murder, the salute or wave of the hand, and thanks, the oath and the sign (*Wink*), *Handwerk* in general. I underscore for reasons that will appear later the allusion to *Handschlag* (the handshake or what is called "shaking on it" with the hand [*dans la main*]) that "grounds," Heidegger says, the alliance, the accord, the engagement (*Bund*). The hand comes to its essence (*west*) only in the movement of truth, in the double movement of what hides and causes to go out of its reserve (*Verbergung/Entbergung*). Moreover, the whole seminar is devoted to the history of truth (ἀλήθεια, λήθη, λαθόν, λαθές). When he says already, in this same passage, that the animal has no hand, that a hand can never upsurge out of a paw or claws, but only from speech, Heidegger specifies that "man 'has' no hands," but that *the* "hand occupies, in order to have in hand, man's essence (*Der Mensch 'hat' nicht Hände, sondern die Hand hat das Wesen des Menschen inne*)."[27]

(2) The second thread leads back to writing. If man's hand is what it is since speech or the word (*das Wort*), the most immediate, the most primordial manifestation of this origin will be the hand's gesture for making the word manifest, to wit, handwriting, manuscripture (*Handscrift*), that shows [*montre*] and inscribes the word for the gaze. "The word as drawn [or inscribed: *eingezeichnete*] and such that it shows itself thus to the gaze (*und so dem Blick sich zeigende*) is the written word, that is, writing (*d. h. die Schrift*). But the word as writing is handwriting (*Das Wort als die Schrift aber ist die Handschrift*)." Instead of handwriting, let us say rather manuscripture, for, don't forget, the writing of the typewriter against which Heidegger is going to raise an implacable indictment is also a handwriting. In the brief " 'history' of the art of writing ('*Geschichte*' *der Art des Schreibens*)" he sketches in a paragraph, Heidegger sees the fundamental motif of a "destruction of the word" or of speech (*Zerstörung des Wortes*). Typographic mechanization destroys this unity of the word, this integral identity, this proper integrity of the spoken word that writing manuscripts, at once because it appears closer to the voice or body proper and because it ties together the letters, conserves and gathers together. I stress this motif of gathering together for reasons that will also appear in a moment. The typewriter tends to

destroy the word: the typewriter "tears (*entreisst*) writing from the essential domain of the hand, that is, of the word," of speech. The "typed" word is only a copy (*Abschrift*), and Heidegger recalls that first moment of the typewriter when a typed letter offended the rules of etiquette. Today, the manuscripted letter is what seems culpable: it slows down reading and seems outmoded. The manuscripted letter obstructs what Heidegger considers a veritable degradation of the word by the machine. The machine "degrades (*degradiert*)" the word or the speech it reduces to a simple means of transport (*Verkehrsmittel*), to the instrument of commerce and communication. Furthermore, the machine offers the advantage, for those who wish for this degradation, of dissimulating manuscripted writing and "character." "In typewriting, all men resemble one another," concludes Heidegger.[28]

The paths according to which the denunciation of the typewriter increased and specified itself would have to be followed closely (I cannot do that here).[29] Finally, the typewriter would dissimulate the very essence of the writing gesture and of writing (*"Die Schreib-maschine verhüllt das Wesen des Schreibens und der Schrift"*). This dissimulation or this veiling is also a movement of withdrawal or subtraction (the words *entziehen, Entzug* often recur in this passage). And if in this withdrawal [*retrait*] the typewriter becomes "*zeichenlos*," without sign, unsignfying, a-signifying,[30] that is because it loses the hand; in any case it threatens what in the hand holds speech safe [*garde la parole*] or holds safe for speech the relation of Being to man and of man to beings. "The hand handles": *Die Hand handelt*. The essential co-belonging (*Wesenszusammengehörigkeit*) of the hand and speech, man's essential distinction, manifests itself in this, that the hand manifests, precisely, what is hidden (*die Hand Verborgenes entbirgt*). And the hand does this precisely, in its relation to speaking, by showing [*montrant*] and by writing, by pointing to, signs that show, or rather by giving to these signs or these "*monstres*" *forms* called writing (*"sie zeigt und zeigend zeichnet und zeichnend die zeigenden Zeichen zu Gebilden bildet. Diese Gebilde heissen nach dem 'Verbum'* γράφειν *die* γράμματα"*). This implies that, as Heidegger expressly says, writing in its essential source is manuscripture (*"Die Schrift ist in ihrer Wesensherkunft die Hand-schrift"*). And I shall add—what Heidegger does not say but which seems to me even more decisive— manuscripture *immediately* bound to speech, that is, more probably the *system of phonetic writing,* unless what gathers together *Wort, zeigen,* and *Zeichen* does not always necessarily pass through the voice and unless the speech Heidegger speaks of here is essentially distinct from all θωνή. The distinction would be strange enough to warrant emphasizing; now Heidegger does not breathe a word of this. He insists, on the contrary, on the essential and primordial co-belonging of *Sein, Wort,* λέγειν, λόγος, *Lese, Schrift* as *Hand-schrift.* Moreover, this co-belonging that gathers them together stems from the movement of the very gathering together Heidegger always reads, here as elsewhere, in λέγειν and *lesen* ("*das 'Lesen', d. h. Sammeln . . .*").[31] This motif of gathering together (*Versammlung*) governs the meditation of *Geschlecht* in the text on Trakl that I shall evoke very briefly in a few minutes. Here, the protest against the typewriter also belongs—this is a matter of course—to an interpretation of technology [*technique*], to an interpretation of politics starting from technology. Just as *Was heisst Denken?* will name Marx a few pages after treating of the hand, so this seminar of 1942–43 situates Lenin and "Leninism" (the name Stalin gave to this metaphysics). Heidegger recalls the word of Lenin: "Bolshevism is the power of the Soviet + electrification."[32] When he was writing that, Germany was just entering into war with Russia and with the United States (it is not spared either in this seminar), but there was not yet the electric typewriter.

This apparently positive evaluation of handwriting does not exclude, on the contrary, a devaluation of writing in general. This devaluation takes on sense within this general interpretation of the art of writing as the increasing destruction of the word or of speech. The typewriter is only a modern aggravation of the evil. This evil comes not only through writing but also through literature. Just before the citation of "Mnemosyne," *Was heisst Denken?* advances two trenchant affirmations: (1) Socrates is "the purest thinker of the West. This is why he wrote nothing (*der reinste Denker des Abendlandes. Deshalb hat er nichts geschrieben*)."[33] He knew how to hold himself in the wind and in the withdrawing movement of what gives itself to be thought (*in den Zugwind dieses Zuges*). In another passage, which also treats of this withdrawal (*Zug des Entziehens*), Heidegger again distinguishes man from animal, this time from the migratory birds. In the very first pages of *Was heisst Denken?* before citing "Mnemosyne" for the first time, he writes: "Once we are drawn into the withdrawal (*Zug des Entziehens*), we are—but completely otherwise than the migratory birds—drawing toward what draws, attracts us by its withdrawal."[34] The choice of example here (an example omitted in the English translation) stems from the German idiom: "migratory birds" is said *Zugvögel* in German. We, men, we are in the drawing (*trait, Zug*) of this withdrawal [*retrait*], *nur ganz anders als die Zugvögel.* (2) Second trenchant affirmation: thought declines the moment one begins to write, *on coming out of* [au sortir de] thought, *in escaping* [en sortant de] thought in order to take shelter from it, as from the wind. This is the moment when thought entered literature (*Das Denken ging in die Literatur ein*).[35] Sheltered from thought, this entry into writing and literature (in the broad sense of this word) would have decided the destiny of Western science as much *qua doctrina* of the Middle Ages (teaching, discipline, *Lehre*) as *qua* the science of Modern Times. This is naturally a matter of what constructs the dominant concept of discipline, teaching, and the university. So one sees being organized around the hand and speech, with a very strong coherence, all the traits whose incessant recurrence I have elsewhere recalled under the name logocentrism. Whatever the lateral or marginal motifs that simultaneously work (over) logocentrism, I would like to suggest that it dominates a certain and very continuous discourse of Heidegger, and does so from the repetition of the question of Being's sense, the destruction of classic ontology, the existential analytic redistributing the (existential and categorial) relations among *Dasein, Vorhandensein,* and *Zuhandensein.*

The economy imposed on me for this discourse prohibits me from going beyond this first reference marking [*repérage*] in the Heideggerian interpretation of the hand. In order to bind better, in a more differentiated coherence, what I am saying here to what I said elsewhere about Heidegger, notably in "*Ousia* and *Grammē,*" one would have to reread a certain page of "The Anaximander Fragment," that is, of a text that also names "Mnemosyne" and in the context of which "*Ousia* and *Grammē*" can be unfolded. This page recalls that in χρεών, which is generally translated by "necessity," there speaks ἡ χείρ, the hand: "χράω means: I handle, I bring my hand to something (*ich be-handle etwas*)."[36] The rest of the paragraph, too difficult to translate since it handles so closely the German idiom (*in die Hand geben, einhändigen, aushändigen:* to hand back to its rightful owner, then to hand over, to give up, *überlassen*), withdraws the participle χρεών from the values of constraint and obligation (*Zwang, Müssen*) and at the same time withdraws from these values the word *Brauch* by which Heidegger proposes to translate τὸ χρεών and which means, in everyday German, "need." So it is not necessary to think the hand starting from "need." In French *der Brauch* is translated by *le maintien,* which, besides indeed some drawbacks or false senses, exploits the chance of a double allusion: to the hand and to the now, the *maintenant,* that preoccupy the specific concern of this text. If *Brauchen* translates well, as Heidegger says, the χρεών that permits thinking the present in its presence (*das Anwesende in seinem Anwesen*), if it names a trace (*Spur*) that disappears in the history of Being as that history unfolds itself as Western metaphysics, if *der Brauch* is indeed "the gathering (*Versammlung*): ὁ λόγος,"³⁷ then, before all hand technics, all surgery [*chirurgie*], the hand does not have no hand in this, it is already implicated [*la main n'y est pas pour rien*].

The hand of *the* man, of man *as such:* no doubt you have remarked that Heidegger does not only think the hand as a very singular thing that would rightfully belong only to man, he always thinks the hand *in the singular,* as if man did not have two hands but, this monster, one single hand. Not one single organ in the middle of the body, just as the Cyclops has one single eye in the middle of the forehead, even though this representation, which leaves something to be desired, also gives rise to thought. No, *the* hand of man, this signifies that we are no longer dealing with prehensile organs or instrumentalizable members that *some* hands are. Apes have prehensile organs that resemble hands, the man of the typewriter and of technics in general uses two hands. But the man that speaks and the man that writes with the hand, as one says; isn't he the monster with a single hand? Thus, when Heidegger writes: "*Der Mensch 'hat' nicht Hände, sondern die Hand hat das Wesen des Menschen inne*": "Man 'has' no hands, but the hand occupies, in order to have in hand, man's essence," this supplementary precision does not just concern, as we saw in the first instance, the structure of "having," a word Heidegger places in quotation marks and whose relation he proposes to invert; it concerns the difference between the plural and the singular: *nicht Hände, sondern die Hand.* What comes to man through λόγος or speech (*das Wort*) can be only one single hand. Hands, that is already or still the organic or technical dissipation [*dispersion*]. So one will not be surprised faced with the absence of all allusion, for example in the Kantian style, to the play of difference between right and left, to the mirror, or to the pair of gloves. This difference cannot be *sensible.* For my part, having already treated in my manner of the pair of shoes, of the left foot and the right foot in Heidegger, I shall not go any further today on this path. I shall content myself with two remarks. On the one hand, the sole sentence in which Heidegger, to my knowledge, names man's hands in the plural seems to concern precisely the moment of prayer, or in any case the gesture in which the two hands join together (*sich falten*) to make themselves only one in simplicity (*Einfalt*). Gathering together (*Versammlung*) is always what Heidegger privileges. On the other hand, nothing is ever said of the caress or of desire. Does one make love, does man make love, with the hand or with the hands? And what about sexual differences in this regard? Heifegger's protest can be imagined: this question is derivative; what you call desire or love presupposes the coming [*avènement*] of *the* hand since speech, and as soon as I alluded to the hand that gives, gives itself, promises, lets go, gives up, hands over, and engages in the alliance or oath, you have at your disposal everything you need to think what you commonly call making love, caressing, or even desiring. Perhaps, but why not say it?

(This last remark should serve for me as a transition, if I had the time, toward this word, this mark *"Geschlecht"* that we should now [*maintenant*] follow in another text. I shall not give this part of my lecture [*conférence*], which should have been titled *"Geschlecht* III" and whose (typed) manuscript has been photo*copied* and distributed to some of you so that discussion of it might be possible. I shall confine myself then, if you would kindly grant me a few minutes more, to a very cursory sketch.)

I just said "the word *'Geschlecht'* ": that is because I am not so sure it has a determinable and unifiable referent. I am not so sure one can speak of *Geschlecht* beyond the word *"Geschlecht"*—which then is found necessarily cited, between quotation marks, mentioned rather than used. Next, I leave the word in German. As I have already said, no word, no word for word will suffice to translate this word that gathers in its idiomatic value stock, race, family, species, genus/gender, generation, sex. Then, after saying the word *"Geschlecht,"* I amended or corrected myself: the "mark *'Geschlecht,'* " I clarified. For the theme of my analysis would come down to a sort of composition or decomposition that affects, precisely, the unity of this word. Perhaps it is no longer a word. Perhaps one must begin by gaining access to it from its disarticulation or its decomposition, in other words, its formation, its information, its deformations or transformations, its translations, the genealogy of its body unified starting from or according to the dividing and the sharing of the words' morsels. We are going then to concern ourselves with the *Geschlecht* of *Geschlecht,* with its genealogy or its generation. But this genealogical composition of *"Geschlecht"* will be inseparable, in the text of Heidegger I should interrogate now [*maintenant*], from the decomposition of human *Geschlecht,* from the decomposition of man.

One year after *Was heisst Denken?* in 1953, Heidegger published "Die Sprache im Gedicht" in *Merkur* under the title "Georg Trakl," with a subtitle that so to speak will not change when the text will be taken up again in 1959 in *Unterwegs zur Sprache:* "Eine Erörterung seines Gedichtes." All these titles are already practically untranslatable. I will nevertheless have recourse, rather frequently, to the invaluable translation published by Jean Beaufret and Wolfgang Brokmeier in the

Nouvelle Revue Française, today collected in *Acheminement vers la pa-role.*[38] At each step the risk of thought remains intimately engaged in the tongue, the idiom, and translation. I salute the daring venture that constituted, in its very discretion, such a translation. Our debt here goes toward a gift that gives much more than what is called a French version. Each time I will have to diverge from it, that will be without the least intention of evaluating, even less of amending, that version. Rather, we shall have to multiply the drafts, harass the German word, and analyze it according to several waves of touches, caresses, or strokes. A transla-tion, in the usual sense of what is published under this name, cannot indulge itself in this. But we, on the contrary, have the duty to do this each time the calculus of word for word, one word for another, that is, the conventional ideal of translation, will be defied. It would be more-over legitimate, apparently trivial, but in truth essential to take this text on Trakl for a situation (*Erörterung*) of what we are calling translation. At the heart of this situation, of this place or site (*Ort*), *Geschlecht,* the word or the mark. For the composition and the decomposition of this mark, the labor of Heidegger in his tongue, his hand and artisan writ-ing, his *Hand-Werk,* these are what the existing translations (the French and, I suppose, the English) tend fatally to efface.

Before any other preliminary, I jump suddenly to the middle of the text, in order to throw light as from a first flash on the site that interests me. On two occasions, in the first and the third parts, Heideg-ger declares that the word "*Geschlecht*" has in German, "in our tongue" (it is always a question of "we"), a multitude of significations. But this singular multitude must gather itself together in some manner. In *Was heisst Denken?* a bit after the passage on the hand, Heidegger protests more than once against one-track thinking or the one-track path. While recalling here that *Geschlecht* is open to a kind of polysemy, he heads, before and after all, toward a certain unity that gathers this multiplicity. This unity is not an identity, but guards the simplicity of the same, even in the form of the fold. Heidegger wants this primordial simplicity to give rise to thought beyond all etymological derivation, at least accord-ing to the strictly philosophical sense of etymology.

(1) The first passage[39] cites the next to last stanza of the poem "Autumn Soul (*Herbstseele*)." I read it in its French translation that will pose some problems for us later on:

> Bientôt fuient poisson et gibier.
> Ame bleue, obscur voyage
> Départ de l'Autre, de l'Aimé
> Le soir change sens et image [*Sinn und Bild*].

> Soon fish and game slip away.
> Blue soul, dark wandering
> Soon parted us from loved ones, others.
> Evening changes sense and image.

Heidegger connects: "The travelers who follow the stranger find themselves immediately separated from 'Loved Ones' (*von Lieben*) who are for them 'Others' (*die für sie 'Andere' sind*). The 'Others,' let us understand the ruined stock of man."

What is translated in that way is "*der Schlag der verwesten Gestalt des Menschen.*" "*Schlag*" means several things in German. In the literal sense, as the dictionary would say, it is *blow* [coup] with all the associable significations; but in the figurative sense, says the dictionary, it is also race or species, the stock [*la souche*] (the word chosen by the French translators). Heidegger's meditation will let itself be guided by this relation between *Schlag* (at once as blow and as stock) and *Geschlecht*. *Der Schlag der verwesten Gestalt des Menschen* implies a *Verwesen* in the sense of what is "decomposed," if it is literally understood according to the usual code of bodily decay, but also in another sense of the corruption of being or essence (*Wesen*) that Heidegger is not going to stop retracing and recalling. Here he opens a paragraph that begins with "*Unsere Sprache*": "Our language calls (*nennt:* names] humanity (*Menschenwesen*) having received the imprint of a striking (*das aus einem Schlag geprägte*) and in this striking struck with/as species determination [*und in diesen Schlag verschlagene:* and in effect *verschlagen* means commonly to specify, separate, cast adrift, partition, board-up, distinguish, differentiate], our language calls humanity . . . '*Geschlecht.*'" The word is between quotation marks. I am going up to the end of this paragraph whose context would have to be reconstituted later: "The word [*Geschlecht,* then] signifies the human species (*Menschengeschlecht*) in the sense of humanity (*Menschheit*) as well as the species in the sense of tribes, stocks, and families, all that struck again [*dies alles wiederum geprägt:* struck in the sense of what receives the imprint, the τύπος, the typical mark] with the generic duality of the sexes (*in das Zwiefache der Geschlechter*)." *Dualité générique des sexes* is in French a risky translation. Heidegger, it is true, does speak this time of the *sexual* difference that comes again, in a second blow (*wiederum geprägt*), to strike (also in the sense that one says in French and English to strike coins) the *Geschlecht* in all the senses just enumerated. My questions will later be concentrated on this second blow. But Heidegger does not say "generic duality." And as to the word *das Zwiefache,* the double, the dual, the dual alliance, it carries the whole enigma of the text that plays itself out

between, on the one hand, *das Zwiefache,* a certain duplicity, a certain
fold of sexual difference or *Geschlecht,* and, on the other hand, *die
Zwietracht der Geschlechter,* the duality of sexes as dissension, war, dis-
agreement, opposition, the duel of violence, and of declared hostilities.

(2) The second passage will be taken from the third part[40] in the
course of a passage that will have indeed displaced things: " *'One'* [in
quotation marks and italics in the German text: *"das 'Ein'"*] in the
words '*One* race' [*im Wort 'Ein Geschlecht':* citation of a verse by Trakl;
this time the French translators chose, without apparent or satisfactory
justification, to translate *Geschlecht* by "race"] does not mean 'one' in
place of 'two' (*meint nicht 'eins' statt 'zwei'*). *One* does not signify either
the indifference of an insipid uniformity [*das Einerlei einer faden
Gleichheit:* on this point I take the liberty of referring to the first part of
my essay entitled *"Geschlecht"*]. The words '*One* race' (*das Wort 'Ein
Geschlecht'*) name here no biologically determinable state of things
(*nennt hier keinen biologischen Tatbestand*), neither 'unisexuality' (*weder
die 'Eingeschlechtlichkeit'*) nor the 'undifferentiation of the sexes' (*noch
die 'Gleichgeschlechtlichkeit'*). In the *One* underlined [by Trakl] (*In dem
betonten 'Ein Geschlecht'*) does the unity take shelter, the unity that,
starting from the matching azure of the spiritual night, reunites (*einigt*).
[The "matching azure" is incomprehensible as long as one has not recognized, as I try to do in the rest of the talk I shall not give, the sym-
phonic or synchromatic reading of the blues or of the blue of the azured
sky in Trakl's poems, and as long as one has not recognized that the
French translators are translating by "*appareillant* (matching)" the
word *versammelnd:* gathering, collecting in the same or the "similar
(*pareil*)" of what is not identical.] The word [by implication, the word
Ein in Ein Geschlecht] speaks from out of the song (*Das Wort spricht aus
dem Lied*) in which is sung the land of the decline [or of the setting or of
the Occident: *worin das Land des Abends gesungen wird*]. Consequently,
the word '*Geschlecht*' keeps here the multiple fullness of signification
(*mehrfältige Bedeutung*) we have already mentioned. '*Geschlecht*' first
names the historial race, man, humanity (*das geschichtliche Geschlecht des
Menschen, die Menschheit*) in the difference that separates it from the rest
of the living (plant and animal) (*im Unterschied zum übrigen Lebendigen
[Planze und Tier]*). The word '*Geschlecht*' next names as well the genera-
tions [*Geschlechter,* in the plural: the word *Geschlecht* names the *Geschlechter!*], tribes, stocks, families of this human species (*Stämme, Sippen,
Familien dieses Menschengeschlechtes*). The word '*Geschlecht*' names at the
same time, across all these distinctions [*überall:* throughout; Heidegger
does not specify "all these distinctions" that the French translation introduces by analogy with the first definition, but no matter], the gener-

ic splitting in two [*die Zwiefalt der Geschlechter:* the French translation here does not name the sexuality nonetheless evident, whereas above it translated *Zweifache der Geschlechter* by "*dualité générique des sexes* (generic duality of the sexes)"]."

So Heidegger has just recalled that *Geschlecht* names, surnames, *at the same time* (zugleich) sexual difference, in addition to all the other senses. And he opens the following paragraph with the word *Schlag,* that the French translation renders by *frappe,* striking, which presents a double drawback. On the one hand, the translation lacks the recall of the Trakl verse whose word *Flügelschlag* is accurately translated by "wingbeat." On the other hand, in using two different words, *coup* (beat) and *frappe* (striking), to translate the same word *Schlag,* the translation effaces what authorizes Heidegger to recall the affinity between *Schlag* and *Geschlecht* in the two verses he is in the process of reading. Such affinity supports the whole demonstration. These verses are extracted from a poem entitled "Occidental Song" (*Abendländisches Lied*). Another is titled "The Occident" (*Abendland*), and the decline *of* the Occident, *as* Occident, is at the center of this meditation.

> O der Seele nachtlicher Flügelschlag:

> O de l'âme nocturne coup d'aile:

> O the soul's nocturnal wingbeat:[41]

After these two verses, colon [*deux points*] and two words plain and simple: "Ein *Geschlecht.*" "Ein": the sole word that, in his whole oeuvre, Heidegger notes, Trakl will have underlined in this way. To underline is *betonen.* The word thus underlined (Ein) then will give the fundamental tone, the fundamental note (*Grundton*). But it is the *Grundton* of *Gedicht* and not of *Dichtung,* for Heidegger regularly distinguishes *Gedicht,* which always remains unspoken (*ungesprochene*), silent, from poems (*Dichtungen*), which themselves say and speak in proceeding from *Gedicht. Gedicht* is the silent source of written and spoken poems (*Dichtungen*) from which one must start in order to situate (*erörtern*) the site (*Ort*), the source, to wit, *Gedicht.* That is why Heidegger says of this "Ein *Geschlecht*" that it shelters the *Grundton* from which the *Gedicht* of this poet silences (*schweigt*) the secret (*Geheimnis*). So the paragraph beginning with *Der Schlag* can be warranted not only by a philological decomposition but by what happens in Trakl's verse, his *Dichtung:* "The striking (*Der Schlag*) whose imprint gathers together such a splitting in two in a simplicity of the *one* race

(*der sie in die Einfalt des* 'Einen *Geschlechts*' *prägt*) and thus restores the
stocks of the species (*die Sippen des Menschengeschlechtes*) and the species
itself in the sweetness of the more serene infancy, that striking strikes
(*eingeschlagen lässt*) the soul with an opening for the path of the 'blue
springtime' [this is a citation of Trakl indicated by the quotation marks
omitted in the French translation]."[42]

Those then are the two passages, still separated from their context,
two passages in which Heidegger thematizes at once the polysemy and
the focal simplicity of "*Geschlecht*" in "our tongue." This tongue, which is
ours, German, is also the tongue of "our *Geschlecht*," as Fichte would say,
if *Geschlecht* also means family, generation, stock. Now what is written
and played out with the writing of this word, *Geschlecht,* in our *Geschlecht*
and in our tongue (*unsere Sprache*) is idiomatic enough in its possibilities
to remain almost untranslatable. The affinity between *Schlag* and
Geschlecht takes place and is thinkable only from this "*Sprache.*" Not only
from the German idiom I hesitate here to call a "national" idiom, but
from the overdetermined idiom of a singular *Gedicht* and *Dichten,* here
that or those of Trakl, which are moreover then overdetermined by the
idiom of a *Denken,* the idiom that passes through the writing of Heidegger. Yes, I say *Dichten* and *Denken,* poetry and thought. You recall that
for Heidegger *Dichten* and *Denken* are a work of the hand exposed to the
same dangers as the handicraft (*Hand-Werk*) of the cabinetmaker. You
also know that Heidegger never places philosophy and science on a level
with thought and poetry. These last two, thought and poetry, although
radically different, are relatives and parallels, parallels that cut across and
breach each other, that cut each other in a place that is also a kind of
signature (*Zeichnung*), the incision of a trait (*Riss*).[43] Philosophy, science, and technics are, so to speak, excluded from this parallelism.

What is one to think of this text? How is it to be read?

But will it be a matter again of a "lecture," in the French or English sense of the word? I am afraid and with you I hope that it is
nothing of the kind. *On the one hand,* it is too late, and in place of
continuing to read the one hundred or so pages I have devoted to this
text on Trakl and whose first French version, incomplete and provisional, has been communicated to certain among you, I shall content myself
with indicating in a few minutes their principal concern, inasmuch as
that can be translated into a series of suspended or suspensive questions. I have grouped them, more or less artificially, around *five* foci.
Now *on the other hand,* one of these foci concerns the concept of reading [*lecture*] that does not seem adequate, without being profoundly
reelaborated, either for naming what Heidegger does in his *Gespräch*

with Trakl or in what he calls the authentic *Gespräch* or the *Zwiesprache* (two speaking) of one poet with another poet or of a thinker with a poet, or for naming what I am attempting or what interests me in this *explication with* (*Auseinandersetzung*) this text here of Heidegger.

My most constant concern is evidently the "mark" *"Geschlecht"* and what in that mark *remarks* the mark, the striking, the impression, a certain writing as *Schlag, Prägung,* and so on. This *re-mark* seems to me to maintain an essential relation to what, a bit arbitrarily, I place in the first place among the five foci of questioning:

(1) Of man and animality (the text on Trakl also proposes a thinking of the difference between animality and humanity), of the difference between two sexual differences, of difference, of the relation between the 1 and the 2, and of divisibility in general. At the focus of this focus, the mark *Geschlecht* in its polysemy (species or sex) and in its dissemination.

(2) Another focus of questioning concerns just what Heidegger says of polysemy and that I want to distinguish from dissemination. On several occasions, Heidegger shows himself receptive to what could be called a "good" polysemy, that of poetic language and of the "great poet." This polysemy has to let itself be *gathered* into a "higher" univocity and into the oneness of a harmony (*Einklang*). Heidegger thus comes to valorize for once a *"Sicherheit"* of the poetic rigor, thus stretched by the force of the gathering together. And he opposes this "security (*Sicherheit*)" both to the errance of mediocre poets that hand themselves over to bad polysemy—the one that does not let itself be gathered into a *Gedicht* or into a unique site (*Ort*)—and to the univocity of exactitude (*Exaktheit*) in techno-science. This motif appears to me at once traditional (properly Aristotelian), dogmatic in its form, and symptomatically contradictory to other Heideggerian motifs. For I never "criticize" Heidegger without recalling that that can be done from other places in his own text. His text could not be homogeneous and is written with two hands, at least.

(3) That question, which I title then *polysemy and dissemination,* communicates with another focus in which several *questions of method* cross. What is Heidegger doing? How does he "operate" and according to what ways, ὁδοί, that are not yet or already no more *methods?* What is Heidegger's step [*le pas*] on this path; what is his rhythm in this text that explicitly pronounces itself on the essence of ῥυθμός; and what is also his *manner,* his *Hand-Werk* of writing? These questions beyond-or-across-method [*outre-méthode*] are also questions of the relation this Heidegger text (and the text I am writing in my turn) maintains with

what is called hermeneutics, interpretation or exegesis, literary criticism, rhetoric or poetics, but also with all the bodies of knowledge
[*savoirs*] of the human or social sciences (history, psychoanalysis, so-
ciology, political science, and so on). Two oppositions or distinctions,
two couples of concepts support the Heideggerian argumentation—
and I am questioning them in my turn. There is, *on the one hand,* the
distinction between *Gedicht* and *Dichtung. Gedicht* (an untranslatable
word, once more) is, in its place, what gathers together all the
Dichtungen (the poems) of a poet. This gathering together is not that of
a complete corpus, of the *œuvres complètes,* but a unique source that is
not presented in any part of any poem. This gathering is the site of
origin, the place from which and toward which the poems come and go
according to a "rhythm." Not elsewhere, not some other thing, and yet
not to be confused with the poems insofar as they say (*sagen*) something, *Gedicht* is "unspoken (*ungesprochene*)." What Heidegger wants to
indicate, to announce rather than show, is the unique Site (*Ort*) of this
Gedicht. That is why Heidegger presents his text as an *Erörterung,* that
is to say, according to the reawakened literalness of this word, a situation that localizes the unique site or the proper place of *Gedicht* from
which the poems of Trakl sing. Whence, *on the other hand,* a second
distinction between the *Erörterung* of *Gedicht* and an *Erläuterung* (clari-
fication, elucidation, explication) of poems (*Dichtungen*) themselves,
from which one must indeed start. I pay particular attention then to all
the difficulties that result from this double starting point and from what
Heidegger calls "*Wechselbezug,*" the relation of reciprocity or exchange
between situation (*Erörterung*) and elucidation (*Erläuterung*).[44] Does
this *Wechselbezug* coincide with what is called the hermeneutic circle?
And how does Heidegger practice or play, *in his manner,* this *Wechsel-
bezung?*

(4) This last formulation, which always aims at Heidegger's *manner* or, as one can also say in French and English, with another connota-
tion, his manners, no more lets itself be separated, no more than the
hand according to Heidegger, from bringing the tongue into play, its
mise en œuvre. Here then from a certain maneuver of writing. This maneuver of writing always resorts in its decisive moments to a resource
that is idiomatic, in other words, untranslatable, if one trusts in the
common concept of translation. This resource, overdetermined by the
idiom of Trakl and by Heidegger's, is not only the resource of German,
but most often of an idiom of the Old High German idiom. In my
manner, that is, following the injunctions and the economy of other
idioms, I retrace and remark all these recourses by Heidegger to Old

German, each time he begins by saying: in our tongue (*in unsere Sprache*); such a word signifies originally (*bedeutet ursprünglich*). Here, in this quick overview, I can only give the list of words, of morsels of words, or of sentences near which I mark a slightly longer stop.

(*a*) First, naturally, there is the word "*Geschlecht*" and all its *Geschlecht,* all its family, its roots, its offshoots, legitimate or not. Heidegger convokes them all and gives to each its role. There is *Schlag, einschlagen, verschlagen* (to separate, partition), *zerschlagen* (to break, smash, dismantle), *auseinanderschlagen* (to separate while striking one another), and so on. In place of displaying here again the whole Heideggerian maneuver and the one to which he binds us, I shall cite, as a sign of thanks, a paragraph that David Krell devotes in English to this word in chapter 11 of his book *Intimations of Mortality* (University Park: Pennsylvania State University Press, 1986), the manuscript of which he was kind enough, after the publication of my first article on *Geschlecht,* to send me. The chapter is titled "Strokes of Love and Death," and I have extracted this:

> "Strokes of love and death": *Schlag der Liebe, Schlag des Todes.* What do the words *Schlag, schlagen* mean? Hermann Paul's *Deutsches Worterbuch* lists six principal areas of meaning for *der Schlag;* for the verb *schlagen* it cites six "proper" senses and ten "distant" meanings. Deriving from the Old High German and Gothic *slahan* (from which the English word "slay" also derives) and related to the modern German word *schlachten,* "to slaughter," *schlagen* means to strike a blow, to hit or beat. A *Schlag* may be the stroke of a hand, of midnight, or of the brain; the beating of wings or of a heart. *Schlagen* may be done with a hammer or a fist. God does it through his angels and his plagues; a nightingale does it with his song. One of the most prevalent senses of *schlagen* is to mint or stamp a coin. *Der Schlag* may therefore mean a particular coinage, imprint, or type; a horse dealer might refer to *einem guten Schlag Pferde.* It is by virtue of this sense that *Schlag* forms the root of a word that is very important for Trakl, *das Geschlecht.* Paul lists three principal meanings for *Geschlecht* (Old High German *gislahti*). First, it translates the Latin word *genus,* being equivalent to *Gattung: das Geschlecht* is a group of people who share a common ancestry, especially if they constitute a part of the hereditary nobility. Of course, if the ancestry is traced back far enough we may speak of *des menschliche Geschlecht,* "humankind." Second, *das Geschlecht* may mean one generation of men and women who die to make way for a succeeding generation. Third, there are male and female *Geschlechter,* and *Geschlecht* becomes the root of many words for the

things males and females have and do for the sake of the first two meanings: *Geschlechts-glied* or *-teil,* the genitals; *-trieb,* the sex drive; *-verkehr,* sexual intercourse; and so on.

(*b*) There is next the noun *Ort.* When Heidegger recalls, from the first page, that this word "Originally . . . signifies (*Ursprünglich bedeutet*)" the point of the spear (*die Spitze des Speers*), that is before everything (and there is much to say on this "before everything") to insist on its value of gathering. Everything *concurs* and converges toward the point (*in ihr läuft alles zusammen*). The site is always the site of gathering, the gathering, *das Versammelnde.* This definition of site, besides implying the recourse to an "original signification" in a determined language, governs the whole course of *Erörterung,* the privilege granted to oneness and to indivisibility in situating *Gedicht* and what Heidegger calls a "great poet," great insofar as he is related to that oneness of gathering and resists the forces of dissemination or dislocation.[45] Naturally, I would multiply the questions around this value of gathering.

(*c*) There is next the idiomatic and untranslatable opposition between *geistig* and *geistlich* that plays a determinant role. This opposition authorizes withdrawing the *Gedicht* or the "site" of Trakl both from what is gathered together by Heidegger under the title of *the* "western metaphysics" and of its Platonic tradition distinguishing between the "sensible" material and the "intelligible" spiritual (αἰσθητόν/νόητον) and from the Christian opposition between the spiritual and the temporal. Heidegger again refers to the "original signification (*ursprüngliche Bedeutung*)" of the word "Geist (*gheis*): to be lifted up, transported outside of oneself, like a flame (*aufgebracht, entsetzt, ausser sich sein*).[46] It is a matter of the ambivalence of the fire or the flame of the spirit, which is at once the Good and the Evil.

(*d*) There is again the word *fremd* that does not signify the foreign, in the Latin sense of what is outside of, extra, *extraneus,* but properly (*eigentlich*), according to the High German, *fram:* forward toward elsewhere, in the act of making one's own path . . . , to the encounter of what in advance lies in store ("*anderswohin vorwärts, unterwegs nach . . . , dem Voraufbehaltenen entgegen*"). This allows saying that the Stranger does not wander [*erre*], but has a destination ("*es irrt nicht, bar jeder Bestimmung, ratlos umher*"),[47] the Stranger is not without destination.

(*e*) There is furthermore the word *Wahnsinn* that does not signify, as one thinks, the dream of the insane. Since *Wahn* is led back to the High German *wana* that signifies *ohne, sans, without,* the "*Wahnsinnige,*" the demented is the one who remains *without* the sense of Others.

It is of another sense, and *Sinnan "bedeutet ursprünglich,"* originally signifies, *"reisen, streben nach . . . , eine Richtung einschlagen,"* to travel, to strive toward, to carve open with a blow a direction. Heidegger invokes the "Indo-European root *sent, set*" that signifies *Weg,* path.[48] Here things get worse, since it is the very sense of the word *sense* that appears untranslatable, tied to an idiom. And then this value of sense is what, governing nonetheless the traditional concept of translation, suddenly finds itself rooted in one single tongue or family or *Geschlecht* of tongues, outside of which it loses its original sense.

If the "situation (*Erörterung*)" of *Gedicht* is thus found to depend in its decisive moments on recourse to the idiom of *Geschlecht* or to the *Geschlecht* of the idiom, how is one to think the relation between the unspoken of *Gedicht* and its belonging, the appropriation of its very silence, to one tongue and to one *Geschlecht?* This question concerns not only the German *Geschlecht* and the German tongue, but also those that seem recognized in the Occident, in Occidental man, since this whole "situation" is preoccupied, I shall say in English/French, with concern for the place, the site, the path, and the destination of the Occident. This brings me to the fifth focus. I multiply the foci in order to "decountrify [*dépayser*]" a bit an atmosphere perhaps a bit too much "in one country [*paysante*]"; I do not say countrified [*paysanne*], even were it for Trakl . . .

(5) What comes to *Geschlecht* as its decomposition (*Verwesung*), its corruption, is a *second blow* that comes to strike the sexual difference and to transform it into dissension, war, savage opposition. The primordial sexual difference is tender, gentle, peaceful; when that difference is struck down by a "curse" (*Fluch,* a word of Trakl taken up and interpreted by Heidegger), the duality or the duplicity of the two becomes unleashed, indeed bestial, opposition.[49] This schema, which I reduce here to its most summary expression, Heidegger claims, despite all the appearances and signs of which he is well aware, is neither Platonic nor Christian. This schema would come under neither metaphysical theology nor ecclesial theology. But the primordiality (pre-Platonic, pre-metaphysical, or pre-Christian) to which Heidegger recalls us and in which he situates the proper site of Trakl *has no other content and even no other language* than that of Platonism and Christianity. This primordiality is simply that starting from which things like metaphysics and Christianity are possible and thinkable. But what constitutes their arch-morning origin and their ultra-Occidental horizon is nothing other than this hollow of a repetition, in the strongest and most unusual sense of this term. And the form or the "logic" of this repetition is not only readable in this text on Trakl, but in everything

that, since *Sein und Zeit,* analyzes the structures of *Dasein,* the *Verfall,* the *Ruf,* care *(Sorge),* and regulates this relation of the "most primordial" according to what is less so, notably Christianity. In this text, the argumentation (especially for demonstrating that Trakl is not a Christian poet) takes some particularly laborious and at times very simplistic forms—which I cannot reconstitute in this schema. Just as Heidegger requires a unique and gathering site for Trakl's *Gedicht,* he must presuppose that there is one single site, unique and univocal, for THE metaphysics and THE Christianity. But does this gathering take place? Has it a place, a unity of place? That is the question I shall leave suspended thus, just before the *chute.* In French one sometimes calls the end of a text *chute.* One also says, in place of *chute,* the *envoi.*

Notes

The following abbreviations are used in the references in the notes:

> *AN*   Johann Gottlieb Fichte, *Addresses to the German Nation;* see note 2.
> *AP*   Martin Heidegger, *Acheminement vers la parole;* see note 38.
> *RN*   Johann Gottlieb Fichte, *Reden an die Deutsche Nation;* see note 2.
> *US*   Martin Heidegger, *Unterwegs zur Sprache;* see note 10.
> *WD*   Martin Heidegger, *Was heisst Denken?;* see note 8.
> *WT*   Martin Heidegger, *What is Called Thinking?;* see note 12.

1. Jacques Derrida, *"Geschlecht:* sexual difference, ontological difference," *Research in Phenomenology* 13 (1983): 65–83.
2. *Reden an die Deutsche Nation* (Leipzig: Philipp Reclam, n.d.), p. 121—hereafter *RN; Addresses to the German Nation,* ed. George Armstrong Kelly (New York: Harper & Row, 1968), p. 108—hereafter *AN:* "whoever believes in spirituality and in the freedom of this spirituality, and who wills the eternal development of this spirituality by freedom, wherever he may have been born and whatever language he speaks, is of our blood; he is one of us, and will come over to our side."
3. *RN* 65; *AN* 55.
4. *RN* 63; *AN* 53.
5. *RN* 64; *AN* 54.
6. *RN* 65–66; *AN* 55–56.
7. Letter of Heidegger to Academic Rectorate of Albert-Ludwig University.
8. *Was heisst Denken?* 3d ed. (Tübingen: Niemeyer, 1971), p. 52—hereafter *WD.*
9. *Qu'appelle-t-on penser?* trans. Aloys Becker and Gérard Granel (Paris: Presses Universitaires de France, 1959), p. 92.
10. *Unterwegs zur Sprache* (Pfullingen: Neske, 1959), p. 252—hereafter *US.*
11. Ibid., p. 253.
12. *WD* 51; *What Is Called Thinking?* trans. Fred D. Wieck and J. Glenn Gray (New York: Harper & Row, 1968), p. 16—hereafter *WT.*
13. *WD* 48ff.; *WT* 12ff.
14. *WD* 49; *WT* 14.

15. *WD* 50; *WT* 16.
16. *WD* 50; *WT* 14–15.
17. *WD* 50–51; *WT* 16.
18. *WD* 51; *WT* 16.
19. Ibid.
20. Elsewhere I shall study, as closely as possible, the developments Heidegger devoted to animality in *Die Grundbegriffe der Metaphysik* (1929–30) (*Gesamtausgabe*, vols. 29–30 [Frankfurt: Klostermann, 1983], part 2, chap. 4). Without any essential discontinuity, these developments seem to me to constitute the base of those I am interrogating here, whether it be a question of (1) the classic gesture that consists in considering zoology as a regional science faced with presupposing the essence of animality in general—what Heidegger proposes then to describe without the aid of this scientific knowledge (see § 45); (2) the thesis according to which *"Das Tier ist weltarm,"* a thesis median between the two others (*"der Stein ist weltlos"* and *"der Mensch ist weltbildend"*)—a greatly muddled analysis in the course of which Heidegger has much trouble, it seems to me, determining poverty, being-poor (*Armsein*), and lack (*Entbehren*) as essential traits foreign to the empiric determination of differences of degrees (p. 287), and explaining the original mode of this having-without-having of the animal that has and does not have world (*"Das Haben und Nichthaben von Welt"* [§ 50])); (3) the phenomeno-ontological modality of the *als,* the animal not having access to the being *as* (*als*) being [*étant* comme *étant*] (p. 290ff.). This last distinction would push one to specify that the difference between man and animal corresponds less to the opposition between being-able-to-give and being-able-to-take than to the opposition between *two ways* of taking or giving: one, man's, is giving and taking *as such,* of the being or the present *as such;* the other, the animal's, would be neither giving nor taking *as such.*
21. *WD* 51; *WT* 16.
22. Ibid.
23. *WD* 51; *WT* 16–17.
24. *Sein und Zeit,* 9th ed. (Tübingen: Niemeyer, 1960), p. 69; trans. John Macquarrie and Edward Robinson, *Being and Time* (New York: Harper & Row, 1962), p. 99.
25. *Sein und Zeit,* p. 68; *Being and Time,* pp. 96–97.
26. *Gesamtausgabe,* vol. 54, *Parmenides* (Frankfurt: Klostermann, 1982), p. 118.
27. Ibid., pp. 118–19.
28. Ibid., p. 119.
29. Ibid., pp. 124ff.
30. Ibid., p. 126.
31. Ibid., p. 125.
32. Ibid., p. 127.
33. *WD* 52; *WT* 17.
34. *WD* 5; *WT* 9.
35. *WD* 52; *WT* 18.
36. *Holzwege* (Frankfurt: Klostermann, 1950), p. 337; trans. David Farrell Krell and Frank A. Capuzzi, *Early Greek Thinking* (New York: Harper & Row, 1975, 1984), p. 51.
37. *Holzwege,* p. 340; *Early Greek Thinking,* pp. 54–55.
38. *Nouvelle Revue Française* 6, no. 61 (1958): 52–75, 213–36; *Acheminement vers la parole* (Paris: Gallimard, 1976), pp. 39–83—hereafter *AP.* Perhaps you will be surprised to see me citing a French translation of Heidegger in a lecture given in

English. I am doing so for two reasons. On the one hand, in order not to efface the constraints or the chances of the idiom in which I myself work, teach, read, or write. What you hear right this moment is the translation of a text I first wrote in French. On the other hand, I thought that Heidegger's text could be still more accessible, could gain some supplementary readability by reaching us thus through a third ear; the explication (*Auseinandersetzung*) with one tongue extra can refine our translation (*Über-setzung*) of the text that is called "original." I just spoke of the ear of the other as a third ear. That was not only to multiply to excess the examples of pairs (feet, hands, ears, eyes, breasts, and so on) and all the problems they should pose to Heidegger. It is also to underscore that one can write on the typewriter, as I have done, with three hands among three tongues. I knew I would have to speak in English the text I was writing in French on another I was reading in German.

    39. *US* 49–50; *AP* 53.
    40. *US* 78; *AP* 80.
    41. *US* 77; *AP* 79.
    42. *US* 78–79; *AP* 80.
    43. *US* 196.
    44. *US* 37–38.
    45. *US* 37.
    46. *US* 60.
    47. *US* 41.
    48. *US* 53.
    49. *US* 50.

Notes on Contributors

Ruben Berezdivin studied at Duquesne and Tübingen and with Derrida at Yale. He has taught at Sonoma State University and at Texas Tech. He has published papers on Heidegger and on Greek philosophy.

Robert Bernasconi was a student and subsequently taught at the University of Sussex. Since 1976 he has been a Lecturer in Philosophy at the University of Essex. He is the author of *The Question of Language in Heidegger's History of Being* as well as of a number of essays on Hegel, Heidegger, Levinas, and Derrida. He has also edited a collection of Gadamer's essays on art and aesthetics which will appear in 1986 under the title *The Relevance of the Beautiful*.

John D. Caputo, Professor of Philosophy at Villanova University, is the author of *Heidegger and Aquinas: An Essay on Overcoming Metaphysics*, and *The Mystical Element in Heidegger's Thought*. He has just completed a book entitled *Radical Hermeneutics: Thinking with the Flux*. He is interested in the relationship of the later Heidegger's thinking to the religious and mystical tradition, on the one hand, and to deconstruction, on the other.

Jacques Derrida currently teaches at the Ecole des Hautes Etudes en Sciences Sociales in Paris. He is also a regular Visiting Professor at Yale and at Cornell. All of his principal texts have been, or are currently being, translated into English. They include *Speech and Phenomena*, *Writing and Difference*, *Of Grammatology*, *Positions*, *Dissemination*, *The Archeology of the Frivolous*, *Spurs*, *Glas*, *Truth in Painting*, and *The Post Card*.

Rodolphe Gasché is Professor of Comparative Literature at the State University of New York at Buffalo. His publications include *Die hybride Wissenschaft, System und Metaphorik in der Philosophie von Georges Bataille,* and *The Tain of the Mirror: Derrida and the Philosophy of Reflection* (1986). A new book, *Rethinking Relation: On Heidegger, Derrida, and de Man,* is nearing completion.

Irene E. Harvey studied at York University and with Derrida in Paris. She currently teaches philosophy at the Pennsylvania State University, where she is also Director of the Center for Psychoanalytic Studies. She is the author of a recent book, *Derrida and the Economy of Différance.*

David Farrell Krell is Senior Lecturer and Chairman of the Philosophy Department at the University of Essex. In addition to his many translations of works of Heidegger, he has published two monographs, *Intimations of Mortality: Time, Truth, and Finitude in Heidegger's Thinking of Being,* and *Postponements: Women, Sensuality, and Death in Nietzsche.*

John P. Leavey, Jr., teaches at the University of Florida. He has translated several texts of Derrida (*Edmund Husserl's "Origin of Geometry": An Introduction, The Archeology of the Frivolous,* and *Glas*) and has written the critical apparatus to *Glas* (*Glassary*). He is currently at work on the translation of *Pas* (in *Parage*).

John Llewelyn studied philosophy at the universities of Wales, Oxford, and Edinburgh, where, after teaching at the University of New England (Australia), he is now Reader in Philosophy. His publications include *Beyond Metaphysics? The Hermeneutical Circle in Contemporary Continental Philosophy,* and *Derrida on the Threshold of Sense.*

John Sallis is the Arthur J. Schmitt Professor of Philosophy at Loyola University of Chicago. His books include *Phenomenology and the Return to Beginnings, Being and Logos: The Way of Platonic Dialogue, The Gathering of Reason, Delimitations,* and *Spacings—of Reason and Imagination.* He is founding editor of the journal *Research in Phenomenology.*

Hugh J. Silverman is Professor of Philosophy and Comparative Literature at the State University of New York at Stony Brook. He is author of *Inscriptions: Between Phenomenology and Structuralism;* editor of *Piaget, Philosophy and the Human Sciences;* and coeditor of *Hermeneutics and Deconstruction, Descriptions, Continental Philosophy in America,* and

Jean-Paul Sartre: Contemporary Approaches to His Philosophy. He has been Co-Director of the Society for Phenomenology and Existential Philosophy since 1980 and is currently Executive Secretary of the International Association for Philosophy and Literature.

Stephen Watson currently teaches at the University of Notre Dame. He is the author of numerous articles published both in the United States and Europe on topics ranging from Kant and German Idealism to hermeneutics to the philosophical implications of "Post-Structuralist" thought in figures such as Derrida, Lyotard, and Foucault.

David Wood holds a Ph.D. from the University of Warwick, where he has taught philosophy since 1971, after graduate work at Oxford. He has written often on Derrida, has edited a number of volumes (including *Derrida and Differance*), and is author of *The Deconstruction of Time*. He has lectured widely in the United States and has been a Visitor at Berkeley, Yale, and Stony Brook.

Index

Abel, K., 87
Absence, 110, 115, 148, 154
Abyss (*Abgrund*), 27–30, 82, 174
Adrift, 35–36
Adroitly (*wendig*), 34, 36
Aletheia, 47, 111
Allegory, 63
Als ob, 80
Alterity, 128
Ambiguity, 9–11
Analogy, 10, 72, 74–75
Animality, 112, 165, 173, 189, 195
Anteriority, 17, 121
Antipodes, x
Antisystematic, 6
Apocalypse, 38; Johannine, 37, 39, 41
Apollonian, 24
Apotropocalyptic, 37
Appearance, 51–54, 84, 110
Arbitrary, 3, 164
Arche-syntheses, 5. *See also* Infrastructures
Arche-trace, 5, 8
Arche-writing, 62, 66, 105
Argumentation, 68, 84; Heideggerian, 190; philosophical, 4
Aristotle, 16, 23, 49, 55, 57, 59, 61, 64, 66–68, 70, 85, 121, 132–33, 136–38, 189
Artaud, A., 81
Articulation, 12; metaphysical, 56

Aufhebung, 13, 24, 37, 42, 88–89, 92–94
Augenblick, 117
Austin, J. L., 81, 84, 147, 152, 160
Authentic, 170–71

Babel, 36–37
Barrier, 29, 31
Beaufret, J., 122–23, 132, 183
Becker, A., 166
Beckett, S., 83
Beginning, 23, 145
Begriff (concept), 172
Being, 49, 53, 88, 122–34; beyond of, xiii; destiny of, 124, 135; history of, 181; meaning of, 17; sense of, 177, 181; truth of, 123
Benjamin, W., 35–39, 41–42
Bernet, R., 113
Beyond philosophy, 84
Biologism, 165, 173
Blanchot, M., 33, 42–43, 54, 92, 148
Body (*Leib*), 171
Bolshevism, 180
Bradley, F. H., 93
Bridge, 29–30, 82
Brokmeier, W., 183
Buridan, 13

Call, the, 153
Camus, A., 154

Care, 116, 194
Castration, 37, 42
Categorical, 17
Christianity, 193–94
Circle (*Kreis*), 162–63
Close of philosophy, 19
Closure, 130; of metaphysics, 150;
    of philosophy, 158
Cogito, 103
Coleridge, S., 28
Completeness, 78, 81
Concealing (*Verbergung*), 34–35
Concept (*Begriff*), 4, 82, 88, 90, 92,
    94, 125, 130, 172
Condillac, M., 23
Consciousness, 61, 65, 68, 102, 155
Constitution, 73, 107
Context, 84–85
Contradiction, 4–5, 11
Copernicus, 76
Correspondence, 170
Criticism, 14, 26, 81, 158
Critique, 108, 124, 130, 136, 173;
    of thematic criticism, 14
Culture, 26

Dasein, 34, 114–18, 153, 168, 171,
    176, 181, 194
Da Vinci, L., 25
Death, 153–56, 159, 191
Deception, xii, 50–59
Deconstruction, 131, 149, 151, 158;
    as accounting, 5; and ethics, 122–
    39; goal of, 3–4, 8; method of, 3;
    and phenomenology, xiii; and Pla-
    to, 47–59; and power, 157
Deductivity, 15
Delimitation, 91, 113, 146, 174, 177
De Man, P., 60–70
Derrida, J., 114–21
Descartes, 23–24, 61, 67, 128, 172
Design, argument from, 77
Desire, 157, 182
Destinerrance, 33–41
Destruktion, xiii, 116–17
Determination, 81, 84

Dialectics, 10, 87
Dialogue, 48, 57
Dichten, 111
Dichtung, 111
Differance, 5, 8, 61–64, 87–89,
    105, 111, 146–47, 155
Difference, 8, 87, 189; sexual, 161–
    96
Dilthey, W., 117
Ding-an-sich, 73
Dionysius, 24, 107
Disclosure (*Entbergung*), 34–35
Discourse, 17, 53, 56–57, 66; philo-
    sophical, 5–6, 127, 129;
    transcendental condition of, 38
Dispatches (*envois*), 38
Displacement, 12, 66
Dissemination, 42, 56, 156, 189,
    192; of *envois,* 39
Dreams, 57
Duality, 56, 185, 187
Duplicity, 56, 61, 63

Economy, 91, 176
Ecstasis, 116
End(s), 21, 23, 118
Entrückung, 116
Envois, 39–40
Episteme, 6, 8
Epoche, 147
Equipmentality (*Zeughaftigkeit*),
    177
Ereignis, 48
Erinnerung, 13
Erlebnis, 101, 103
Errancy (*die Irre*), 34–35, 39, 151
Essence (*Wesen*), 7, 25, 118, 170,
    175, 185
Ethics, 122–39; of philosophy, 25
Ethos, 132
Everyday, 133
Excess of syntactic over semantic,
    11–14
Exemplarity, 60–70
Existence, 56
Explanation (*Erklärung*), 84

False, 49
Falsehood, 47, 50. *See also* Deception
Fascination, 54
Feuerbach, L., 90, 95
Fichte, J. G., 162–64, 188
Fiction, 50–51, 58–59, 65
Finitude, 6, 82, 114–21, 134, 138
Forgetfulness, 82
Foundation, 21, 28, 79, 176
Fragment, 6, 35–36
Freedom, 162–63, 194
Freud, S., 33, 37, 42, 87–88, 93,
    117, 152
Fulfillment, 17
Fundamental ontology, 115–17,
    123, 136
Future, 114–21

Gadamer, H. G., 73, 83, 85
Gasché, R., 112, 160
Gathering (*Versammlung*), 118, 163,
    178, 180, 182, 190–92
Gedicht, 187, 190
Geheimnis, 34–35, 187
General system, the, 7–19; discourse
    of, 8
George, S., 110, 150
German Idealism, 107
Geschlecht, 161–96
Gestell, 56
Gewesen, 118, 121
Gift, 174, 176
Given, the, 78
Glas, 92
God, 131
Gödel, K., 9, 20
Gödel's theorem, 9
Godot, 80
Granel, G., 15, 20, 166
Ground (*Grund*), 4–5, 19, 21, 25–
    28, 78, 80, 116, 178

Hand, the, 34–35, 38–40, 168–69,
    172, 182
Handwerk, Hand-Werk, 170–72,
    175, 184, 188–89

Heart, 22–23
Hegel, G. W. F., xiii, 4, 11, 23, 37,
    61, 67, 87–95, 128, 138–39,
    158
Heidegger, M., x, 4, 17, 20, 23–24,
    27, 32–34, 39–41, 47–48, 54,
    59, 68, 85, 110, 114, 139
Heraclitus, 50, 123, 132–36
Hermeneutics, 68, 190
Heterogeneity, 73
Historical unconscious, 67, 70
History, 26, 128, 149, 159
Hobbes, J., 85
Hölderlin, F., 138, 165–66
Horizon, 116
Humanism, 168, 173
Humanity, 163–65, 185–86, 189
Hume, D., 93
Husserl, E., 4, 7, 9, 13, 20, 81, 84,
    99–113, 116, 147, 155, 157; and
    Derrida, 14–18
Hymen, 11, 13

Idea, 15, 80; transcendental, 72
Ideality, 49
Illusion, 78
Images, 53–54, 56–57
Imagination, 107, 155
Imitation, 53
Immanence, 72–73
Immediacy, 62, 67
Impossible, the, 124, 130, 135
Indecidable, 23–25. *See also*
    Undecidability
Infinite regress, 57
Infinite will, 163
Infinity, 91, 127–28, 131, 134
Infrastructures, 5, 7, 9, 12–14, 17
Inner time-consciousness, 101, 103,
    110
Inscription, xii; of philosophy, x
Insight and blindness, 69
Institution, 111
Intentio, 36
Intention, 129
Intentional fulfillment, 16

Intentionality, 16
Intuition, 24, 73, 101, 104–6

Jankelevitch, S., 162
Judgment, 71

Kafka, F., 107
Kant, I., 25, 33, 37, 71–86, 93, 121, 182
Knowledge, x, 6, 8, 15–16, 23, 38, 41, 50, 73, 80, 83, 92, 173
Kolakowski, L., 138
Koyré, A., 88
Krell, D. F., 191

Lacan, J., 33
Language, ix, 11–12, 17, 35–36, 38, 65–66, 89, 102–103, 113, 129–30, 137, 147, 150–51, 163–65, 185; detour of, 36
Law, 74, 82, 123, 125, 130; of reason, 75
Learning, 169
Leibniz, G. W., 36, 89
Lenin, V. I., 180
Levinas, E., 81, 124–39, 148, 153, 159
Liberation, 108
Libertson, J., 138
Light (*Lichtung*), 25–26, 171
Limit, 7, 174
Literature, 3, 180–81
Locke, J., 23
Logic, 19, 79–80, 135, 193
Logocentrism, ix, 60, 181
Logos, 21, 31, 48–49, 52–53, 57–59, 80, 127, 178
Love, 22, 37, 191

Macbeth, 127, 133
Macleish, A., 149, 159–60
Madness, 75
Mallarmé, S., 5, 12, 14, 39, 93
Man, 166, 168, 174, 178–79, 182–83
Manifold, 4–5

Margin, 53
Mark, 39, 189
Martineau, E., 42
Marx, K., 158, 180
Meaning, 12, 17, 155
Memory, 70
Merleau-Ponty, M., 25, 113
Metaphor, 25, 145–46, 172
Metaphysics, 6, 23, 105, 108, 112, 127, 155, 173–74, 181, 192, 194; beginning of, 49; closure of, 150–59; decline of, 50; end of, 71; and exemplarity, 60–70; history of, xii, 70; inception of, 47–59; and physics, 23; Platonic, 48–59; of presence, 64; topology of, 58; tradition of, 68
Mohanty, J. N., 112
Montaigne, 23, 64
Multiplicity, 9–10, 55–6, 184
Music (*musike*), 24
Mystery (*Geheimnis*), 34–35, 187

Name, 41
Nancy, J.-L., 85
Nationalism, 161–62, 165, 168
Nature, 23, 72–74, 77, 85, 94
Necessity, 181
Negation, 149
Newton, I., 76, 85
Nietzsche, F., x, 24, 29, 150, 165, 168
Non-knowing, xii
Non-presence, xiii
Non-sense (*Unsinn*), 105

Off-scene, 38, 40
O'Leary, J., 113
One and Two, 54–55, 59
One, the, 186
Ontico-ontological difference, 40, 131
Ontological, 68; difference, 49
Ontology, 122, 128, 135, 177, 181
Opinion, 50

Opposition, 4, 10, 12, 24, 157, 175–78, 193
Origin, 4, 150, 190
Original, 38–39, 56, 123
Other (capitalized), 8, 10, 19, 55, 126, 130, 148, 153–56, 192, 196; absence of, 148; relation to, 148, 154, 159
Other, otherness (lowercase), xii, 53–55, 58, 61, 65, 152, 154

Pain/pleasure, 51–52, 156
Paradox, 37
Parmenides, 34, 47, 53, 59, 126–27, 129, 177
Parricide, 126–27
Pascal, B., 22–23, 32
Passion, 23
Path (*Weg*), 29, 193
Phaedo, 48
Phaedrus, 61, 64, 70
Phenomenology, xiii, 4, 108–9; discourse of, 18; Husserlian, 14; and metaphysics, 14; transcendental, 103
Phenomenon, 110
Philebus, 52
Philosophy, 29, 90, 128, 149, 188; as bridge, 30–31; closure of, 158; death of, 125, 159; end of, 23; essence of, 25; first, 8; fundamentals of, 4; limit of, xii, 94; national-socialist, 172; and other, 10, 31; responsibility of, 31; text of, 31
Physics, 55
Pierrot, 47
Place, 48, 170, 184
Plato, ix, 4, 15, 24–25, 48–50, 54, 58–59, 61, 64, 66–68, 81, 93, 131, 192–93
Play, 3, 10–11, 91, 169, 182
Playroom, 54
Plurality, 5
Poetry, 188
Politics, 172, 180
Polysemy, 184, 189

Possibility, 9, 15
Praxis, 11, 176–78
Presence, xii, 9, 38, 61, 64, 67, 101, 109–10, 115, 143–44, 146, 155, 159, 176, 181; deconstruction of, ix–x; as form, 11; metaphysics of, ix–x; *Praesenz,* 115; and substance, 18
Principle, 4
Protagoras, 50
Protention, 101–2
Proximity, 102
Purely logical grammar, 14–17, 104
Pythagoras, 55

Reader, 145–46
Reading, 62, 64, 91–92, 145–46, 148, 157, 188
Reason, xiii, 21–25, 27, 71–86; limits of, 30; transcendental, 75, 79
Reduction, 100–108, 111
Reference, 112
Reinscription, 17, 19, 56, 58, 155
Relation, 135, 148, 154, 179
Re-mark, 5, 12–14, 18, 40
Repetition, 63, 68, 105, 193
Representation, 58, 73, 101–2
Republic, 50, 52
Retention, 101–3, 108, 111
Reversal, 33
Richardson, W., 33–34, 41
Rosenberg, A., 165
Rousseau, J.-J., xii, 60–70, 155

Sallis, J., 23, 25, 33–34, 113, 177
Same, the, 67, 128, 152, 184
Sans, 42–43
Sartre, J.-P., 81, 144
Saussure, F., 4, 67, 147
Schein, logic of, 71, 75, 82
Scheler, M., 85
Science, 181, 188
Searle, J., 82, 146
Self, 126
Self-identity, 68, 101
Semantics, 11

Semblance, 52–53
Sense (*Sinn*), 17, 105, 193
Sexual difference, 161–96
Shem, 41
Sign, 67, 99–113, 164, 167–68
Signature, 40
Signification, 5, 12, 42
Signifier, 99, 106–7, 111, 151
Simulacrum, 10, 12, 37
Site (*Ort*), 184, 190, 192–94
Slippage, 66–67
Socrates, ix–xi, 22, 57, 70, 108, 180
Soliloquy, 100
Sophist, 52–54
Sophistry, 53–54, 58
Space, x–xiii, 56, 58, 94
Spacing, 12, 58
Speech, 103–4, 143, 169, 174,
    178–79, 182
Spirituality, 162–63, 194
Stalin, J., 180
Stiftung, 111
Stoicism, 154
Strategy, 160
Structure of exemplarity, 60–70
Substitution, 10, 23
Supplement, 12, 17, 61, 64, 132,
    136, 150, 155
Supplementarity, 5, 62, 64
Symposium, 22
Syncategoremata, 13–14, 18
Syntax, 11–12, 14, 18
Synthesis, 79
System, 4; formation, 6; of knowl-
    edge, 8; non-unitary, 7
Systematicity, 7–8

Teaching, 168–69, 181
Technics, 169, 172, 188
Technology, 165, 180
Teleology, 56
Temporality, 114–21
Tenere, 102–3
Text, 38, 58, 81, 90–91, 129, 158,
    173

Textuality, 62–63, 65, 69, 82, 91
Thanking (*Danken*), 32
Theaetetus, 50, 57
Theology, 83, 193
Theory, 26, 52, 176–78
Thing, 177
Thing itself, 109–10, 113
Thinking (*Denken*), 32, 49, 91, 123,
    132, 146, 169–71, 175, 177; task
    of, 111; topic of, 111
Thought, 52–53, 84, 127, 135, 168,
    171, 174, 181, 188
Threshold, 48, 54, 59; of meta-
    physics, 47–59
Timaeus, 55
Time, xiii, 114–21
Totality, 6, 81, 127
Trace, 38, 181
Tradition, 127–30, 174; of meta-
    physics, 68, 174
Trakl, G., 59, 118–21, 161, 167,
    180, 184, 186, 190
Transcendental analytic, 74
Transcendental deduction, 74
Transcendental dialectic, 71, 75
Transcendental ideal, 72–73
Transcendentalism, 79–82, 88, 127
Transcendental logic, 71
Transcendental reason, 75, 84
Transcendental signified, 110
Transgression, 75–76, 79
Translation, xii, 33–41, 68, 157,
    184, 190, 193, 196
Trivia, 16–17
Truth, 34–35, 39, 49–50, 53, 56–
    59, 123, 132, 134–35, 159, 178;
    essence of, 47; *Scheinung* of, 82

Umschlag, 47
Undecidability, 63, 82, 88. *See also*
    Indecidable
Undecidables, 9–13, 18
Unhappy Consciousness, 92
Unheimlich, 87, 91, 166
Unity, 75, 80, 88, 184, 186

Universality, 82
Urgrund, 115
Ursprung, 79, 89

Voice, 102, 136, 171, 179
Void, 55–56
Vorhandenheit, 176–78
Vorhandensein, 181

Wagner, R., 24
Way (*Weg*), 29, 193
Whole, 84
William of Shyreswood, 13

Wisdom, 22
Withdrawal, x–xi, 72, 82, 179–80
Wittgenstein, 93, 147
Wonder, 23
Woraufhin, 115
World, 17, 107, 111, 115
Writing, x–xi, 4, 38, 49, 61–62, 64–67, 88–89, 91, 94, 143, 148–49, 151, 154–55, 159, 179–80, 189–90; in withdrawal, xi, xiii

Zarathustra, 92, 101, 119
Zuhandenheit, 176–78
Zuhandensein, 181